# ANARCHIST ATHEIST

## *A MEMOIR OF STRUGGLE, GRIEF, PHILOSOPHY AND HOPE*

**By DaN McKee**

Published by Earth Island Books
Pickforde Lodge
Pickforde Lane
Ticehurst
East Sussex
TN5 7BN

www.earthislandbooks.com



First published by Earth Island Books 2023



ISBN 9781739363833

Printed and bound by Solopress

*Contents*

# <u>ANARCHIST ATHEIST PUNK ROCK TEACHER</u>

*A MEMOIR OF STRUGGLE, GRIEF, PHILOSOPHY AND HOPE*

**By DaN McKee**

*To Lucy, who I couldn't have done any of this without.*

*'How can the bird that is born for joy*
*Sit in a cage and sing?'*

**'The Schoolboy', William Blake**

*'Dear XXXXXXXXXXXX,*

*After a lot of thought, and many happy years at XXXXXXXXXXXXX, I have decided it is time to move on to pursue other professional opportunities. While I intend to stay on in my current position until the end of the summer term, I would like this academic year to be my last at the school. I ask, therefore, that you accept this email as my letter of resignation. Hopefully two terms gives plenty of time to find a suitable replacement.*

*Many thanks, and happy new year.*

*DaN'*

**Author's letter of resignation, sent as a 'New Year's Resolution' 01/01/22**

## 1.
## *I'll Give It Until Christmas*

It is important to know that I hated school when I was a student. And I don't just mean that I hated *my* school, with its particular teachers, specific buildings, and the classmates I didn't get on with (although there was that too). I mean that I hated school in general. School as an institution. The whole damn concept. Being forced to learn things you couldn't see the point of learning, in uniform you'd never choose to wear, from teachers who had done nothing to demonstrate they were worth listening to, yet who seemed to demand complete obedience and unearned respect. The punk band my best friend and I formed together at the age of fourteen was named 'Academy Morticians' *precisely* because we hoped our music would somehow prepare the very concept of the academy for burial. An early song I wrote at the age of fifteen, 'The Forbidden Curriculum', showed my eventual anarchist leanings by summing up school as a capitalist con, there merely to mould us into a semi-educated workforce, fit only for exploitation:

*Propaganda decorates the walls, we're taught to fear our masters*
*It's in the rules that we don't complain, if we do it is a disaster*

*Is this place Nazi Germany?*
*No it's just my school*
*Subservience is taught to me:*
*The government's prime tool*

*We're taught only what they want us to know,*
*Worthless 'facts' not education*
*Punished when we speak out loud*
*Creating a slave-nation*
*School!*

*National curriculum/National restriction*
*You can no longer use your brains*
*If you don't go along with their marking-schemes you'll never get the grade!*

*Curriculumized, bastardized*
*School bores me, it's no surprise*
*Creativity ain't worth a hill of beans*
*With government-approved marking schemes*

*We're taught only what they want us to know,*
*Worthless 'facts' not education*
*Punished when we speak out loud*
*Creating a slave-nation*
*School!*

So you can imagine the surprise from everyone who knew me when, in the Spring of 2010, a few years after completing – and doing nothing with – my PhD in Philosophy, I announced that I was thinking of becoming a teacher.

'Oh, DaN, *no*!' was my mother's actual reaction when I told her over the phone I had been accepted onto a teacher-training course. The sense of tragedy in her voice was palpable. She herself had only recently re-trained as a teacher after decades of life as a successful freelance journalist. For mom, her former career part of the collateral damage of the breakdown of her marriage, teaching had been a lifeline with which to earn a living on both sides of the ocean as she carved out a fresh existence for herself, post-divorce, with a new American husband. Mom was American herself, and had fallen in love with the romanticism of teaching adult classes on Cape Cod in the summers as my stepdad worked on the beaches of Provincetown as a lifeguard. In the winters though, back in England, no one would let her into a classroom without the proper qualifications. Thinking she was doing something which would both bring financial security and ensure long summer holidays in which she could return to the Cape, mom found any joy that teaching had once given her in the States drained away as the brutal training year in a British classroom introduced her to the previously alien systems and standards of UK schooling, so very different from the far freer American equivalent. That first year of unexpected misery, combined with early jobs in unsupportive and demanding schools, left her deeply regretting the late-life career choice she had made and, a few years later, when she got terminally ill with the cancer that would eventually kill her, she would always blame the years she spent teaching as one of the primary causes of her sickness. An unrelenting disappointment and stressor on her body which left it vulnerable to attack from within.

But that was still two years away when I called her with my 'good' news. She didn't think teaching would kill me, but she did believe teaching might take away much from my life that made it worth living.

'You'll have no time for music!' she gasped. 'Or to write. No time to be creative at all!'

It was funny, because most parents, upon hearing the news that their twenty-eight year old layabout son – a man who had, at this point, never actually held a full-time day-job, either being in full-time education and living off loans, savings, and grants, or taking time off to 'figure things out and write a novel' while living off a small inheritance from his grandmother and leftover loan and grant money from seven years at university spent without drinking alcohol – would be thanking God that he was finally growing up and taking on adult responsibilities. That's how my dad took the news. Although he was sceptical at the sudden change of heart towards schools after remembering the years he'd actively had to *bribe* me to do well at my GCSEs (one hundred pounds for every A* and fifty quid for every A) he himself had put his hand to teaching for a stint following his own PhD back in the day, and his own mother had been a very happy teacher for many years until my granddad's multiple sclerosis forced her to give up her career and become his carer. 'Sounds like a plan,' he'd ultimately said, in his understated, Northern, way. Though there was something in his voice that suggested he didn't think that plan would be long-term. I think he was glad I was finally getting around to something loosely resembling employment after my year or so as a failed novelist. Something to finally put on my CV. However, he still assumed, I'm sure, that I would eventually find something more fitting elsewhere. Dad always sort of just hoped things would work out. That was one of his many failings, and a key reason – besides his many infidelities – why his and mom's marriage didn't last. When she finally asked for a divorce after nearly thirty years of his cheating, he was genuinely surprised, despite all the times he'd broken her heart.

Mom's concerns, meanwhile, came from a place of genuine knowledge about the job and of the sort of person she knew me to be. A dreamer. A thinker. Someone a little too much like *her*. And worst of all, I knew she was right about how tough and life-consuming teaching would be, especially in the training year. My own wife had already been teaching English for three years when I decided to join her in the profession, and I had watched first-hand the late nights, stunted social life, and soul-stealing stresses of her own induction into the career. That year was probably the toughest one we'd gone through in our entire relationship, and mom's words merely echoed the truth of that experience: teaching puts everything else in your life on hold. It's hard. It's frustrating. It's thankless. Especially at the start. But I had the arrogance of thinking my prior understanding of this gave me some sort of advantage over the two of them. Both my mom and my wife had arguably gone into their training years with rose-tinted glasses about teaching, only to have those glasses stomped on by the brutal foot of reality. Not me. Unlike them, my eyes would be *wide* open. There would be no shock to *this* system because I already knew the training would be hard. I was *prepared* for it. Not only that, but unlike either of them I would be living with a fellow teacher as I became one myself, not a civilian free on evenings and weekends and wondering what had happened to the fun-loving partner they used to spend time with. My wife's first-hand understanding of what I was going through would make her far better placed to support me through it than I, in my ignorance, had ever been for her.

I also was going into teaching with a secret up my sleeve. I *still* hated school. I still thought the system was bullshit. The PhD I had completed on anarchism only hardened the embryonic, punk rock critiques of schooling I had made in my youth. The role schooling played in ideological control and oppression was part of my doctoral thesis, identified as something which needed to be overcome if we were ever to live in the anarchist society I argued as being the only legitimate system of political organisation we ever ought to accept. I would be taking everything they taught me as I trained with a pinch of salt. Running it through a well-honed anti-propaganda and anti-government bullshit detector with a mantra that would bring me solace if times ever got too tough: I could walk away from this whenever I wanted.

I suppose I should pause here and quote someone else's lyrics. Those of anarchist punk band, *Propagandhi:*

*I recognise the irony that the very system I oppose affords me the luxury of biting the hand that feeds. But that's exactly why privileged fucks like me should feel obliged to whine and kick and scream – until everyone has everything they need.*

My family wasn't rich, but they weren't poor either. It was a completely undeserved advantage of privilege that allowed me my carefree mantra as I signed up to be a teacher. I had always been comfortable, despite a lack of serious income, thanks to my parents' belief – and the belief of both sets of my grandparents – in the value of education. Although I'd been careful with their generosity and saved well, my life thus far had been heavily subsidised. My wife was also working full-time and was happy to support me while I figured out what I wanted to do with my life. More privilege. More undeserved luck. The gift I'd been given of time, and *options* of what to do with my life, is far more than many have ever received, including those wonderful people in my life who, themselves, gave me that privileged gift. I will forever be grateful for their generosity and selflessness in those years and acknowledge the envious advantage of my position was entirely thanks to their support and love. It certainly gave me an extra layer of comfort as I considered embarking on this new journey. Whereas both my wife and my mother had spent their training years with the high stakes worry of trying not to fuck up a career they really wanted, I was coming at this strange new challenge from a fortunate place of economic stability.

I hadn't avoided employment because I was work-shy or incompetent. My avoidance had been brewed out of misguided punk rock rebellion. I had been taught from an early age in the music I listened to that paid work was a scam, and jobs were exploitation. I stayed in postgraduate education because I legitimately wanted to do further philosophical research after my undergraduate studies, but I stayed also because, like an American student during the Vietnam draft, I knew it gave me justifiable deferment from throwing my life away for a cause I didn't believe in. While the money and avoidance strategies were now starting to run out, and I had conceded that I needed to do *something* to put money *into* the bank instead of merely taking money *out* (realising, finally, that those same bands who had complained about their jobs in their music could only do so because they actually *had jobs* about which to complain), I was going into teaching knowing that if it *wasn't* something I enjoyed, I could always quit and do something else to pay the bills. I wouldn't be any worse off starting again a few months down the line than I was already in terms of my limited work experience. In fact, with *something* now on my CV, even briefly, I would probably be *better* placed than I was currently with the yawning chasm of unemployment that put an immediate question mark next to my name. It wasn't like it would mess up any great career trajectory I was building. At this point, despite all the privilege that got me there, I needed to work just like anybody else. But if this first attempt at doing something didn't work out, I would simply start again and try something different. My plan was to take things term by term. Dip a toe in and see if I could then slowly cover the whole foot in the water of education. Step in up to my knees, only taking the complete plunge when I truly felt it was worth it. *Knowing* it would be difficult, *expecting* it to be time-consuming, and feeling the freedom to tap out on the whole thing at any moment if it all got too much.

I therefore felt that mom's concerns could be ignored. I had an exit strategy if everything went pear-shaped and was bizarrely excited at the prospect of becoming a teacher, despite my antipathy towards the whole business of *schools*. Although I hadn't technically held a proper job at any point in my life up until now, I *had* worked a little while at university, and the main part-time work I had done alongside sporadic admin stuff and occasional lecturing was as an undergraduate tutor for the Philosophy department, teaching first year students. When I made the decision to quit academia at the end of my PhD – the default career plan I had been reflexively following as I slowly figured out what I wanted to do with my life – it was those weekly seminars with my students that I missed most. I didn't regret the decision not to seek a job as an academic philosopher, having seen that the discipline at that time was more concerned with linguistic analysis and navel-gazing at the meaning of words than the actual conclusions of those words and putting ideas into action (a real problem if, like me, your philosophical focus was on practical politics and ethics, not merely the *language* of politics and ethics), but I did regret not being able to continue teaching philosophy to young people. As my wife came home from work each day with funny and inspiring stories about her own adventures in the classroom, it made me crave once again to have a class of my own. While I hated *school* as a child, the moment I was liberated from schools and did the rest of my learning in sixth form colleges and university, *education* came alive. Free to focus on subjects that actually interested me and finally treated like an adult, or at least as an individual, I flourished. Self-directed and no longer micro-managed, I have never doubted the power of *education*, and the pleasure of guiding people towards that discovery was something that never stopped appealing.

There was only one small problem – whereas my mother and my wife each had expertise in English, a useful subject area taught in every classroom in the country, my specialism was in *Philosophy*, a subject taught only at A-level, and only then at *some* schools. My expertise in anarchism and political teleology may have been an asset on a university course (and even then, only maybe), but it wouldn't do much good in a secondary classroom looking for outstanding GCSE and A-level results in everyday subjects.

Luckily for me, the decline in religiosity in the UK since my own school days, combined with the antiquated legal requirement that all schools in England still had to teach Religious Education, meant that, by happy coincidence, just as I was looking for a way into teaching, Religious Education departments had started to call themselves departments of Religion *and Philosophy* in a bid to attract better uptake at GCSE and A-level and more specialist teachers. The exam boards jettisoned old-fashioned analysis of scripture from the specifications, replacing it with more appealing ethical and theological exploration, and RE departments were looking for *philosophers*.

However, there still remained a hitch – I was not only an anarchist punk rocker who hated school and disagreed with much of what it stood for, I was an *atheist* anarchist punk rocker. It was one thing to return to the same institution I spent my whole childhood yearning only to escape bolstered by some idealistic belief that I could somehow transform the broken institution from within, but quite another to go there each day to teach people about a God I not only didn't believe in but felt was responsible for some very harmful things in society through the religions set up in its name. Truth be told, the entire reason I had discovered philosophy in the first place was through my friends and I being a nuisance to the Christian youth outreach programme that visited our own school each Thursday lunchtime looking for young souls to save. Their evangelical fishing nets were coming up empty, so my friends and I, noticing the smattering of Christian teachers chatting amongst themselves in a vacant classroom without any students to convert each week, started visiting the group to ask tough questions of the faithful. At some point the word 'philosophy' came up as a label for the sort of questions we were asking, and my friend noted that the local college we were all eyeing up to make our escape from our awful school had a course by the same name. I signed up to study Philosophy with the grandiose idea I would one day write a world-shaking thesis disproving the existence of God once and for all. Instead of that, within a few weeks of discovering the existence of ethics and political philosophy – philosophy about things which actually *mattered* – I abandoned all plans of wasting my time thinking about non-existent deities, stopped worrying about theology entirely, and developed a brand new obsession with anarchism. (It turned out there was a lot more to it than was suggested by Johnny Rotten's simplistic caricature). While occasionally my studies brought me back to thinkers or ideas surrounding religion over the years, and I was always fascinated by the attempts to justify belief in something so obviously false, I found most theological arguments I encountered weak and intellectually lacking. It was hard to take seriously the people who still held such beliefs the older they were, and the occasional social gathering at university would meet with great awkwardness if the topic ever came up around me. I was one of those annoying people who bought Dawkins' *The God Delusion* in hardback as soon as it came out and didn't even notice its strident tone or possibility to cause offence. One of the first songs I ever wrote had the chorus '*God is the socially acceptable imaginary friend*' and the last song I wrote about God explicitly called him a '*cunt*' at the end. A lyric I regret solely because it ruined the ongoing joke of merely *alluding* to the word at the end of each verse without actually saying it – *con*tinuation, *con*sidering, *can't*... I felt no guilt about calling God one of the most arguably offensive words in the English language – blasphemy wasn't what bothered me, nor – then – even the possible misogyny of the word. Ruining the *comedy* did. By really saying the word (not even *saying*, group-*shouting* it, repeatedly, at the climax), we killed the joke and cleverness of the writing for far less powerful shock-value that undermined the whole thing.

*Now, how can I put this without hurting your feelings?*
*I really don't want to hurt you, you know*
*But truth knows neither timing nor emotion.*
*You can go to church on Sunday, hell,*
*You can go there any damn day you want,*
*Read your bible each night, fondle your rosary...whatever.*
*You can drink holy water 'till your piss is blessed,*
*Genuflect and all your sins confess,*
*Obey the bible word for word and live your life by the*
*ten commandments,*
*And pray, pray, pray as much as you want.*
*It changes nothing.*
*Now, how can I put this to you without being so blunt?*
*The God you worship is a...*

***Con****tinuation of stale ideas.*
*Capitalism, patriarchy and fear.*
*All that talk of peace and love is just a white-wash to the truth*
*That it serves only to keep you in line,*
*for your bible swap your human rights.*
*See the trouble religion causes?*
*How can you still keep your faith?*
*Even if we accept this fiction of theism, and allow existence of God,*
*All-knowing, All-loving, All-present He cannot be, look at the evidence.*
*Your all-powerful God sits idly by*
*Just watching His children die*
*Then He blames it on our free-will which He created in the first place!*
*The God you worship is a...*

***Con****sidering his actual existence or lack there-of*
*Isn't even necessary for me to make my point*

*Because empirically...*
*The starving people starve whether God exists or not,*
*The planet is still dying and the death-rate's going up.*
*Blame humanity if you wish but surely in your myth*
*It claims God is all-knowing (that is if He does exist!)*
*So surely He knew this outcome from the start?*
*The God you worship is a...*

***Can't*** *you see real life contradicts your beliefs and definitions of the deity?*
*What all-loving God leaves us to suffer in this way?*
*And your free-will defence can't cope with natural disasters or why bad shit happens to good people.*
*Take your blinkers off for a moment and think!*
*The only coherence between reality and your faith is either most likely*
*That God just doesn't exist, or sadly if He does...*
*If He does, then, the God you worship is a...*

... Well, you all know the word we shouted next to ruin the whole thing. How could a person who had written *those* lyrics stand in a classroom and teach children with a straight face about God?

But teacher after teacher I spoke to about my concerns said that atheism was actually a strength these days in teaching RE. As an outsider, with no horse in the race, I would be unbiased and open-minded. I could teach about different religions without trying to proselytise, and obviously it would be an advantage for all the critical, philosophical stuff too. So long as I didn't make it my mission to convince students there was no God – something I never felt the need to do being as it was always, to me, so self-evident that belief in a deity was untenable and something I assumed every reasonable person would one day grow out of (like belief in Santa Claus or the Tooth Fairy) – my atheism apparently only *helped* my application. In fact, the song I worried so much about was a pretty perfect outline (albeit a very sweary one) of what the exam specifications referred to as 'the problem of evil' and demonstrated my depth of subject knowledge in the area. While the specific language used might not be appropriate for the classroom, the issue itself was standard stuff every student needed to cover in school.

The final obstacle standing in my way of becoming a teacher was that I had left it fairly late in the year to make a last-minute career choice. It was nearing the end of April when I booked a meeting with the head of academics at my wife's school to discuss what I would actually need to do if I wanted to get qualified, and his advice, though encouraging about what I might bring to the table as a teacher, was lacking in any practical next steps once it was clear there was no job for me going *there*. As I lamented that fact with my own former A-level teacher a month later, he mentioned that his daughter had trained 'with a consortium' to get her own qualification. I had no idea what that meant, but Googled it when I got home and found a 'consortium' near me. It was now late May, but I sent them an email anyway, still not really understanding what such a 'consortium' did. As it happened, they were still looking to fill a training space for a teacher of RE. The Training Manager of the consortium (what I then found out to be a collection of schools working together to train new teachers) called me to say that they would not be willing to give me a place without my having at least *some* work-experience in an actual classroom. Teaching undergraduates was all good and well, but a completely different experience from teaching a room full of *eleven*-year-olds, or thirty hormonal fifteen-year-olds. The fact that I had written a gushing application about what I thought about teaching and yet had not set foot inside a school classroom since my own schooldays was a red flag to her; most applicants for teacher training have done at least some work experience before applying, ideally in both primary *and* secondary settings so they can make an informed choice about what they are letting themselves in for.

They must have been desperate though. The consortium gave me the details of two schools I could contact directly *that day* for work experience placements where they had already greased the wheels for me in advance – one a Church of England school in Walsall and the other a local comprehensive. The consortium interviewed me on May 28th, and by the end of June I had managed about four days in the two schools before the June 28th interview at my own placement school where, having never taught a lesson before and still not quite sure that Religious Education was my calling, I was asked to teach a fifty-minute lesson on 'the value of RE in the school curriculum' to the first teenagers I had spoken to since being one myself. It must have gone OK because the school accepted me for the job, and on June 30th, the training with the consortium began.

A whirlwind.

In three months I had gone from *maybe* thinking about *possibly* exploring this as a *potential* option *perhaps*, to officially becoming a new trainee teacher for September 2010. As July whizzed by with new obligations to meet and greet people at my new place of employ – and complete the remaining days of my original work experience at the other schools – I faced the summer break with a lot to do. Namely, research everything I could about the religions I had been completely ignoring since becoming a teenage atheist. I bought a Torah, a Bible, a Qur'an, the Bhagavad Gita, some Buddhist texts, and many general books on religion, and settled in for a long summer of reading.

On August 15th, Torah, Bible, and Qur'an conquered, and mid-way through the Bhagavad Gita, my world changed forever with a single phone-call. A familiar number on the caller ID, which I didn't place at first as the landline of my childhood home, and an unfamiliar voice of a police officer asking me if I was the son of Robert Andrew McKee…

My dad had died at a conference in Sweden. The years of neglecting his health, eating too much, drinking *way* too much, and sleeping far too little as he commuted each day from Coventry to London for his job as Chief Executive of the Chartered Institute for Library and Information Professionals (CILIP), along with the stresses he was facing on the frontlines of the profession since the 2008 economic crash and battling the recent coalition government's imposition of austerity on library – and other public – services, had finally caught up with him. Heart failure at fifty-nine. Dead. Alone in a hotel room. He had died on Friday the 13th and not been found until the following morning when he missed some important meetings. It took another day for the message to get to the UK embassy, and then to the local police, who had to break into his house to find the number of his next-of-kin. With the divorce, that meant *me*, and suddenly, a few weeks before I was meant to start this demanding new career, I found myself with a funeral to plan, a body I needed to get back from Gothenburg, probate to deal with, and the emotional pain of having my father unexpectedly die (as well as having to break that news to, and be there for, my sister, my mother, and my dad's own ninety-three-year-old mother, who was still alive and wondering why her son hadn't called each night at six o'clock the way he normally did, even when he was away at a conference in another country).

A sane person would have deferred their training year. That's what my wife told me to do, my sister, my mom…it's what the consortium suggested too. Everyone would understand. The school would even hold my placement until the following September. Teaching could wait a year while I got my head and my life back together. But I am an idiot. I find it very hard to deal with suddenly changing plans. Dad had been excited about me becoming a teacher and never liked to cause a fuss. If you want an example, my gran only found out that he and my mother were divorced, and mom was now remarried, *after* dad died. This is because dad insisted we would still get together as a family to see her a few times each year. Mom and dad driving up the M6 from different homes, then parking their separate cars at the pub around the corner from gran's house and quickly debriefing each other in the car park with the latest ins and outs of each other's lives before jumping in the same car to drive the final few yards to gran's front door together and arrive as the seemingly happy couple. Gran had worked it out, of course. When she called me the day I confirmed it to her, it was to merely to corroborate what she already suspected as she updated her will – '*your mother and father, were they just separated or had they actually divorced before he died?*' Whatever the answer, she knew they weren't married, but dad had learned not to make a fuss from the master – neither mother nor son chose to shatter the illusion and disrupt the image of marital bliss with anything as shabby as the truth.

We McKees made plans and *stuck to them*, even when doing so made absolutely no sense. So I told the consortium, and the school that hired me, that I intended for nothing to change, but conceded I may need a day off here and there for minor nuisances such as his funeral.

Amazingly, they agreed. And on September 1st I attended my first INSET training day, learning the ropes of my new department and new job whilst also chasing up the repatriation of my father's body from Sweden and finalising the order of service for the church. My first full week of school I observed lessons in the day, and at night was writing my father's eulogy. It was also around this time at some point a message came through Facebook revealing to my sister and I that dad had another daughter with a random woman we didn't know about; a half-sister we didn't even know existed coming forward to add another shock to our already shaken world. I had a day off for the funeral on Thursday and was back to work again on the Friday. Ridiculous. But I was determined to stick to 'the plan'. After all, I could always walk away whenever I wanted, couldn't I? What was the harm in giving it until Christmas?

To be fair, I think I wrote a fairly good eulogy under the circumstances:

> *It is impossible to express in words here today how shocked I am to be making a eulogy to my father at just 28 years of age. We always know that one day our parents will die, but I always*

*imagined that I would be an old man myself before I had to deal with anything like this.*

*Taken in the prime of his life, just three days before his sixtieth birthday and two months before the retirement he had been looking forward to for so long, dad was not only taken long before his time, but he was taken at a time when I was only now, after twenty-eight years, really beginning to feel like I was starting to know him.*

*That may sound strange, because I knew dad all of my life, but dad and I always had a fairly complicated relationship. Growing up, he tried his best, and so did I, but we didn't exactly make it all that easy for each other. The great love of his life was football – specifically: Bury FC – and from a very early age he tried to get me to share in that passion. But while you can bring a horse to water, you can't always make it drink, and despite the many Saturdays spent at Gigg Lane and other cold and dreary club grounds around the country, watching his beloved Shakers win and lose in equal measure, there came a point in our relationship where I had to break his heart.*

*'Dad', I told him one morning, when the new application forms for our Bury season tickets came through the door. 'This year, maybe you don't get one for me...'*

*Without a shared love of football over which we could easily bond, and with dad's dedication to his work meaning that he wasn't around as much as I would have liked in those early years, from childhood until the time I went to university, dad and I did the best we could with each other, but we both knew our best was far from perfect. That's not to say he wasn't a good father – he was. When I needed someone to teach me how to ride a bike, it was dad who took me to the empty school playground and followed me around as I slipped and wobbled my way to balance.*

*When I needed encouragement – or sometimes even bribes – to do well at school, it was dad who usually gave me the stern lectures, or crisp ten pound notes, that made me do better. When I was ill, long before I'd read my first Stephen King novel, it was dad who used to bring me home piles of the teenage 'Point Horror' books that I used to love reading from Solihull library each day, and when I started up my teenage punk band, and we finally became really serious about recording something, it was dad who gave us the finances to release our first proper album, 'Shallow Permanence'.*

*But like many fathers and sons, ours was a relationship that – although warm enough – was often fraught with awkward stiffness: not quite knowing each other well enough to find more common ground for conversation than the obligatory parent/children topics of school, homework, the trouble I had been in that week, and pocket money. Specifically – how much the trouble I had been in that week would affect my pocket-money.*

*We loved each other – but it was a very British, very undemonstrative and repressed kind of love. No hugs and kisses for dad and me – just the occasional knowing high-five and well-nodded slap on the shoulder. For the most part, we just kept out of each other's way – each of us in our own respective corners of the house, tucked away behind closed doors, blaring music out loudly to ourselves as we got on with our lives: for dad, Springsteen, Bowie, or the Rolling Stones. For me Green Day, Bad Religion, and the ever-present cacophony of my own bass guitar.*

*When I got older and moved away to university though, dad's and my relationship finally began to change. Something about moving away from home and starting my own life in Cardiff allowed dad and I to forge a brand-new dynamic together as adults. As the miles meant that we now had to make a special effort to see each other, and couldn't just continue our previous laissez-faire arrangement of occasional banter at home, we both began to make much more of an effort, making the most of the sporadic moments in the year when I would venture back to Balsall Common – or he to Cardiff – and we would drink tea together and catch up. Soon, those catch-up sessions became one of the highlights of my trips home, and the more we talked, the more the conversation came easy. We would sit and talk for hours – about life, about university, about music, about politics, about libraries – and as our relationship matured into this comfortable new phase, after years of not really feeling like we had much in common, suddenly we could barely shut each other up.*

*I know that my sister felt a similar shift too when she went to university and began her own weekly catch-up sessions with dad. For whatever reason, it was like he was making up for lost time. He knew he hadn't been there for us as much as he should have been when we were growing up, and now he was making amends. Starting again and getting it right.*

*A few years ago he added a new string to his fatherly bow and began calling us too if the time between visits got too great. Long Sunday conversations that made me wonder why we hadn't done it before. And when I moved back to Birmingham in 2008, and our visits became much more frequent, those phone-calls continued anyway – excuses no longer needed: we just knew it was nice to talk.*

*After so many years of awkwardness and perfunctory parenting, over the past few years dad not only became the father I had always wanted him to be, he became a friend. But just as that friendship was really starting to blossom – just as we had finally found our groove together as father and son – it was all suddenly taken away.*

*The last conversation I had with dad was on August 1st, two weeks before he died. We were making plans for his birthday and talking about his retirement, and about how much he was looking forward to going to Sweden. Like all phone-calls with dad – as anyone who has ever spoken to him at length on his aging house-phone would know – after about ten minutes, our conversation started to be interrupted by these annoying little beeps.*

*The phone is old, and its battery is dying, but we'd all gotten used to just ignoring the beeps over the years and carrying on talking with the understanding that, at any second, our conversation could abruptly cut out mid-sentence.*

*Dad and I talked about my new job that was starting in September. We talked about the coalition government and their destruction of public services. We talked about [my sister] and how proud we both were of her dedication to becoming an actor. And we talked about the film Born on the Fourth of July, which [my wife] and I were in the process of watching when he called, and which he had randomly watched himself just the night before.*

*And then, just as always, right in the middle of the conversation, the phone suddenly went dead in my hand.*

*That day, of course, seconds later dad called me back on his mobile to say a proper goodbye. My phone rang again, he apologised for his rubbish landline, and we signed off the call with the telephone equivalent of a knowing high-five and a well-nodded slap on the shoulder.*

*Little did we know though, that, as we said goodbye, there were other beeps we were ignoring in the background. Not a broken phone battery this time, but the inaudible beeps of something wrong inside his heart. And the next time our conversation would be cut abruptly short, there would be no other line on which to say a proper goodbye, just a thousand conversations left forever uncompleted, and a million unsaid things we'd always wish that we could say.*

*Dad may not have been perfect, but he was the only dad we had. And though he was taken from us all far too early, I thank him today for all the good years that we did have together, and all that he did to make me the man I am today, and [my sister] the woman that she is. Our time together in this life may have cut out all too suddenly, but the memories that we have of him, and the way he shaped our lives, will live on in us both forever.*

*I don't think I said it enough to dad when he was alive. Then again, I don't think I needed to: it was so obvious that it didn't need speaking out loud. But now the time for knowing high-fives and well-nodded shoulder slaps is over, and there's no other way I can say it. I love you Dad. You will be sorely missed, and I can't believe you're gone.*

Somehow, barely, I survived that first term. Learning the basics of how to put together a lesson, get a class to listen to you, craft and understand meaningful assessments, get to know your students, remember names, help out a trip or two, all while adjusting to life without my father, taking on the responsibility of looking after my gran a hundred miles away in Manchester, figuring out how to deal with lawyers and estates, packing up our old family home and getting it ready for sale, taking DNA tests to see if this random person contacting us on Facebook actually was our sister (she was – we met her once for pizza, gave her some of dad's money, and never saw her again), and seeing greed and lingering heartache add further strain to my always troubled relationship with my mother as her fury at discovering dad had not left her what she believed to be her 'fair share' of his death-in-service benefits soured her feelings towards the children (us, and the secret sister) who got what she felt should be hers.

I almost tapped-out at the halfway point. I remember October half term, flying to New Jersey in the United States to see an old friend from university get married and realising the book I read on the plane,

*The Girl with the Dragon Tattoo,* was the first thing I'd had time to read simply for pleasure since becoming a teacher. Two nights spent in New York after was the first time I felt I'd felt human in months. No books to mark, no trainee assignments to finish, no lawyers to talk to or dad-stuff to deal with – just me, my wife, and the forty-eight hours of completely free time even made the crushing jet-lag worth it as we zombie-shuffled back to work the following Monday. The break reminded me of everything life used to be before teaching and made the thought of quitting tempting, but it was also the recharge I needed to make it through the few more weeks until Christmas.

Christmas, though, I was ready to quit. Even if I'd been learning the job at the best school in the country it would have all been too much, but this school I had landed in was far from the best school in the country, despite the stamp of 'outstanding' from Ofsted. Like I said, the anarchist in me was always going to take my training with a pinch of salt, and that included arbitrary deference to the questionable judgments of a problematic inspection regiment, around which my entire training programme seemed based. Besides the logical problems of an entire profession making 'outstanding' the expected norm (and thus negating the entire notion of 'outstanding'), if *this* school was 'outstanding' then I could see that something was deeply flawed with the measurement. The shouting teachers barking orders at students; the silly rules that had little to do with education and everything to do with control; the classes all set into ability groups which limited the opportunities of those in the lower sets by assuming their failure before the students even had the chance to prove them wrong. They might have ticked the right boxes for an inspector once upon a time, but combined with a generally unsupportive environment in which to learn how to teach RE and Philosophy (there was no sixth form, so no A-level teaching at all, and my so-called 'mentor' was not a subject-specialist and held only rushed, very public, meetings with me on the edge of her desk in the middle of the History lessons she prioritised; their purpose seeming only to be to remind me to lower my expectations of what I thought my students could do), I was disappointed daily at such an impoverished idea of what education could be. I was proud I had made it to Christmas, but part of the relief of the December holidays was knowing that the first day back at the consortium training sessions in January I planned to quit and never have to do any of this shit again.

On my particular training course, however, you got sent to a different placement school the first few weeks of the new year to give you a taste of a dissimilar educational context. My first day there, at a selective girls' grammar school, would be a Monday, the day before my planned resignation at the consortium during our weekly Tuesday training sessions. That was fine. I decided I could spend one more Monday in a school before breaking free on Tuesday morning. What could it hurt to wait twenty-four hours?

Within thirty seconds of walking through the doors of my second placement, however, I realised something profound: it wasn't *teaching* that I was hating, but merely the *school* in which I had been teaching. This new place was a completely different world from the other – friendly staff and happy students, an assumption of success for all and ambition that every student would do well in life instead of separating some into groups destined only for failure. My first lesson I watched was a Year 7 session about the crucifixion of Jesus. I had to swallow back a laugh as I saw the teacher use words like 'salvation', 'atonement', and 'reconciliation' with her eager eleven-year-olds. Words I had just a few weeks before been actively *told off* for using with my more advanced GCSE class at the other school because such words were, according to my mentor, 'beyond their vocabulary' and 'not necessary for the exam'.

The next day, rather than quitting teaching, instead I quit that first school and asked for asylum in the second. On our induction day at the consortium the previous July, our Training Manager had told us there was a box of tissues in her office and, at some point over the next year, each of us would need it. I had scoffed at the idea, especially as the weeks went by in the wake of my father's passing and, even then, my eyes stayed dry. But that Tuesday morning in January, a third of the way into my first year of teaching, telling her how I had felt over Christmas and what I had planned on saying today before seeing the difference between the two schools, I felt my chin start to wobble, my voice grow thin, and suddenly found myself reaching out for those foreshadowed tissues.

Arrangements were made and I was able to stay there. The new school was a much better fit, and I finally found myself being able to teach *Philosophy* as well as RE. The dad stuff was still there in the background, but even that was made easier by feeling happier about the teaching side of things. The February half term, knowing I would not be returning to my previous placement, was the first school holiday I enjoyed without a growing dread of how quickly it was passing; I was even excited about what the next six weeks would bring. Drawing on that bit of my dad that always assumed everything would somehow work out, just as this new school had saved me from my first placement, I fantasized about never having to leave it. Maybe they would like me so much they would just give me a job in September and I'd be set for life, without even having to do interviews?

I admit: that it was a *grammar school* did clash with my political sensibilities. Having gone to a comprehensive school myself as a child and done OK, I had all the usual leftist qualms with systems of selection which cherry-pick the best and brightest from the primary schools in an area and take them out of the comprehensive cohorts, creating a two-tier system of education. However, I am also a realist. While the social-mission of the comprehensive school is ostensibly worthy – an education for all – (though even that is not without its concerns if, as the anarchist in me suggests, the education on offer is more of a process of accreditation and indoctrination into a questionable state-system than a real attempt to meaningfully educate), if I were honest with myself I had never claimed to be getting into education for the pure social-mission of helping children. Of course, you can't be a teacher without wanting to help children, but I wanted to help children only in one very specific way: by teaching them Philosophy. While some teachers may feel their subject knowledge is merely the McGuffin which allows them access to the classroom where they can act as parent, friend, and social worker to a group of young people in need of their care, others, like me, really are in love with our fields of knowledge and want to teach only for the intrinsic value of passing on a love of our subjects. There are comprehensive schools where you can do that too; I had visited several during my training and knew people who had worked in places like that. The only difference between my first placement school and the second was the *attitude* of teachers and students, not the selection process (although the selection process certainly helped bolster the attitude). *Because* it was a grammar school, the assumption was of success, whereas the particular comprehensive school in which I served my first placement lacked the self-confidence to share in that assumption. Not all do, and many comprehensive schools share that same self-belief my second placement did. Politically, I agree that grammar schools should not exist – especially *single-sex* grammar schools, which were a ridiculous anachronism in contemporary society even before gender fluidity became mainstream enough to make a mockery of their commitment to that easily rejected binary – and that fee-paying independent schools should exist even less. However, as an anarchist who does not live in an anarchy, I am used to the ideal of what *ought* to be falling far short of what *is* and the pragmatic need for ideological compromise in much of my life. The grammar school system remains inherently flawed, but it was the educational system into which I was thrust by my training consortium, and my experience in doing so was that the grammar school environment I had found myself working in was allowing me to focus on the thing I actually wanted to focus on – *Philosophy* – and treated the students there with the respect they deserved in a way that the comprehensive school I had worked in had not. While not an inevitability or truism, personally I didn't have the motivation or ambition to change course, become a Headteacher, and campaign to run my own comprehensive school one day where we could do things as they ought to be done (because then I would be a manager, not a teacher, and what I wanted to do was *teach*). Though not ideal, the easiest way to find job satisfaction in a world where every job is a form of alienating exploitation and life was too short, I decided, was to find a school – any school – which would allow me to do what I loved, even if it was a grammar school. Ignoring their ideological role in creating a compliant workforce, many comprehensive schools were comprehensive only on paper, with elaborate setting systems that segregated students into different streams of potential achievement within the same four walls. Many comprehensive schools were also now becoming part-privatised as business-sponsored academies with their own competing agendas beyond the idea of universal education. Others were off-rolling difficult students to make their numbers look good in league tables and equally undermining the ethos of education for all. I was not prepared to be a martyr for comprehensive education when I could see that, in the problematic UK education system, it wasn't that simple anyway. I had to make my peace with the fact that twelve weeks in a bad school had nearly killed me mentally, and just one single day in a good one had brought me back to life. It didn't matter if the place was comprehensive, grammar, or independent – I could campaign for a better world in my free-time, one where all schools were equally fantastic, but in my working hours, if I was going to sell my soul to pay the bills, I had to do it somewhere where I could stay sane and feel fulfilled.

Unfortunately, while most schools who took on trainees did so precisely *because* they had a job they needed to fill and wanted the opportunity to train someone up to do it, this school I was now at had not asked for a trainee. I had been allowed to stay there longer than the initial five-week placement, remember, merely as an act of mercy. While I watched my initial placement school put a job ad in the Times Educational Supplement for the role they had probably hoped I would eventually be filling, no one at this lovely new placement was thinking of leaving anytime soon and once my training year was up, my services would no longer be required. I would have to look for my first job as a newly qualified teacher somewhere else.

That was if I even wanted to *be* a teacher. Because I still wasn't sure. This new school was better than the first, but there were still aspects of the job that bothered me. As well as the unease about the inherent inequality of it being a grammar school, there was the po-faced formality of all schools. The endless stupid rules. The over-emphasis on exams and teaching students how to jump through the hoops of arbitrary mark-schemes and success criteria instead of learning for learning's sake. The forced competitiveness and entrenched lionisation of the individual over the success of all. And I still hadn't sold my dad's house. Gran was getting frailer too – we'd organised her some homecare and *Meals on Wheels*, but the first murmurings about her maybe preferring to move into a care-home were beginning to emerge when I asked her how she was doing on one of our regular (but not regular enough) phone calls. I still wasn't talking to my mom either (oh, and she had been *right* – since becoming a teacher I *didn't* have time to write, to play music, to do much of anything except the grinding business of *teaching*). And did I mention that my wife and I had decided to add moving house to our list of things to do? Still traumatised by my experience at my first placement, as my fellow trainees began applying for – and getting – their new jobs for September, I decided I would only apply for a job that felt right; a school that was the right fit, or a job I felt would give me the time I needed to sort out all the chaos in my life.

I therefore only applied for two jobs. I didn't get the first, at a comprehensive school in walking distance from our new house, and the second came up so late – at the end of May – that I had already made peace with the fact I wouldn't be teaching in the 2011/2012 academic cycle. It was only part-time, but it was in a school – another grammar school unfortunately; this time for boys – which I had been intrigued about since I started my training year. It was the school the only other RE trainee on my course was placed at, and about which she complained every time we got together. 'They teach too much

*Philosophy* there!' she'd sniff, as if it were a swear-word. 'I mean who teaches things like Kantian ethics and utilitarianism to *thirteen-year-olds?*' Me, I hoped. But like I said, schools tend to take on trainees to groom them for a particular job. If the amazing philosophy-heavy school who taught high-level, non-religious, ethical theories to their key-stage-three students had a job going next academic year, first dibs would obviously go to their trainee.

Except, she didn't want it.

Which is why they advertised it in the first place.

Whereas I got into teaching RE for the *Philosophy*, she got into it (far more sensibly) for the *religion* side of things, and she wanted a job somewhere where there was more focus on that aspect of RE. So I applied, and I got it. Part-time, starting in September. Days off each week to maybe start writing another novel, pick up the guitar again, or just deal with the ongoing dad stuff, or gran stuff, or secret-sister stuff, or mom-stuff, or any other *stuff* which might come up. Days in which I could catch my breath before returning to the classroom. And if it didn't work out, well, it was only part-time.

I said yes and decided I would give it until Christmas...

Today, I am writing this first chapter of what I hope to be part memoir, part useful guide for teachers and other educators, and part polemic about education, and I'm a few weeks away from the end of my eleventh year at the same place. My thirty-third term here. Eleven Christmases have passed and, somehow, I went from being the oppositional outsider not even convinced I wanted the job, to becoming part of the school's furniture. The part-time gig quickly became full-time when my Head of Department got promoted to Deputy Headteacher at the end of my first year and I found myself becoming her replacement as Head of Department. However, as I write this, it is also my *last* term at the school and, perhaps, even in teaching.

I have seen – and thought – a lot during my career of over a decade and have decided I need some time to reflect and review.

The day I went for my interview at that first placement school at the start of this journey I observed a lesson about euthanasia and religious ethics. The teacher wrote the day's date on the board as I sat at the back of the room, taking notes, followed by the lesson's title for students to jot down in their books. Not really knowing what I was looking for yet when observing a lesson, I just aimlessly copied what she had written into my notepad: *June 28th. The End of Life.* That whole first year of teaching the phrase haunted me as I said goodbye to my former ambitions of being an epoch-shattering anarchist philosopher, a professional punk rocker, or a successful novelist, and found myself settling for the far more pedestrian life of merely being a teacher. My dad was dead, there was no longer any time to do any of the things that I loved; *The End of Life* seemed about right.

Today, all these years later, I'm still here and it is June 28th again. As a philosopher, I believe very strongly in Socrates' reported claim that the unexamined life is not worth living and I think the role of school in all of our lives is a fascinating one. It is a place we all go to, in one way or another, and which shapes us all in so many ways – for good and for bad – and yet as students we have no say at all in the kind of institution it is or education it provides us; as parents we get only the illusion of choice along some fairly limited parameters, based on fairly flimsy knowledge and hearsay, about the kind of place we will send our children to be inevitably shaped and moulded far beyond our own meagre influence; and as teachers we find ourselves bound by professional codes and obligations to conform to norms and circumstances we often know are damaging at worse or, at best, inadequate for the task of true *education*. Schools, by their nature, are inherently political establishments which, despite our purported democracy, usually leave those actually entangled with them powerless to meaningfully transform them. We are either a school's students, and the school protects itself with its inbuilt authoritarianism and hierarchy, decrying any critique as insolence; the parents of students at a school, where school protects itself with esoteric systems and procedural mysteries which leave us reliant on interpretation and translators of policy (always with the underlying threat that we could send our children elsewhere if we have a serious problem with the way things are being done and, if we rock the boat too much, the knowledge that it may be our child's future we are putting in jeopardy with our concerns); or we are a school's staff, beholden to the protocols and directions of the Department for Education and the managerial accountability-measures our leadership teams are burdened with which create hierarchies of cowardice, blame, and fear for those who ask too many questions.

But schools are also where we learn important lessons. Not just the obvious subjects within the curriculums taught, although there can be some value there too, but lessons about friendship, equality and its lack, how and when to break the rules, the fragility and fiction of authority, and who you are as a person. Schools shape us and schools scar us, and for those of us privileged (or foolish) enough to have been shaped and scarred on each side of the classroom – both as student and as teacher – there is a lot to think about – to *examine* – and in this book I hope to do just that. We teachers love a good self-assessment. Written targets about what we did well and what could have gone better. Performance-management; mini plenaries; end of year reports. After so many years at what people bizarrely still call 'the chalkface' despite the long-time absence of both blackboards and chalk, I decided it was finally time to pause for breath. I handed in my notice in January, the next month will be my last one here, and I haven't got another job lined up. I have no idea what will come next.

Maybe this project will become the book I want it to be and maybe it won't? There's a lot to say and yet also that nagging concern any writer has when writing about their own small life that maybe none of this will be interesting or worthwhile to anyone who isn't *me*? We all have our feelings about schools and our own experiences and mine is just one story amongst many.

But I do think I have something worth saying and a unique perspective to share. It's June 28th again, twelve years later, and *The End of Life* is once again looming as my resignation becomes real once we break up for the summer. I still have not decided if I want to carry on as a teacher or become just another statistic to add to the one-in-three teachers currently considering leaving the profession at any given time in this country. But I do know that writing about things has always been the way I've helped organise my thoughts and make big decisions. I also know that whatever the posterity of this project, histories are important. Personal histories especially. And histories of dissent even more so. Putting my thoughts and memories down on paper, therefore, just seems right. If one-in-three teachers are thinking about quitting, maybe this might shine a light on why? So I'll dip a toe in. See what comes from it. Write a chapter or two. See if this thing goes anywhere interesting. After all, if it doesn't, I can always quit and do something else.

I think I'll give it until Christmas...

## INTERLUDE – PHILOSOPHY UNLEASHED POST - 02/12/19:

*Philosophy Unleashed is a free weekly philosophy blog and teaching resource I have been writing since 2019. Between each chapter of this memoir I have decided to share a relevant post from it to give further insight into my thinking at a particular time (although sometimes the role of Philosophy Unleashed is to play devil's advocate with my own thoughts).*

### BREAKING THE CODE OF POLITICAL SILENCE - On Why Teachers Ought To Share Their Political Beliefs With Their Students

Elections are a strange time to be a teacher. The most significant political event in the country is happening all around us, dominating the headlines of every news outlet and the conversations of most staff-rooms and, understandably, students are curious to know our thoughts.

"Sir," they ask me, "who are you going to vote for?"

The same way they always ask me, as an RE teacher, what my religious beliefs are. Or as their Philosophy teacher which theory of mind I think is the best. In those other situations I am happy to tell them my views. If I am asking them to share their religious beliefs with their class and myself each RE lesson, the least I can do is do the same when asked by them. If I am asking them to evaluate the ideas we are discussing in philosophy classes, it makes sense they will want to see me doing the same thing.

Yet, for some reason, we teachers are not supposed to make our political beliefs overtly known to our students. The argument goes something like this:

1) Being a teacher puts you in a position of authority: students *listen* to what you have to say. In most classroom cases, students not only listen, but *follow* your advice, as you are the perceived authority on the issue.

2) If a teacher, therefore, shared their political allegiances with their students, they would have undue influence on that student's political thinking. A teacher telling their classes they support Party X, for example, has the potential to indoctrinate their students into similar support.

3) Therefore a teacher should not tell their students who they are voting for in an election.

Personally I take great issue with this idea. Because,

4) Teachers have a duty to not only teach their subject content to their students, but to socialise them and facilitate their growth into productive and contributing members of society.

As a result, I would argue,

5) In a democracy it is vital that the citizens of a democratic country are politically engaged, not only with those who share their own beliefs, but with *all* political views so that a truly informed choice is made at the ballot.

Therefore it is my contention that,

> 6) A teacher therefore has a duty to model democratic engagement to their students. A teacher *not* discussing an upcoming election or *not* having an opinion on the current political situation sends a negative message to their students that political engagement is not important.

And that, furthermore,

> 7) The more students hear their different teachers' differing views on the political issues of the day the more likelihood there is of them *not* being indoctrinated by any one view and being forced to make up their own minds from the range of views they encounter.

And if it happens to be the case that, uniformly, every teacher in the school shares the exact same view of the upcoming election (not that this has ever actually happened in any school I have worked at), then that perhaps sends an important message to the students. Either:

> 8a) If every teacher shared the exact same view regarding who to vote for then it is highly suggestive, given their levels of education, that perhaps there is only one worthwhile candidate to vote for and the pupils are therefore being correctly socialised.

or

> 8b) If every teacher shared the exact same view regarding who to vote for then it is highly suggestive some sort of deep bias in that

particular school community, or educational class, which in turn educates the students that certain economic or social groups tends to vote similarly, independent of objective facts. Another important lesson for them to learn.

Meaning:

9) Even if 8a or 8b occurs (a very unlikely and rare scenario anyway) there is still important educational value in sharing voting intentions with students.

We are encouraged in many other branches of PSHE and school life to share real life experience with our students and be role models. It is also one of the teacher standards all British teachers are supposed to abide by, in the "personal and professional conduct" section (the same section where this resistance to sharing such things with students actually comes from when it reminds us to ensure "personal beliefs are not expressed in ways which exploit pupils' vulnerability"), to uphold the "fundamental British value" of "democracy".

I do not believe my sharing my personal voting intention with my students exploits their vulnerability any more than their parents or carers equally sharing such intentions with them. Or the many *friends* of the family who pass through their home and pass comment on the politics of the day. I think it is vital in a functioning democracy that open political discourse takes place all over the place, and believe that teachers are well placed to model such discourse to their pupils and start them on their own political journeys. I absolutely do not think a teacher should say something like "you ought to vote for X or else" or "intelligent people vote Y not Z", but I do think a teacher sharing their own reasons for voting and who they will be voting for - and listening, in turn, to the scrutiny of their students - would have the following impact on society:

i) A politically engaged youth, entering voting age with experience of political campaigns and political discourse.

ii) The normalisation of political conversation and openness of discussion regarding political differences of opinion, leading to discourse instead of division as the way of solving dispute.

iii) The possibility of adult voters (teachers) hearing from those disenfranchised members of our society unable to vote but still affected by the outcome of elections (students), and therefore being influenced to vote with their interests in mind as well as their own.

iv) An expectation of teachers of the next generation to be politically engaged citizens who can model and pass on what it means to be a good citizen to their students. (If your students ask you who you are voting for and your ideas aren't really informed or defendable it would be fairly embarrassing!) This means our teachers modelling political engagement and good citizenry would be the best models.

Leading to my conclusion,

10) As outcomes i-iv are all desirable in a functioning democracy which truly cares about ensuring the continuing function of that

democracy, I believe it should be part of a teacher's job to share their personal voting intentions with their students and discuss, openly, what each election means to them, so that students get to hear from a cross section of society (their teachers, parents, family and friends) and make up their own minds in readiness for the day they turn eighteen and the vote becomes theirs to use.

## 2.
## *Wrestling with the Basics*

When you are a student, the person at the front of the classroom seems like they have all the answers. But it was only once I became a teacher that I realised this was true only in the same way it might be considered impressive to hit a bullseye with a dart you have thrown first, and only drawn the target around afterwards. When you can retroactively position a dart that lands anywhere as being dead in the centre, you create the illusion that your aim is true. Teachers generate the same illusion. By setting their questions carefully, they can appear to know far more than they actually do. It can seem amazing to a class how easily certain names and concepts fall from your lips because, to them, these names and concepts are something so difficult to grasp. Difficult yet vital: the keys to accessing much-vaunted qualifications which depend entirely on their ability to memorise these names and concepts and regurgitating them under restrictive exam conditions. Only you, their teacher, will know that the information you shared was first learned by you only the night before. And, in many cases, that it is largely worthless. Perhaps debunked by something better which came along later but is omitted from the syllabus? Or perhaps it covers only a lesser figure in your subject-area because those more accomplished in the field – or those non-white and non-male voices which have been historically marginalised and therefore not been taught to the people determining the specification content – have ideas too difficult to condense simply enough for a seventeen-year-old to understand? Teaching is in many ways a *performance*, and a significant part of that performance is about gaining the trust of your students to feel that it is worth giving you their time and attention for an hour. For some teachers, that trust is gained through projecting an illusion of omniscience, using knowledge as a sort of a con. Something to pull the wool over their students' eyes.

In my first weeks of teacher training, worried I had to be an expert in everything I was teaching and fearing the killer question from one of my students which would expose me as the fraud I felt I really was, I remember the disappointment I felt, rather than comfort, when the Head of Department I was working for assured me my fears were unfounded.

'As long as you're a chapter ahead of them in the textbook you'll be fine.'

It was like having the curtain pulled back on a magician's trick and discovering the trapdoor which enabled the deception.

'Sometimes,' she continued, only making it worse, 'when I haven't had time to plan, especially in a subject I don't know a lot about, I get the kids to do all the work for me. I set them the thing I don't know as a "research task" and get them to teach each other. As they do that, I can learn along with the class.'

'But what if they get it wrong?' I asked. 'How would you ever know?'

'You Google it while they're working. Then check properly if you have time before their next lesson. You can always pretend you planned it all along if you find out they got it wrong. Start the next class by saying you were disappointed no one spotted each other's mistakes and that you had given them *the whole lesson to do it* so everyone had the opportunity to correct it. Now it's *their* fault, not yours, that they got it wrong. Even better, set the research for homework so you have time to check *before* they feed back.'

Overburdened with everything else going on in my life and the demands of the training in those first few months, I have to admit I tried this approach a few times and, sadly, she was right. I had no idea what I was talking about as I confidently asked my students to do my work for me, or I spoke like an expert on something I had only just learnt myself the night before, and somehow I got to the end of the lesson with my pupils none the wiser that I was completely winging it. However, I hated the feeling of tricking them. I felt it was sloppy.

And just a few months in, something happened which made me decide such lazy short-cuts were no longer acceptable.

We were teaching one of the younger years – Year 7 or 8 I think – about religion and the environment, and I was assigned a lesson on someone called Chief Seattle. Not being an expert in religion yet, I responded the way I did to all those early lessons I was asked to takeover: accepting on face value that the things in the scheme-of-work must make sense and be, in some way, acceptable 'canon' for the topics being taught. I had never heard of Chief Seattle, but as an American citizen whose hippy mother had held a lifelong fascination with all things Native American, I knew a little bit about Native American spiritual practices and could see their great relevance to thinking about the environment. (The night my mom decided it was finally time to leave my dad, she did so after a sort of vision-quest downstairs alone in our lounge, banging what she called her 'moondancer' drum, given to her in her journalism days while interviewing an indigenous tribe, howling at the night sky along to the rhythm until clarity came.) I also remembered the small section we had studied on Native American religion during my own GCSE History lessons on American expansion. I knew they centred around the earth and nature and that most indigenous Americans believed we shouldn't monetise and haemorrhage resources from this thing which wasn't ours. I remembered how even when they killed an animal, they ensured they used every part of it to try and guarantee the life they had ended was not wasted. I knew a few things but had never studied the main resource for the planned lesson before – Chief Seattle's letter – so I did my due diligence.

It appears no one at the school, who had been teaching this lesson for years, ever had.

The next day I met with the Head of Department.

'You know that Chief Seattle speech you want me to teach actually comes from a Hollywood screenwriter? It's not the real words of a

Native American at all. Do you want me to find something better?' I asked.

She looked at me with pity, and the slight suggestion I was being a nuisance.

'Does it really matter?' She responded curtly. 'It still makes the right point.'

I was shocked. Of course it mattered. We were supposed to be *educators*, allegedly dealing in *knowledge* and *facts*. It was we who were supposed to be teaching our students about how to discern good sources from bad when researching. One of my major motivations for entering the profession had been seeing the poor level of critical discourse in the country during the 2010 General Election and thinking something must be done to combat the deluge of false but appealing soundbites that took the place of meaningful political debate. All of us, adults and children alike, needed to be taught how to go beyond superficial slogans and sort fact from fiction, and yet here we were knowingly attributing words to a historical figure who did not say them. Wasn't she *concerned*?

At the same time, we were the *Religious Education* department. In a way, questionable historical attribution was our bread and butter. I almost would have respected her attitude if the next thing she had said to me was: 'news flash – Jesus Christ might not actually have said any of those things in the Bible either.' But she didn't say that. She just said: 'don't overthink it. It's a good lesson.'

I wasn't happy, so I sought a second opinion. The class-teacher whose lesson I would be taking over had a free period and I asked her if she was aware of the fact the Chief Seattle speech she'd asked me to teach was bogus? Shrugging her shoulders, she simply paraphrased Peter Venkman from my favourite film, *Ghostbusters*: 'well…the kids love it.'

The good thing about being an anarchist is we don't take well to authority figures, especially when we can see that what they are asking us to do is wrong. So the next day I went rogue. I taught the lesson as they wanted, but told the students that the resource was questionable and not to be considered historically accurate. I supplemented the speech with some actual Native American environmental thought and realised that although we teachers *could* get away with gaps in our knowledge and tricks, I no longer thought that we *should.* I had been told that one good way of dealing with the feared moment a question might come from our students which exposed a lack of knowledge was to put the onus back onto *them*: 'great question – can anyone here answer it?' And if not, add it to their homework. 'First right answer next lesson gets a merit.' But I realised there was another thing you could do too: be *honest.* Be *authentic.* 'That's a great question,' you could say, 'and I don't actually know the answer. I'll look into it and get back to you... unless anyone else in the class knows?' After all, every teacher wants their students to know that learning doesn't end the day they leave school. We should *always* keep learning. Showing that even you, the teacher, have a lot more to learn, and are willing to do so, is the best way of demonstrating that message that I can think of.

As a trainee teacher though, it is hard to overcome the ego when you're afraid of not being taken seriously by students already looking to test you. If the teacher is supposed to have all the answers, admitting you don't is a pretty scary step. And this fear is especially heightened if, like me, you are knowingly walking into the classroom to teach something unfamiliar. My grandfather had been a Methodist minister, so I grew up with a basic understanding of Christianity, and my mother's side of the family was Jewish – making me technically Jewish myself – but that family background was also the soil in which my atheism took root. The holocaust loomed large for my Jewish grandmother, who proudly told us about how grandad – a talent-agent for classical musicians and opera singers – wouldn't represent any male German who had served during the war (because 'if your side had won I'd be a lampshade by now') and how he once caught pneumonia walking across Manhattan in the rain because he refused to take a lift in a friend's German-made Volkswagen. She told the stories proudly, despite their suggesting to me merely a lingering xenophobia and stubbornness that was less than laudable. But my granddad was unable to defend his actions himself because he was dead long before I was born. Cancer. Meanwhile, on my dad's side, his father, the Methodist minister, wasn't dead as I grew up, but was suffering from multiple sclerosis, a disease which had brought his preaching career to an end. Not only was I raised in this two-religion household with the concept of religion shown demonstrably to be something non-absolute – a *choice* one could make (Jewish or Christian) rather than a truism set in stone – but I was shown that the reward for staunch faith in the divine seemed to be either suffering or death. The devout were afflicted with pain in return for their devotion, shown most starkly in the six million 'chosen people' God let die in concentration camps during World War II. The less I knew, therefore, the better. Until suddenly I was told to stand in front of a group of children and pretend I was an expert on the very subject I had been ignoring the details of for my entire life.

So I balanced out the honesty of admitting I didn't know a lot with the tough work which meant such honesty wouldn't be a frequent issue. I committed myself to further learning so that, rather than having to admit to my ignorance about a religion, or use cheap tricks to hide it, I simply *wouldn't be* so ignorant anymore. If I wanted to stand in front of a class and ask students to listen to what I had to say, I ought to *deserve* my spot at the front of the room. I didn't need to be an expert in everything there was to know about faith, but if I was teaching a lesson on something specific, I decided I should at least be an expert on *that*.

Being honest and authentic with your students, not only about your strengths but also about your weaknesses, is, in my opinion, one of the most transformative things a teacher can do in the classroom in terms of building relationships. Over the years I have seen new colleagues come and go from the profession, citing classroom management as the issue – they just couldn't get the students to *listen*. Talk to the students about those same teachers though and the reviews are always honest and brutal: 'I didn't feel their lessons, sir', 'their lessons were dead', and, most damningly, 'they didn't care – why should we?' A bit more digging and what this means becomes all too clear: the person standing before them was just an empty placeholder for the word 'teacher', not an actual person they could see any reason to give their attention to. There needs to be give and take in the relationship. Too many teachers merely come to take, expecting a respect they do nothing to earn.

Personally, I'm not a great fan of what Paulo Freire calls the 'banking' concept of education anyway – the idea that a teacher is merely there to transmit the knowledge they have into the minds of their students. I believe in something more Socratic: students using tools from a teacher to discover the answers for themselves. But I can't get students to do that if I can't get students to listen to my instructions, advice, or feedback. Like any performance, without that relationship with your audience, the performance of a teacher is doomed to fail. And let's be clear: to be honest and authentic with students is not to ignore the important performative aspects of teaching. Sometimes agreeing to a shared illusion remains crucial. A class might *like* you, *respect* you even for your honest and authentic approach…but that doesn't mean that they will *listen* to you. It is just as common to hear a student say of a colleague that 'they really love their subject, but they just can't *teach* it', or 'they're a nice person, but they can't control a class', as it is for them to rave about the lessons they enjoy.

I remember understanding the performative nature of teaching in an early training session. We were shown a new technique the trainer called 'odd socks'. On each desk was a small card. On one side of the card was a picture of a sock. On the other was a piece of information related to the topic we were learning that day (different activities for ‘engaging learners’). Each ‘sock’ had a corresponding pair somewhere in the room. A card with identical information. It was our job to find the matching pair to the odd sock we’d been given. The process of finding our other sock meant talking to a bunch of people first to see what was written on the back of their card, sharing nuggets of new information as we searched. Then, once paired up, we now not only had a partner to work with for the next task, but that partner would have heard *different* information on their way to finding us so we could share *all* the new stuff we had learned beyond the singular bit of writing on our own matching individual cards.

‘Oh,’ I said after running around the room franticly with my fellow trainees looking for my pair and sharing dry details about pedagogy with something akin to excitement as I did. ‘I get it. It’s about creating the *illusion* of fun.’

‘That’s right,’ said our trainer, ‘although I wouldn’t quite put it like that. Hopefully the activity really *is* fun. But if it’s not, the illusion of fun is sufficient to get the class engaged in doing it.’

I still use that stupid odd socks activity in the classroom to this day because the illusion works. The first time I tried it on a Year 8 class learning about Bar and Bat Mitzvahs in Judaism, I did so cynically, rolling my eyes as I prepared the cards and expecting the whole thing to be a waste of time. But I sold the task as fun to them, and they bought into it wholeheartedly. In fact, if I had been honest and authentic here, telling them that I was just using these silly props to get them to do some reading they wouldn’t do if I just gave them a handout with the same information on it, the activity would have been a disaster. The pretence of fun, the *illusion*, was important.

Luckily for me, I have been a fan of the ultimate spectacle of illusion since the age of ten: professional wrestling. Say what you will about the cartoonish antics of grown men and women pretending to hit each other in a square that pretends to be a circle (a ring) – and about the baked-in exploitation and questionable politics of the entire industry – but what wrestling really is all about is *character*. Getting your character *over* with the fans. Good guy or bad guy, the art of wrestling is not just the art of making cooperative athletics look like a competitive fight, it is about being able to tell a story simply through mannerism, action, or tone of voice. A simple hand-gesture; a raised eyebrow; a stomp of a foot. And as a fan of the pseudo-sport, I have read many books and interviews on wrestling and learned how, in so many cases, the person in the ring usually started with some personal deficit – something they struggled with or couldn't do – and turned it into an asset by simply fabricating the reality that they *could*. The shy introvert becoming an arrogant camera hog, the quiet mathematician a feared brute, the bookish loner a flamboyant entertainer, the girl who was bullied at school becoming the bully herself… Or, in other cases, the illusion was a matter of what legendary wrestler, Dwayne 'The Rock' Johnson, once called 'turning up the volume' on your existing characteristics or interests. The person who talks a little too much sometimes becoming an overbearing loudmouth, the comic book fan becoming a real-life superhero, the horror movie afficionado becoming something from one of their nightmares, the real-life boss becoming a fictional tyrant… Wrestling is all about *selling* something, whether it be an emotion, another match, a big event, or a sponsor's product. Every match or TV segment has its purpose, and if you know what it is then your job is not only to get your character over, but whatever idea you were selling over to an audience too.

Wrestling is not widely respected as an artform, but when you consider that there are really only a finite number of wrestling moves you can ever do, and that the basic setup of two or more people having some sort of conflict and wanting a fight to settle it is all there is for the business to go on, that this artform has been with us for so long, and generates so many hours of new television content each week, means it really should be. We've seen this dance before, week after week, and yet they still make us believe we're seeing something different each time. If there was a single thing outside of teaching which I attribute to my success in the classroom, it would be my understanding of what wrestlers call 'ring psychology'. How to get the crowd to understand what you want from them and take them on a journey from whatever is going on in their lives that day to the emotional destination you need to get them to without them realising, or at least without them being *bothered by the fact,* they are being manipulated. Subtle turns of phrase that can make an audience boo or cheer, or both depending on your needs; a nuanced understanding of when maintaining the illusion of 'reality' was crucial to enjoying the match, and when the fourth-wall and conceit could be dropped and the intelligence of the audience respected without the whole construct falling down. Getting an audience to trust you enough to *willingly* and *knowingly* allow you to manipulate them in that way because they know there will be a pay off in the end.

That's really important. Only the most naïve wrestling fan watches the show believing that it is real. The majority of fans either in the arena or watching at home are entering into a willing agreement with the wrestlers and wrestling company that for the payoff of entertainment they will *allow themselves* to be manipulated for the duration of the show. Likewise, in a good classroom, the relationship between students and their teacher should be one of willing agreement, for the payoff of education, to allow themselves to be manipulated for the duration of the lesson. In both cases, if the payoff isn't there – the entertainment or educational outcome – then the agreement stops. The fans stop watching. The students misbehave.

Returning to honesty and authenticity, being honest (at least implicitly) that everything you are asking the student to do is to ensure a desired educational outcome in the most enjoyable way possible, is vital for motivating them to do it. No one wants to be manipulated against their will, but we are happy to *allow* ourselves to be manipulated if we trust that the manipulator has our best interests at heart. Any piece of good literature, cinema or theatre manipulates our emotions, with our consent, so we go on the journey the author intends for us. In a happy classroom it should be an open secret that we could all sit in silence reading a text – or sit at home doing the same – to learn whatever it is that we are learning, but doing it *this* way, with this weird task, collaboratively, is a more enjoyable way to reach the same end. And just as we sometimes see a film, a play, a TV show, that doesn't quite work from a screenwriter we trusted, it does not have to be the case that the lessons always fulfil their goals of mixing enjoyment with learning; only that the *intention* was honestly there. This is what allows your class to trust you next lesson to try again once more.

Hence the importance of authenticity. In my life as a wrestling fan, I have seen a wide range of different people attempt the same task in the ring over the years, perform the same moves, say the same words, and yet while some of those people became legends, inducted into a Hall of Fame and filling arenas with screaming fans wanting to buy their merchandise and watch them wrestle their latest foe, others, doing seemingly the exact same thing, faded away into obscurity, the fans using their appearance in a match as an opportunity for a bathroom break. Likewise, in teaching, I will never forget the week I spent observing an experienced teacher hold her classes in the palm of her hand right at the start of my career. I was due to take over some of these classes the following week so took notes as she made behaviour management look so easy, merely counting down from three to one and achieving total silence from her students every time, or standing at the front of the room and quietly saying 'okay' in order to get their attention. When it came time for my own first lesson with one of those same classes, I remember the students entering noisily to their desks and feeling my confidence swell as I knew I had this secret weapon in my arsenal.

'Three…two…one.' I counted, just as she had. Only, as the 'one' came out of *my* mouth, the noise still continued. Got louder, even.

'Okay…' I said, confused that the students still chatted amongst themselves, and growing even more confused as the chatter continued. 'Okay?'

I didn't understand. I had done the exact same moves my colleague had done but the students hadn't responded in the same way. And then it hit me: I was just some nameless new guy running into the ring in the opening match at Wrestlemania and hitting a Stone Cold Stunner on my opponent, surprised that the crowd didn't roar in delight the same way they would have done if the move had been hit by 'Stone Cold' Steve Austin. If it were me at home watching some *nobody* go through the motions of my hero I would, rightly, roll my eyes and wonder who this jabroni thinks he is? Importantly, *even if that nobody was Steve Austin himself, a few years too early for his character to have connected with us*, like the years he had floundered in WWE as 'The Ringmaster', or the time before that in WCW when he worked as 'Stunning' Steve Austin, I wouldn't have bought what he did because he wasn't *that guy* yet. It wasn't about the *moves* – although doing the moves with confidence was an important step. (Better I was at least trying the 'three, two, one' countdown than screaming at the class for quiet like some of my equally inexperienced peers.) But it was about the moves *in combination with* something even more important: a relationship with the audience. In this case, your students. The teacher I had observed had, in wrestling terms, *gotten herself over* with her classes, and that was why her moves worked for her but didn't work for me. The class respected and trusted her, meanwhile they had no idea yet who the hell I was.

You can plan the most fun lesson in the world (or at least a lesson with the greatest *illusion* of fun), but if your students don't want to give you that willing agreement to do what you ask of them, if they don't trust you will take them on a journey worth taking, then you're just a nobody at Wrestlemania falling on your ass to silence. Your *authenticity*, allowing your students a glimpse of *who you really are*, is what will make them decide to give you their attention or not, which is why the second most useful thing I learned about teaching that wasn't from teaching at all, comes from the world of comedy.

At a very early age I fell in love with the movie *Ghostbusters* because the haunted building in the film known as 'spook central' (where Dana Barrett and Louis Tulley live) was, in real life, the apartment building on Central Park West where my grandmother lived (and, eventually, died). The early exposure to Saturday Night Live and SCTV alumni Bill Murray, Dan Ackroyd and Harold Ramis, led me down the pre-internet equivalent of a rabbit-hole back when you couldn't just check IMDB for someone's credits and watch a bunch of clips on YouTube. A lot of my early years were therefore filled with obscure cultural quests and detective work as I tried to reconcile my American heritage with my British one, and Saturday Night Live seemed to hold a lot of answers I was looking for with its American pop-culture references and parodies. I would keep an eye out for anything SNL-related in the UK, and when we visited America for vacations, I would watch whatever I could of the show and follow the trail of names and faces both my relatives, and people on TV, would unwittingly lead me to. Stand up, sitcoms, films, theatre, books, improv – I devoured it all. Still do. And, as in wrestling, many take a chance under the spotlight of a comedy club's unforgiving crowd and not all who try their hand at stand-up succeed. The same jokes out of one person's mouth may kill, while from another they play only to stony silence. A set which has the audience rolling on the floor one night may have a different audience bored to tears the next. Just like in wrestling, it is not only about the moves, but about who is doing them and the relationship they have with the audience at any given time. As I researched everything Saturday Night Live-related that I could find, I learned that producer, Lorne Michaels, had a tendency to give new cast members the opportunity to show the audience 'who they are' alongside the usual skits and character work. Usually this was direct to camera during the *Weekend Update* segment of the show. He did this first with my favourite Ghostbuster, Bill Murray, new to the cast in its second season and trying to overcome the audience's disappointment that he was not Chevy Chase, and the trick continues to this day each time a new face joins the crew and has trouble connecting. Michaels also did it on another show he produced, *The Kids in the Hall*, which I grew up adoring too. The cast were able to take far more chances and take their audience on some very strange rides, simply because they'd taken the time across the shows to introduce *themselves* as well as their comedy. Speaking as a fan, some of their sketches weren't even funny, but you watched them anyway because it was nice spending some time with them. I feel the same way about my favourite author, Stephen King. Many of his books are fantastic. The vast majority. But even though some aren't as good as my favourites, even a bad Stephen King book is enjoyable to me because I love his *voice* as an author. It's like hearing from an old friend. Even if the conversation isn't one of your best together, it's still a great way to pass the time.

Comedian (and also a Saturday Night Live alumni), Billy Crystal calls it 'leaving a tip'. You could go to a comedy club one night and see ten people do jokes and all of them make you laugh, but if you leave the audience a tip – a little *something* that reveals a bit about who you are to them – it makes them leave the club specifically wanting to hear *you* make them laugh again. You share a connection and they become invested in *you*.

In a way, I am using this technique with you right now. I said at the start of this book that it's hard for a writer to know if the things they write about their own small life are interesting to other people. From the start you know I'm a teacher – so you already know something about me which might make you a little bit interested in what I have to say – but there are loads of teachers who could write a book, so why me? If the anarchist, atheist, punk rock bit didn't appeal, or you were heartless enough to remain untouched by the dead dad and soon-to-be-dead mother angle of the first chapter, in this section I have thrown in a few new details to try and win you over. I'm a wrestling fan. Maybe you are too? I like comedy. My gran lived in the Ghostbusters building in New York. I am a dual US/UK citizen (I'm actually a triple citizen, as I have Irish citizenship too!). I couldn't get the first class I taught to be quiet. I'm a fan of Stephen King. Each of these little things are 'tips', something extra about myself which might make you feel like you know me a little better and may, hopefully, persuade you to give me the benefit of your time. I've also said I like to be honest, which is why I'm revealing this explicitly to you right now as an overt, but honest, attempt to manipulate you. The 'tip' is authenticity; a glimpse of what is true. (And all of those things about me are true). The reason it works is because it affords the audience a look at the human being behind the title – teacher, comedian, wrestler, writer – which makes us respond to them as a *person* and not merely as a cipher for the role.

Think back on your own time as a student. Which teachers did you respond to? For me it was my own RE teacher, also my form-tutor at the time, when she saw I was interested in politics and gave me a bunch of old *New Internationalist* magazines she subscribed to which told me everything I needed to know about her own political leanings. Or my Physics teacher who I learned had studied once to be a priest and who openly struggled reconciling his faith with his chosen subject. It was the Maths teacher who let down his guard long enough to show compassion for me and my misfit friends and find us a classroom to spend our lunch breaks in because he remembered what it was to be an outcast at our age with nowhere to go himself; the English teacher who lived down the road from one of my friends and whose young son sometimes played with us during the holidays, much to her annoyance; the French teacher we discovered was into amateur dramatics and who my best friend and I once went to watch perform in a gender-swapped production of Neil Simon's *The Odd Couple*; the art teacher who gave up his evenings several times at a minute's notice to be a member of staff on hand for the early punk gigs we used to put on at the school, coming to our aid as the school tried to thwart us with last minute health and safety regulations they didn't think we could meet; the drama teacher who revealed to us an ongoing grudge against the music department when he let us rehearse in his studio after his rival department disowned us because we accidently blew up one of their amps; the stern Deputy Head, a chemistry teacher, who disclosed he sang a mean version of 'Johnny B Goode' and asked if he could do so at our next school gig, accompanied by our band; and the history teacher who may have been a total arse politically but who threw in jokes and very dated pop culture references alongside his clear passion for his subject, as well as his trademark Polo mints and moustache, that made me at least recognise that he was trying, even if I can never fully forgive him for the time he tried to get me banned from our school-leavers photo because he thought my hair was too spiky (though the Head of Year who smuggled me back in behind his back once he was sitting left me, perhaps, the greatest 'tip' of all, when she rolled her eyes and described him as 'just a silly old man'). All of this was decades ago, and I can remember it still because the connection – the glimpse of the person behind the profession – is the opening of the door to everything.

Leaving a 'tip' in teaching is not about trying to win students over with gimmicks and having them like you (although that's nice if it happens). It is about treating students with respect, as fellow human beings, and letting them know who you are so that they can choose to give you back that respect in return and see what you have to say. In much the same way we are expected to know our students, not simply see them as bodies taking up space behind desks. We know as educators, from experience, that getting to know our pupils as *people* makes us invest far more in their success or failure, so why wouldn't the same be true in reverse? I may not have *liked* all of the teachers listed above, but, grudgingly for some, happily for others, I could see they were all trying their best to teach me *something* and I respected at least the *effort* of what they were trying to achieve.

The weird thing about being a subject-specialist in a secondary school is that you will often find yourself teaching your subject to people who have absolutely no interest in it. Until you have those small A-level classes of people who have actively chosen to study it, most of the time you are simply something timetabled and mandatory, the bane of many students' day. Leaving a tip when you're teaching means that the students in such classes who don't really want to be there won't necessarily hold it against you. You might not be their favourite lesson of the week, but they know enough about who you are and why you're asking them to do what you're asking them to do that they will give you that willing agreement you need for them to go on a learning journey with you regardless. (Seriously, think about it. Every period of the timetable these children walk into a room and have no idea what fresh lunacy awaits. Will the teacher ask them to write a timed essay today? Make a movie? Work on a group project with people they hate? Write a poem and perform it? Sing a song? Draw a picture? Devise a boardgame? Read an article? Read *out loud*? Perform a mini play? I have asked students to do all of the above and a million things more. When you really break it down, from a student's perspective, the school day is generally *insane* and requires a lot of trust from them that all this chaos they are being instructed to engage in is somehow worth doing.) In the language of students – your subject might be dry, but you're *alright.* Leave them a tip and they'll at least give you a chance.

## INTERLUDE – PHILOSOPHY UNLEASHED EXCERPT - 01/06/20:

### A LIFE WITHOUT SANCTIONS - Thinking About Consequences And Their Lack In An Age Without Punishment

It has been quite the week for thinking about sanctions, punishments, and consequences. The week began, in Britain, with Dominic Cummings' clear breach of the Covid-19 lockdown guidelines with his cross-country drive with infected family members and his own suspected illness (anyone living with a suspected Covid sufferer here in the UK is meant to self-isolate for 14 days), not to mention his further breach of lockdown to "test his eyes" with a drive to Barnard Castle before the long drive back to London. As thousands isolating around the country had loved ones die, alone, from the disease and found themselves unable to find comfort in their usual support networks to grieve; as millions have been separated from family and friends for months, struggled with their own childcare arrangements, missed out on weddings, the birth of children, and all the other many sacrifices people have made to follow strictly the lockdown rules which Cummings himself authored, it came as a slap in the face to so many to discover that he had not only breached the rules they had doggedly followed, but that, in attempting to justify his actions, he was essentially telling them that they probably should have broken the rules too and that they had been fools to suffer alone for the sake of a public health policy the *writers of the policy* weren't even taking seriously. A further face-slap came as Cummings, despite cross-party condemnation, refused to resign, was protected by the Prime Minister, and failed to apologise for what he did. No punishment, no sanction, and seemingly no consequences. For *Cummings* at least. The consequence for the rest of us will likely be a significant second wave of the coronavirus as his actions have weakened public support for the lockdown (something Cummings and Johnson actually *want* in order to restart the economy, so potentially their actual *strategy* here) and eroded public will to stay home and keep the virus from spreading. Today, as this post is published, some primary schools will be re-opening their doors against union and scientific advice, many businesses are re-opening, people are returning to work, and, without any medical consensus that we should do so, or any clear reason why it is *safe* to do so, the lockdown is easing. The predicted second wave which will likely come is one consequence of Cummings' actions, *but* who knows how this breach of public trust will further erode the seriousness with which we make take a *second* lockdown later in the year once the number of infections rise again? The consequences of Cummings actions for *us*, if not for him, may well be fatal.

Across the ocean the week ended with a fatality that is not in dispute as it was recorded for us all to see. It seems hard to believe at a time with over 100,000 deaths in the country from Covid-19 a single death of a single American would be so significant to the entire world, but the brutal murder of George Floyd by police officer Derek Chauvin, caught on camera in all its horror, was a stark reminder that while the coronavirus may have changed much about day-to-day life in our world, we are still living in the same broken system which existed before the quarantine. Another black man murdered by a white police officer. The world, or those who could stomach it (I couldn't, I have merely read the multiple reports), watched as Derek Chauvin crushed the life from George Floyd, callously ignoring his pleas to live; another strangled black voice joining the shameful chorus of all-too familiar last words: *I can't breathe*.

At first there was no sanction. Another failure of the police to bring justice against themselves, another reminder that, in America, black lives *do not* seem to matter as much as non-black lives. And people decided they were fed up with business as usual. Uprisings* spread across the country. Eventually Chauvin *was* arrested and charged with murder, albeit third degree *manslaughter* (as if his brutal actions could be considered somehow *accidental*), but as I write this the uprisings continue. Why? Because *that* sanction, that *punishment*, isn't enough. Not just because Derek Chauvin has not been taken directly into life imprisonment and branded an unequivocal *murderer* instead of this quibbling about degrees of culpability, but because Derek Chauvin is just a symptom of a wider problem of systemic institutional racism in America (and, let's be honest, elsewhere too - it's just the US cops have guns and a more prominent legacy of violence. In Birmingham, England, where I live, this week also marks the start of an IOPC investigation into the West Midlands police use of excessive force on black men across the city. We had our own uprisings in the UK in 2011 after the killing of Mark Duggan by the London Metropolitan Police.) The rioters know that whether Chauvin is exonerated or locked away, his arrest or lack of arrest isn't going to solve a problem which runs so much deeper than this single incident. The consequence here *is* the death of George Floyd. It is the consequence of *centuries* of racism in America and the continued sweeping under the rug of a systemic problem which has killed too many innocent black people. Remember, when the #blacklivesmatter movement came to prominence in 2013 after the death of Trayvon Martin in Florida *that* was already a consequence of too many black lives lost to this institutional racism. It is now seven years later and nothing has changed.

Perhaps this is why people furious about Dominic Cummings are as angry as they are? It is not about one self-serving politician living by one set of rules while we are forced to live by another, but about the continued, *systemic*, self-serving hypocrisy and unjustness of successive UK governments? Cummings, and his escape from justice, becomes, like George Floyd becoming representative of all that is unjust for black people in America, representative of *every* lie and deception we have been told in a *lifetime* of being lied to and deceived. It is a symbol of every hypocrisy. A symbol of our lack of trust in leaders. A symbol of these people continuing to live without consequences to their actions. Whether it is Tony Blair lying the country into illegal and unjustified wars; Gordon Brown deregulating the economy as Blair's Chancellor only to act surprised as the markets crashed *because of such deregulation* in 2008; Nick Clegg's broken promise on student tuition fees; David Cameron, George Osborne and Theresa May's deadly policies of continued austerity politics masquerading as economic necessity instead of the ideological *choice* that they were; or Boris Johnson's many demonstrable falsehoods on Brexit and the EU both during the referendum campaign and in his bid to become Prime Minister...our leaders continue to lie with impunity. Cummings was just the latest straw to break even further the already broken camel's back. Even if he *had* been punished, arrested by Durham police or fired from government, it might've felt good for a moment (as it did to hear Derek Chauvin had been taken into custody), but after the initial visceral sense of justice wears off we are left with the realisation that removing one piece off the chessboard is not enough to end the game of chess. Until the bigger underlying problem is resolved, there will be other Derek Chauvins and other Dominic Cummings. (Apparently all human synecdoches of wider systemic abuses have the initials D.C?)

Sanctions, punishments, threats...these may bring some short-term sense of comfort that justice is being done, but true justice comes when we no longer need such threats to ensure good behaviour. When the logic of the *genuine consequences of an action* is enough to make people make better choices. When police aren't racists and politicians aren't liars *because the obvious wrongness of being a racist or a liar, and its logical consequence in the death and suffering of innocent people, is sufficient to not want to be racist or lie.*

One of the things I have loved about online teaching since schools closed in March has been the fact that I, like every other online teacher, have been robbed of our punitive ability to punish our students for bad behaviour. Bizarrely, as someone probably considered one of the strictest teachers at my school, punishing students for bad behaviour has always been my least favourite aspect of my job. In fact it was the area I most worried about in my training year - how could I, an anarchist anti-authoritarian, be an "authority figure" in the classroom? My initial idea that I would *just not bother and see what happens* was undermined not only by facing classes of children trained with a lifetime of sanction and reward to respond only to threat, but also by the fact that behaviour management - so-defined by whatever school policy it is you are working under - is one of the Teacher Standards a trainee teacher is bound to meet or else they will not be qualified to work in a British school. Thankfully, however, I had two things going for me to square the circle of my cognitive dissonance surrounding telling my students off. Number one, I had read some Richard Rorty while at university, and remembered his strange advocacy of being a "liberal ironist" as a postmodernist who did not believe in objective truths yet still wanted to endorse a particular political position as the "right" one. Rorty says, fully aware there is no "right" view, we can still act as if there is anyway and fully commit to our liberalism despite knowing it to be essentially baseless. Secondly, as a lifelong fan of professional wrestling, I knew what it was to play a "heel" character and be the bad guy. The best heels in wrestling were those who infuriated crowds by their clear hypocrisy and self-righteousness, claiming to have acted honourably when clearly they are a dastardly villain. I was reminded of a childhood form tutor of mine who was once deeply feared by me until I realised his teaching persona was entirely an act, largely done for self-amusement (he eventually quit the profession and became a vicar).

So combining these influences I began to play an "authoritarian ironist" heel character in the classroom, rigidly sticking to *all* the ridiculous rules of whatever school I worked in *to the letter* in the hope that not only would classes used to such strict disciplinarianism work for me, but that the ludicrous hypocrisy of the rules that I enforced would be exposed and their absurdity made clear and undermined through their enforcement…Teaching became a form of performance art wherein doing my job well became its deepest subversion. Especially combined with occasional glimpses behind the persona when the curriculum allowed me to discuss my real feelings about authority and rules imposed from on high. Teaching religion, as I do, the discussion is fairly frequent, most major religions being built on some notion of a set of rules which must be followed or else a deity, deities, or force of karma, will sanction you with some form of torment for your transgression.

But despite squaring my classroom authoritarianism with my anarchist conscience in this way, it does bother me that to do my job in the contemporary British classroom I am required to enforce not only so many arbitrary rules, but an entire way of thinking about rule-following and obedience. In most cases, underwriting school rules, are the sanctions that come as a consequence of not following the rules: detentions, exclusions, suspensions. Emails and phone-calls home. Threats of deeper failings - a test, an exam, a university application, a job… But what the online classroom has done is completely remove those threats. If I ask a student to do something and they don't do it, I can't make them stay behind at break time or keep them back after school. I can't meaningfully add a black mark against their name which will be held against them at some future date (after all, in these strange times who knows how many valid reasons there may be for a piece of work not being done). I can't point to a future exam they will fail (currently all exams are suspended). I can't even point to the future career they won't have if they fail my class (currently many *careers* have been suspended too!) Calls can be made home, and emails sent, but communication with home has always exposed the cracks in a teacher's authority. *If* the parent sides with the teacher, they may be able to change their child's behaviour (many can't, and kind of think schools are magic buildings where their defiant teenager suddenly becomes compliant), but often the parent is fully aware of whatever their child has done and *simply doesn't care*. "Your son missed a deadline", "your daughter hasn't logged on to her Teams account in three weeks". "Yes, I know. They've been in their rooms watching Netflix. What about it?" End of conversation.

The point is, working from home has given our students permission - whether we want them to or not - to say no without any obvious sanction or punishment.

I say *obvious* sanction or punishment because there are still consequences. While teachers may bluster with threats which ultimately prove empty (I can think of certain Y11 students this year warned year after year that their poor behaviour and lack of revision would come back to bite them in their exams only for there to end up being no exams and no fabled comeuppance) it does still remain true that in many cases *not* doing certain aspects of schoolwork, just because of the set-up of society that we live in, *will* put students at a disadvantage. Maybe it will be the piece of work which ended up being the highest tariff question in an exam two years down the line (or, in this year's case, the piece of work which, though unbeknownst to the student, or teacher, at the time, ended up contributing the most to the centre-assessed grades derived in lieu of exams.) Perhaps it will simply be some crucial piece of knowledge that will impede them in life by not knowing it (I think myself of the French lessons I messed around in as a child, and my deep regret every time I travel that I can't speak a second language.) It may even be about something beyond academia: the teacher whose work you didn't bother doing ending up one day being someone who could have really helped you through some personal or professional crisis but, because of developing a combative relationship with them in your younger years rather than one of mutual respect, you miss out on that opportunity or goodwill. I'm sure there are several students who have passed my classroom door over the years and left it hating me for whatever reason and, as a result, I never got to know them that well. In the meantime, there are others who I have literally been a lifeline to in dealing with home issues, personal issues, academic issues, and even issues in later life as adults. Consequences can be strange and unpredictable beasts, but up until now teachers haven't really had to meaningfully discuss *real* consequences with their students because our jobs have revolved around enforcing artificial ones. We discuss the *detention* tomorrow or the *bad report* we'll send out at the end of term and tough *parents' evening* looming ahead. Online, without these synthetic tools, we are forced into being honest and open: *I have set you some work which I want you to do. I know you could get away without doing it and if you don't do it it is highly likely nothing will happen to you. But here's why I want you to do it and why I think it will be beneficial...* and we have to hope our rationale is sufficient to motivate our students.

We have also had to be far more flexible. Gone are fixed and frequent deadlines, replaced instead with flexibility - *I'll set it for you on Monday and give you until Friday to do it. If that will be a problem let me know in advance and we can work out an extension.* We have had to *listen* more. No longer able to dismiss explanations for missing work as "excuses", students have come to us on a level playing field: *my uncle has been in hospital with Covid-19...my mother is a nurse and hasn't been around to make me work and, honestly, I've fallen behind... I've been finding it hard to get motivated to do any school stuff.* Their stories suddenly matching our own experiences in this strange new world we have found ourselves quarantined in and hitting home: maybe there *are* good reasons to prioritise things *other than schoolwork*?

And what has warmed my heart the most is seeing how, despite the self-evident lack of meaningful threat or sanction for transgression, so many students around the country are still doing the work. Doing it not because they are scared not to, but because they have rationalised with themselves and come to the conclusion that the work is worth doing (and likewise, many *not* doing the work are likely doing it because they have *rightly* concluded the work set to be inessential. Sometimes a school curriculum can be like one of those old pre-streaming US TV shows where they had 22 episodes to fill each season whether they had a story to tell or not. Teachers stretching a topic across six weeks because they have six weeks in which to teach it, not because it actually needs six weeks to be taught. Students who could see that in the old world, are now able to act on their instincts in this new one.)

As teachers we have had to actually *justify* the requests we make on our students' time and resources. If there is only one laptop in the house and you are sharing it with your dad and your sister, who needs it the most? Is my assignment actually worth your time? If so, I have to show you why without merely telling you off for not doing it. And what's more, I have to *reassess my own beliefs about the work's importance* and be part of a dialogue instead of a monologue. The old canard of doing it *because I said so* no longer flies.

Personally, I am excited about taking this approach back into the real world classroom whenever I return. I have grown weary of playing the heel and would like to turn what in wrestling parlance is called "babyface" - the good guy. Playing the ironist has worn out its welcome. I want to experiment with a classroom of *meaningful consequences*. No detentions. No sanctions and threats. Just a genuine dialogue of my rationale for what is needed to be done, and why, and the eventual likely consequence of a student's legitimate success or failure within the subject. It is highly unlikely any school will allow such an approach without a fight (*why wasn't this student reprimanded? Why haven't their parents been called in? You're not following our school policy!)* but it will be an interesting experiment to attempt.

That said, and the problem with such unilateral experiments, is that so much can be undermined by the way the wider world treats people. If all we know is threat and reward then we are far more likely to respond to such approaches. It then becomes a legitimate moral question to ask (and how I have justified my previous approach to behaviour to myself for so long): *if the majority of students will not know how to act responsibly without the threat of sanction and, as a result, may end up failing or in trouble elsewhere down the line, am I not obliged to do what is 'best' for the majority and do what works, even if that means threat and sanction?*

The good thing about so many months of online learning is that it has changed the game for everyone and given every student a taste of this different approach to behaviour management. Hopefully enough that students, used to their recent independence and this different way of doing things, will be receptive to the new approach? May even flourish with it?

Ultimately, what it comes down to is this: you can fire Dominic Cummings, jail Derek Chauvin, and stick the misbehaving students in a detention. And, short-term, it may even make us feel better. But what we really need to aim for is a world where Cummings, Chauvin and misbehaving students have no reason to, and no benefit in, existing at all. The sooner we realise that it is *consequences*, understanding how and why things are done, and the *reasons* why someone thinks something ought or ought not be done that must motivate us to make real changes - whether this be in the classroom or in the country - and not just sanctions, punishments and their threats, the sooner we live in a world where people are good because they *want to* do good, not just because they are scared to do bad. Until then we must continue to experiment. Or, if the experiments fail, rise up.

---

* In the original post I used the word "riots", unthinkingly parroting the reporting at the time I was hearing despite being a Birmingham resident all-too aware of the media framing of things like the Handsworth Uprising as the Handsworth "riots". Using the word "riot" is usually an attempt to criminalise and delegitimise justifiable political rage. Here, in reproducing parts of the post, I have corrected the original and replaced references to "riots" with referencing to "uprising" or "rising up", and apologise to anyone who felt the original post mischaracterised those events.

# 3.
## *ANARCHIST: Subverting from Within*

Being open and honest with my students means that, even before I published a book advocating the political philosophy of anarchy (*Authentic Democracy: An Ethical Justification of Anarchism*) it was no secret in my school that I was an anarchist. Although I am not sure anyone but my most curious students knew exactly what anarchism entailed. The curious ones would ask big questions, go away and do lots of reading, and come back the next week with more questions to ask. Some even tracked down my PhD thesis online and would trawl through it for answers. Most, however, would simply treat the anarchism I sometimes talked about like a strange curiosity whenever it came up, or even as a joke. After all, how could I, one of the strictest teachers in the school, be someone who doesn't believe in rules and laws?

Yes – that's right. One of the strictest. But we need to back up a bit to get to that…

I had asked myself the exact *opposite* question when I first decided to become a teacher. While I could square the circle politically with myself of why I wanted to get involved in *education* even while maintaining multiple ideological objections to the specifics of contemporary *schooling*, I was intrigued to see how I would cope with the seemingly intrinsic need within such schools to be an authoritarian when every instinct in my body went against the enforcement of ridiculous rules. As I watched teachers during my weeks of work-experience obsess about whether someone had their tie on straight, the length of a student's skirt, the kind of earrings a child wore, the presence of *trainers* instead of school shoes, make-up, and other jewellery, I seriously wondered how any human being could waste the energy to care about such things. In my own schooldays I had got into trouble all the time over these pointless uniform infractions. Growing up with an American mother and obsessed with American TV shows,

I would see a whole country of students learning happily in their own clothes and wonder why such freedoms were not given to us here in the UK. Once, during my GCSEs, I got into trouble when I asked the latest teacher to nag me about tucking in my shirt – the Polo mint sucking guy with the moustache we met earlier – what exactly the educational benefit of doing so was.

'Do you want to ask that of a senior member of staff?' he'd asked. The subtext a threat that doing so would get me in further trouble.

'Yes please.' I replied eagerly, genuinely wanting to know.

Swiftly, I was put into detention for my open curiosity.

A few months later, still unsatisfied with the answers I had been given (lofty but incoherent ideas about equality, belonging, and better behaviour) and now doing pre-exams work-experience at a local newspaper (remember them?), I decided to write an article interviewing the local Director of Education, and several local headteachers, including my own, about why they felt school uniform was so important. The answers they gave echoed those given to me the day I refused to tuck in my shirt, and were all easily countered by the fact that other countries educated their children just as well, if not better, without uniform; that belonging did not have to be dependent on clothing (and many bullied or marginalised students at a school *still* did not feel that sense of belonging despite wearing the same uniform as everybody else); and that equality over clothing wouldn't be an issue if we weren't so messed up as a society about consumerism and social status in the first place. When the underlying inequalities still remain, and are talked about openly on the school playground, people all wearing the same school uniform as each other can, and *do,* continue to belittle each other over their appearance. Furthermore, in the places we were all told to aspire to want to learn at the highest level – universities – uniform wasn't worn. Why was a uniform an essential requirement to education in some settings, but not in other, even more academic, ones?

Writing the article didn't achieve anything, but I enjoyed giving the schools the opportunity to give school uniform its best defence and see them all coming up short. It had always seemed so obvious to me that, despite the seemingly egalitarian rhetoric, uniforms are, and have always been, really about conformity and control: subsuming your individual identity to the collective and wearing what you are told to wear *simply because you have been told to do so*. If they were truly about equality alone, every child in the country would wear the same uniform and it would be provided for free. Never forget, the poorer parents the argument suggests benefit from not having to have their child wear their own clothes to school each week *still* have to clothe their child for all the other days they are not in school *and buy an extra school uniform on top of that*. Jeans and a comfortable top, if worn by all, could just as easily be a uniform as a suit and tie, but the formal 'business attire' approach of our uniforms are all about learning from an early age that in the workplace you will be expected to bury any semblance of personality and wear whatever nonsense your bosses require you to wear. As soon as rules about uniform move from 'everyone wears X' to 'and X must meet specific criteria A, B and C', with sanctions doled out for *not* meeting that criteria, then unless there is a legitimate independent reason for that criteria (such as safety requirements, or job necessity) it is merely about control. In some schools they even send students home for not wearing the 'right' uniform, demonstrating that obeying these arbitrary rules about appearance is more important to the people running the school than any education ostensibly provided. As I thought about becoming a teacher, I hated the idea of being any part of that garbage, let alone having to be the enforcer of other bizarre policies of control, such as getting people to stand behind their chairs before the lesson began rather than just sit down, or for them to sit silently as other students filed in for another tedious assembly. The shushing in assembly halls particularly bothered me because it was so unlike the behaviour we would expect any of these students, or ourselves, to display at any other public space before something begins. At the theatre, at the cinema, at a music venue, at a public *lecture*, for example, we chat happily amongst friends as we wait for the agreed signal to be silent – the dimming of the lights, the end of the trailers, the first note of music. A signal that only asks us to be silent *when it is important that we be silent.* We don't sit in eery silence for five to ten minutes *before* the things get going which require our undivided attention. In fact, if any of the above signals happened and the action *didn't* begin fairly promptly, no one would be surprised at all by the audience getting restless and the chatter starting up again. So why do we expect young people to remain 'seen and not heard' as they sit waiting on uncomfortable seats, or even on the floor, to hear – or yawn through – another list of administrative messages and moralistic missives they have no personal interest in hearing in a school assembly?

The answer, again, is obvious. It is not because the silence, or the standing behind chairs is important in any objective way. As with wearing uniform, it is important because it is a rule, laid out by an authority, and the real lesson we are teaching, *behind* the overt academic curriculum, is the lesson that *authority must always be obeyed*, even if obeying that authority's rule makes little to no sense. It depressed me upon my return to the school environment as an adult that, despite the passage of time, no one seemed to be budging on their commitment to uncomfortable uniforms. That teachers so infrequently questioned the wisdom of doing these coercive things, and blindly enforced clearly meaningless procedures as if to break their edicts would be to commit some sort of criminal act, was something that had bothered me as a child and disturbed me even more as an adult intending to become one of these awful people myself. I really didn't know if I could do it – tell a child off for doing something that harmed no one and merely broke a rule which made no sense to begin with?

I remember one school assembly in my own childhood: the usual rigamarole – sitting in silence, and then, because it was what we did, standing in unison as the Head Teacher entered the room. Except this time a group of my friends in the row ahead of me decided not to stand. Just to see what would happen. The Head marched down the aisle between our chairs as he always did, the rest of us stood as *we* always did, and these four or five brave social-scientists embarked on their daring, improvised fieldwork, staying calmly sitting as the short walking man glanced furiously in their direction, distracting his stroll to the stage.

It is one of my life's biggest regrets that I did not join them. To me, they will always be heroes simply for reminding us all that you can always say no. And the telling-off they received afterwards only served to further expose how empty the silly rule was, as no better rationale for why they ought to have stood was offered other than *because it's what we do here.* As an adult, who still admires the intellect of such mutiny, how would I be able to tell similar students off with a straight face if something like that happened in a school where *I* was the teacher now, tasked to offer the reprimand?

This is not to say the anarchist classroom is a lawless one. Those who understand the theoretical underpinnings of anarchism and don't just know the word from its common, incorrect, conflation with chaos and leering images of snarling punks yelling 'destroy!' know that anarchists are quite comfortable with following rules they agree are necessary. The difference between an anarchist rule and a non-anarchist one, however, is that the anarchist's rules are agreed to by all who choose to follow them, not merely imposed on them from above, and they are temporary and contingent – the rule is followed because we want to achieve X and doing so allows us to achieve X. If X can be achieved without the rule, or X is already achieved, we no longer need the rule. So, for example, as an anarchist teacher I would have no problem with enforcing a rule that we be quiet when people are speaking so that we can hear what they have to say. Such a rule makes sense and ensures that everyone can learn together without impediment. Note also that the rule doesn't simply say we are quiet when *the teacher* is talking, because I don't think such a rule is justified. If the students need to be quiet when I speak so they can hear what I have to say, we all – including me – ought to be quiet when they speak so we can hear them too. This is especially true when a lesson is discursive, and everyone's contribution is equally valuable to the overall learning. However, at the same time, we might also agree in the anarchist classroom to give a teacher some more authority than their students, strictly limited to their role in facilitating learning and the specialist knowledge they may have on both the subject being studied, and on pedagogical strategies, which might make them better placed to make judgements about how best to achieve the learning goals being sought. So, while we might justify the rule of being quiet when people are speaking, we might also allow that the teacher can have the special privilege of calling time on a group discussion, or noting, or even silencing, contributions which are off-topic or inaccurate. All of this is consistent with anarchism *so long as the authorities and privileges agreed to don't step outside the bounds of relevance on which consent to them was justified.* In other words: in my classroom, to help you learn a certain topic, we might agree to grant me the temporary and purposeful authority to ask for quiet at times, and direct what activities we do, *but once the lesson is over, that authority is over too*. And even then, if the same agreed ends can be achieved without that – say, for example, by the students themselves taking control over what activities we do and telling me how they would like a lesson to be taught rather than me telling them – then such authority is no longer justified. Remember – the rules have to be agreed to, not simply imposed. And if I ask you to do something which *doesn't* lead to the agreed end of our educational goal, then you would be free to refuse to comply.

So while the anarchist teacher's classroom may have a range of rules and procedures to be followed without contradiction if they aid in the learning, and I felt no personal tension at the idea of ensuring my classroom was a productive and purposeful one, the idea of *discipline* was something else entirely. After all – my asking you to read a handout or be quiet so we can hear someone speak theoretically serves a legitimate educational purpose, my giving you a detention and asking you to give up your free time serves only a punitive one. The argument is that the punitive consequences of consistent sanctions ultimately mean students learn the need to follow the teacher's instructions, but this is where my anarchism and traditional UK schooling come to odds. The use of punitive sanctions to 'encourage' compliance is *not* based in student learning, or at least not their *academic* learning, it is teaching students only that if they do not do as their teacher tells them, *even if they have good reasons for not doing so*, they will be punished. My desire, therefore, was to enforce the rules anarchically, not by threat of punitive sanction but by rational explanation of the negative consequences of not doing what was asked. i.e. failing the course or not learning the topic at hand.

This was actually how my parents disciplined me once I was old enough to join them in rational discussion. I can't remember exactly what age I was, though I must have been at least six years old because I was that age when we moved to the house in which the conversation happened. Mom and dad used to be smackers. Not frequent smackers, and never repeated smackers, just a single quick smack on the bottom if my sister or I did anything really bad. It was the top level of punishment in our house and used only very rarely. I have very few memories of being hit and none of them are traumatic, at least not in a way that I am aware of (yet). While I had friends whose parents would sadistically ask them to fetch a special slipper or belt for certain transgressions, and who would literally tremble in fear at the prospect of being caught for doing something naughty, my smacking parents gave me little to fear from their restrained and uncommon assaults, and usually only resorted to parental violence when my own safety was in danger from my stupidity. A smack accompanied with the healing concern of: 'you could have been *killed!*' This is not to excuse them. Abuse is abuse and corporal punishment is still unjustifiable bullshit, especially when it comes from people who are supposed to show you unconditional love. It was a different time, sure, but they still could have chosen not to follow the herd.

Eventually, and happily, they did. Dad sat me down and told me that they weren't going to be smacking me anymore. I was old enough to make rational choices and be responsible for my actions and therefore, he said, rather than hitting me to show me something was wrong, the new approach would be that they would use reason with me instead. *Tell* me why what I did was a problem and why I should make better choices next time. Telling me off would become, literally, *telling* me off. They would let me know when I had disappointed them, scared them, infuriated them, annoyed them, and why, and they would hear my side of the story about why I did it. If appropriate, there might be some further consequence, like a loss of pocket-money or a cancelled playdate with a friend, but even that would be done only where relevant; the pocket-money paused to pay for something broken, the visit to a friend stopped so I could think about what I had done. That would be it. Words only. And while, like any kid, I, of course, got into my fair share of trouble, the approach worked pretty well. In terms of the conventional markers for juvenile delinquency, to this day I have never touched a drop of alcohol or taken any drugs. I haven't even smoked a cigarette. I got into no fights and joined no gangs. I got no one pregnant, either accidently or intentionally (let's face it – this is no world in which to bring in a new life against its consent) and I achieved a decent set of GCSEs and some fantastic A-level results. My major stint as a thief occurred *before* the talk with my father. The first theft being that of a single penny-sweet from a local newsagents while I was in Year 1 at primary school. I felt so guilty about taking the sweet, an act I believe I undertook only to see if it could be done, that I ate it with no joy, asking to go to the toilet at school and hiding shamefully in a stall to smuggle the chewy contraband into my trembling mouth where no one else could see. My second, far more terrible, theft occurred a few months later, now in Year 2 and on the cusp of my father's new experiment in discipline; a crime he never knew about. We had moved house to another town and, new to the school, I couldn't understand why my new teacher kept a toy on her desk. A 'Rock Lord'. A terrible brand of knock-off Transformer which, instead of cool robots transforming into even more exciting motor vehicles, saw not-so-cool robots transforming into…rocks. I had foolishly bought one myself the previous summer and had yet to find anyone else stupid enough to join me. My Rock Lord sat in my bedroom, a lumpen green blob of plastic, doing nothing, with no one to play with. And yet here was this strange new teacher in this strange new school with her own Rock Lord just sat there doing nothing like my own. She had clearly made the same mistake that I had. Maybe she left it on her desk as a reminder to never again buy such a rubbish plaything? I had never heard of a teacher before who still bought *toys*, especially a teacher as old as this one, and every day that I saw the Rock Lord sitting there gathering dust was a day I grew more and more determined to liberate it. It wasn't like she was doing anything with it. She didn't seem to be playing with it, or even ever acknowledge it. Meanwhile my Rock Lord was there at home without a playmate. So, one lunchtime, I pretended I needed to get something from the classroom and, instead, I took the red Rock Lord from my teacher's desk so I could pair it with my green one at home.

Except I didn't go straight home in those days because both my parents worked. I had a childminder we went to, and she had a daughter. Sometimes we played together, her daughter and I, other times I played on my own while the daughter played with my sister. With a new Rock Lord burning a hole in my pocket, this day I let my sister enjoy the company while I sat on the sofa by myself, staring at my new toy and looking forward to getting it home.

The next day I learned that this school did something my previous school did not: confiscate items from students. My teacher sat us all down and told us that something terrible had happened. The toy she had confiscated from one of my classmates previously – sometime when I either wasn't there or hadn't noticed – had gone missing from her desk. Someone had *stolen* it.

I realised my mistake. I hadn't liberated an unused toy from an unplayful adult's desk, I had stolen a fellow student's toy which had been sat on the desk for safe-keeping. At this school, apparently, teachers were allowed to steal things and call it *confiscation,* but it was clear that students were not and whoever did this would be in big, big trouble.

I sat tight and stayed silent as the teacher asked if anyone had any information. My plan was simple: I would bring the Rock Lord back to school in the morning and it would be like nothing ever happened. Only, as I mapped out in my mind how I would return the toy to the desk unseen, the classroom door opened and there stood the teacher from next door and next to her, my childminder's daughter.

'Daniel McKee', she said, not looking at me but looking at my teacher. 'Daniel McKee', my teacher echoed back, turning her head in my direction as she spoke. She looked at me, the disappointment clear in her eyes. Worse, the student whose Rock Lord it was looked at me too, the small friendship we were forming in those early days at a new school instantly dead in the water thanks to my unwitting betrayal.

We didn't tell dad about it because mom was worried having a thief for a son might make him leave home again. We had, after all, moved house to this new town to make a fresh start after a recent affair of his had got so serious he had considered ending the marriage. Both she and the Deputy Head I was reported to could see how mortified I was at what I had done, how theft had never been my intention, and I learned, without any punishment, not to just take things from another person's desk, no matter how underused they might seem.

The only childhood thievery I committed after the change in my parents' approach to discipline was the petty theft everyone at my secondary school was doing at a certain point: pocketing the odd bread roll or chocolate cracknel instead of paying for it in the overpriced school canteen. They were left exposed and unguarded on a tray near the till, and it was easy enough to distract the person meant to be keeping an eye on them by wrapping them up in the job of ringing up your items, or while they were busy with the person paying for their meal ahead of you, so you could grab some food and pocket it while their eyes were diverted.

What I find instructive about this was the recognition that even this most blatant stealing seemed to me to be entirely justifiable at the time. The canteen prices were too high. We all complained they were ripping us off anyway, so we were only taking back some of what they had already stolen. And my own additional rationale: any money I saved from lunch could go towards buying music when I'd saved up enough. I was denying myself lunch pretty regularly at that point to feed my growing punk rock habit. The pocketed freebies were therefore very welcome alongside an otherwise sparse plate.

Even this explicit bout of teenage criminality was short-lived, however. After a few weeks of regular five-finger discounts in the dinner queue, I was literally caught bread handed (worst pun ever, but impossible to resist). As I slowly lowered the bread-roll I had picked up surreptitiously into my right pocket while my left hand offered money to the person on the till for whatever was visible on my tray, another hand grabbed my right wrist.

'There's another roll here which Mr McKee needs to pay for', said the teacher who had rumbled me. 'And a chocolate cracknel,' he added, pulling from my pocket the sticky orb of cornflakes, chocolate, and golden syrup that they apparently only sold in my childhood school and not anywhere else in the world, and tossing it accusingly onto the tray.

Bizarrely, that was all that came of it. I handed the woman on the till the right money, the teacher smirked, and then he walked away shaking his head. Like I said – everyone was doing it (and don't forget the 5p sachets of ketchup hidden under our plates, or the occasional slice of pizza you'd try to bury under salad leaves and hope no one noticed). I guess he knew I meant no harm and just wanted to remind me that what I was doing was still wrong on some abstract level.

Again though, it worked. No sanction. No punishment. Not even a telling off. But confronted with the realisation that it may be what everyone is doing *but it's still stealing*, I decided it was no longer something I should do. If I wanted to buy music, I would go without the freebies. If I wanted to eat a chocolate cracknel or bread roll, I would pay for it from now on.

Of course, there is a problem with the idea of rational discourse in the classroom instead of punitive sanctions. Sometimes the student is right – the rule is stupid or the lesson is not worth doing. In a world where curricula are imposed by exam boards, or school 'strategies' aim at ends divorced from education, all too often the only answer we have as to why we have asked our students to do something is 'because you have to'. Why? 'Because *we* have to.' And then there's the issue of numbers. My mom or dad could easily pause their day to have a one-on-one chat with me or my sister if we'd done something they thought was wrong. But can teachers overseeing classes of thirty or more students answer each individual rebellion with thoughtful discourse and discussion without impeding their ability to teach the rest of the class? The punitive sanctions are there to be a quick solution in time-sensitive circumstances within a problematic education system juggling the simultaneous needs of multiple students we simply do not have the time to engage with as humans: comply or else. So, recognising the structural impediments to bringing my parents' rational discipline approach into my classroom (though incorporating aspects of it, where I could, in whole-class discussions where such topics could be raised within the context of the lesson) I went the opposite direction to subvert from within. I decided to, in wrestling parlance, 'turn heel'. Become the bad guy. The one who does everything in their power to get you to hate them and everything they stand for. Instead of letting freedom reign in my classroom, I would enforce *all* the school's stupid rules, to the letter. I would intentionally become one of the strictest teachers in the school in order to highlight how preposterous, unfair, and open to corruption the rules were and – hopefully – foster a more deep-seated revolt against *all* such ridiculous rules in the minds of my furious students. I would do this explicitly – enforcing the rules and playing my heel character, while simultaneously calling out how dumb they are as I did it. I would be a heel who *knows they are playing the heel.*

Soon, I became one of the only teachers in the school making students stand in silence behind their desks before the lesson would begin.

'But why sir?' students would ask. 'No one else cares.'

'I know,' I would tell them, 'but apparently the school thinks it is important enough that it is still written down as one of their rules. They put it in the staff handbook that we have to do this and they induct new teachers to the school like me by telling us that this is what we do here, even though it isn't. Weird, huh?'

'But why do it – no one else does?'

'Because the strange thing is that this total waste of time at the start of the lesson which you should all complain about – look, it's taken up at least two minutes of potential learning time to get you all to do it – is something I can't actually be told off for doing with you as the school has explicitly stated that this is how all lessons *should* start at this school.'

'Why though?'

I pointed out that every new question meant a longer delay on starting the lesson (then also pointed out that if they did that intentionally to delay the start of the lesson in the hope of shortening the lesson I also, quite unreasonably, had the power to take away their recess or lunch break at the end of the lesson and make up the lost time then even though there wouldn't have been any lost time if I hadn't decided to enforce this stupid rule in the first place). Then I answered the question anyway.

'Because the idea is that by getting you all to stand silently at the start of the lesson it resets you, like machines, so that any energy or potential for misbehaviour that you enter the classroom with is diffused. It's meant to be calming and remind you that this is a brand-new lesson so you leave behind any baggage that may be lingering from last lesson or the corridors.'

Genuinely interested, the class is silent as they listen to my response, so I allow them to sit down and begin the lesson. At any point in the next forty-five minutes where someone misbehaves, I don't have to point out to the students that the magical 'reset' idea clearly doesn't work. They point it out for me. The demonstrable failing of standing silently at the start of the lesson is self-evident to them. Nevertheless, next lesson we do it again.

'Why this again, sir?'

'I know. Awful isn't it? But it's the school's rules and we're meant to follow them even if they make no sense.'

'But that doesn't make any sense sir?'

'Exactly.'

By flagging up the stupidities, my hope was to raise a nagging voice inside my students' heads about rules in general. At some point my school brought in an utterly awful system of 'behaviour-points' and 'achievement-points' which allowed us to log onto the computer system every instance of good or bad behaviour our students displayed. Staff were told it was merely for information purposes at first – recording incidents across the day so that we could all be aware if any of our students were having any issues and praise those who were doing well – but soon, and inevitably, it became punitive instead of informational. Three behaviour-points in a day and you get a lunchtime detention. Too many across a week and you get an after-school detention and get put on 'report'. And while the list of categories for bad behaviour were endless, there were only ever a handful of positive behaviours which would warrant an 'achievement' point, stacking the deck purposefully towards sanction rather than praise.

One particularly ambiguous behaviour category was 'refusal to comply' – a behaviour-point which, for some reason, meant an immediate afterschool detention (the reason being: the biggest crime of all was *not doing what a teacher tells you to do*). I gave out that particular behaviour-point frequently, in order to show how ill-defined it was. If I asked a student to do some work and they didn't, was that 'refusal to comply'? If I asked them to stop talking and they continued, was that? If they hadn't done the homework I had set? The reason I asked – and discussed the ambiguity openly with my students – was because there were other distinct behaviour-points for all those other things. 'Insufficient work', 'disruptive behaviour', 'homework not done', but all of these behaviours which might actually be considered legitimate concerns (as they suggested the student was not properly accessing the education they were ostensibly there to get) through the refusal to comply with our instructions did not, apparently, merit the immediate sanction of a detention in the way that the distinct 'refusal to comply' behaviour-point did. Because *that* offence was disrespectful to the *teacher* and not merely an impediment to a student's learning. Because we *teachers* needed to be respected…or else.

Where my school made a mistake with this policy and enabled me to abuse it and make it teachable was that it wasn't the class teacher who handed out the afterschool detention for the 'refusal to comply' behaviour point, it was the Head of Year, such was the supposed severity of the crime. I would therefore clearly explain to my students how they had refused to comply when they didn't do something very minor I had asked them to, and leave it to the Head of Year to have to explain to the student why they needed to have an afterschool detention for their tiny infraction. The eventual realisation would dawn that this wasn't *actual* 'refusal to comply' but merely 'insufficient work' or 'homework not done' or 'low level disruption' or some other low-level crime and the Head of Year would have to somehow explain why one form of 'refusal to comply' was apparently much worse than all the others. The student would avoid the detention but also recognise that, as a school, we seemed to be far more concerned with enforcing respect for our teachers than we were with the quality of the education the students were getting. After all, if a student *hadn't* engaged with the work, bothered with their homework, or decided to chat with a friend instead of do what the teacher asked of them, one way of reading their behaviour was that maybe the teacher wasn't properly challenging or engaging them with their lessons. Maybe it was *our* fault, not theirs?

All of this would be discussed openly with my students. I would explain that I was showing them the faults with the behaviour system and using them to make a point. I would explain that even my doing so demonstrated the unjustifiable power disparities between students and their teachers because I was basically playing with their free-time and causing them stress to show them how bad the system of rules and sanctions were simply because I *could*. But, as well as doing my best to simultaneously try to show them that a note on a computer or a lost recess or lunch-time wasn't exactly the end of the world, I would also treat very differently those actual moments where real responses were needed to behavioural issues. Actually talking to the students who disrupted lessons about why they were doing it; discussing my own lesson-planning with my students to give them a proper say in what we were doing and make lessons more enjoyable if they found they were switching off; even setting fun or educational tasks in detentions, such as poetry, short stories or art projects, rather than the expected punitive sanctions they were used to if forced by the school's behaviour policy to run one. Every good wrestling heel also knows when it's time to turn 'babyface' and finally be the good guy.

Of course the 'achievement-points' got the same treatment too. Instead of making them a holy grail towards which students had to strive, I would reward them gratuitously. Ten points here, twenty points there. I had an issue with these records of behaviour for entirely different reasons. I could see from the start of their introduction that students were now doing work not for the intrinsic motivation of the work itself, but for the instrumental motivation of the reward. If behaviour-points were the stick, achievement-points were the carrot, with the end of each term culminating in a 'rewards afternoon' for those who had earned enough. It did not take long for the desire to spend an afternoon watching a movie or playing paintball to lead to students finding as many ways as possible of gaining precious points. Soon every positive behaviour – a door held open, tidying away resources after a lesson, passing a message onto someone – would be followed by the request: 'can I have an achievement-point for it?' We were using Pavlovian training methods on these children and it worried me. The only lesson it really taught was to do whatever was needed to get a reward and to *only* do it if a reward was being offered. Better motivations, such as the genuine desire to help out or be kind to each other, were crowded out by the promise of pizza or entry into a raffle to win an iPod. Achievement-points were also harder to transform into a teachable moment. If you withheld them for good acts then students, quite understandably, would think you unfair and ungenerous. If you gave too many, as I did at the start to undermine the system and devalue the currency, then they just wanted even more and, seeing that you were game for possible windfalls, would soon bombard you with even more choruses of 'can I have an achievement-point for that?' at every turn.

There was one benefit to achievement-points, however. When a parent would send me an angry email complaining that I had given their child a behaviour-point they disagreed with, I would have a standard reply: 'I will be happy to erase any behaviour-point I have given your child so long as you are also happy for me to erase any achievement-points I have given them too, given your lack of faith in my professional judgement in such matters?'

I was always surprised when these emails arrived in my inbox that the parent hadn't simply assured their child that the click of a mouse against their name on a teacher's register was utterly meaningless and they should just forget about the so-called 'behaviour-point' they had received because behaviour-points *are not real*. They are just an institutional invention which have no bearing on the real world. Rather than parent and child bonding over the ridiculousness of the whole system, as was my hope, the parent would reply to my offer by telling me that, on further reflection, they would be happy to let the behaviour-points, and the achievement-points, stand.

The problem with my performance-art approach to teaching students about the stupidity of school discipline, however, is that the reality of the power imbalance I was trying to make a mockery of meant that, whatever my intended subversion, most students missed the subtext, experienced real sanctions, and just thought I was a prick. While I might have harboured grand ideas about my detentions inspiring future revolution and rebellion, for the students detained it was just an irritating and unjust denial of their freedoms. And many of the sanctions they received happened beyond my classroom and were not part of my intended parody. Stern words and tellings off from form-tutors and Heads of Years as those silly marks against their names on a computer were read by others, in higher positions of authority than me, who still bought into the system and interpreted the data as an objective affront. Who knows how many groundings and locked away games consoles at home were caused because of my stupid attempts at making a point? Let alone the possible beatings from parents who still, behind closed doors, acted as if it were another era? For all my philosophising about behaviour points simply being notes on a computer, most adults had been long trained to interpret those invented marks as something real and, unsurprisingly, they therefore did. My personal mission to lampoon the wider system might, one faraway day in the future, cause the victims of my pantomime to rethink their relationship to authority, but it didn't stop it a jot in the here and now. In the here and now it caused nothing but harm.

It also, at some point, became hard to separate the performance from the reality. We were told from day-one in teacher training about the need for consistency in behaviour management, as well as the importance of following through on any threats we might make. Once a teacher tells a class if they don't do what has been asked of them there will be consequences, and then there are no consequences, a class learns very quickly that they can get away with anything. So, committed to my character, I would lay out my expectations to the class, be clear I would be following the school policy to the letter, and, in doing so, end up having to dole out far too many actual punishments to students who had only committed the most minor of infractions. This often *escalated* their misbehaviour and occasionally led to some genuine hostility and bad feeling. I wanted to show how inhumane the behaviour system was by demonstrating that, if actually followed in the way it was written (but which no one followed in practice), it descended into absurdity. Instead, I found myself unable to be humane myself. I became the personification of the inflexibility of the system.

I became an *actual* prick.

Lost in the role I was playing, I realised there was no meaningful distinction between pretending to be a strict disciplinarian to make a point and *actually being a strict disciplinarian*. Some students were genuinely frightened of me and my erratic and unpredictable behaviour. Would I be the joke-slinging, wacky voices, take-nothing-too-seriously version of me I sometimes was if they asked me a question, or would I be the asshole? Some days even *I* didn't know as I found the frustrations of the job boiling over, and what would begin as a performative attempt at showing annoyance at a student for failing to do a piece of homework became a genuine channel for venting actual anger. I would hear my voice echo that of my mother, when she would take all her irritations about her failing marriage out on me and my sister, ostensibly telling us off about a spilt drink or untidy bedroom but, in reality, just raging against her miserable life. The million little exasperations of a teaching career would be projected onto my students in angry tirades about their shortcomings and I would end the day hating myself a little more, regretting becoming the very thing I hoped to be fighting against. I had become a monster: not merely a teacher, but a *horrible* teacher. The sort of teacher I had always hated when I was at school. And, in the name of consistency, I was getting trapped in that role.

Of course, I would call myself out about it. Apologise to the student. Acknowledge the hypocrisy and unfairness. Seek reconciliation and try to reset the relationship and start again. But even when the students forgave me, *I* never really could. Some days it was hard to look in the mirror. They say 'hurt people, hurt people' and one of the big lessons I got when I first started out teaching, sitting in a freezing school hall on some INSET morning and listening to safeguarding training about the signs of domestic abuse, was that my own childhood had been full of it. Emotional abuse and neglect. My parents' marriage was a long cold-war in grim détente, and my mother's coping strategy was to take it out on us, not in violence, but in verbal cruelty. My sister and I were frequently called idiots. Stupid. Dumb. So much so that it just became normal. I didn't recognise it as abusive at the time because it was just the way she talked. The way life was. Teacher training also taught us that we should never call a child stupid. The same way they taught us never to say 'shut up' when asking a class to be quiet. And I, the anarchist who was also an unwitting victim of my own sad childhood, was naturally suspicious of the supposed wisdom of authorities. I was called stupid and told to shut up loads when I was a kid and it didn't do me any harm, I reasoned, not yet seeing the irony. So found myself intentionally saying it to students to prove a point against those who claimed to know better. 'Shut up' I would say when the noise levels got too high, and when they did shut up, without incident, I fooled myself into thinking there was no difference between asking nicely for quiet and being rude. But I could see the sense of shock in some of my students' eyes, as if they had been slapped, and began to question whether the way my mother spoke to me as a child really *had* left me unharmed. Words, it turned out, were powerful things. And sometimes wisdom was given authority because it was truly wise and deserved to be listened to.

'*You* shut up you fucking prick.'

The student who said that back to me one lesson did not get into trouble for doing so because he was absolutely right. I *was* a fucking prick. Like the student I called a 'moron' in the heat of the moment another lesson who utterly lost it and refused to do any work for the rest of the day because 'I'm such a moron I wouldn't know what to do anyway, sir'. I was humbled by their righteous outrage and ashamed at how I had made them feel just because I couldn't handle my own shit.

Hurt people, hurt people.

When I was at university, I was always interested in the psychology behind philosophical theories. Thomas Hobbes, writing after experiencing the chaos and brutality of civil war, wrote a political philosophy in fear of descending back into such violence that he hoped would ensure such wars never happened again. Jean-Jacques Rousseau was a socially awkward individual, uncomfortable around others, and so he formulated his own version of the social contract which attempted to limit the impositions and interactions of the masses on individual sovereignty. I sometimes think about my own anarchist leanings and wonder how much of it is really based on intellectual conviction and the power of compelling evidence and argument, and how much of it just stems from growing up in a family where the figures of authority were so poor. A cheating, largely absent, father; an abusive and insecure narcissist of a mother. *Of course* I am suspicious of authority. Take it a little further and we find that, before he worked for CILIP, my dad worked in local government and my mom was a journalist. My American grandparents were in publicity, working with the media, and, as I already said, my UK grandad was a priest and my grandmother a teacher. Am I railing against the system, or am I railing against my childhood?

All I know is that this conflict between having to enforce problematic school behaviour policies and stay true to both who I was, and what I believed, was the toughest element of becoming a teacher. Although I was often a go-to colleague for people to come and observe for my so-called 'excellent' classroom management skills, I don't believe I ever got it right unless it was the times I was actively ignoring the policy (or any misguided aspiration to lampoon it through strict adherence) and just working horizontally *with* my students instead of hierarchically against them. Relationships, as I have already said about 'leaving a tip', are key, and rigidly enforcing stupid rules only ever acted as a barrier to having successful relationships. When I dropped the act and opened up a dialogue with my classes as equal partners in their own education, even the students who thought I was an asshole happily opened up too. They worked better than they ever had before. When given the freedom to set their own parameters in the classroom, either on the topic they were studying or the approach they were going to take to learning, time and time again students thrived.

My favourite example of this approach was a lesson I did each year on the concept of authority. Students were given a definition of authority as 'someone who tells you to do something and you feel you have to do it' and asked to come up with a list of all the people they thought had authority over them. Once a list was collected on the board of all the people who have authority over us (parents, teachers, police, government, God, doctors, aunts and uncles, grandparents, etc…) I would ask students to come up with a question they thought would be worth asking about that list. I showed them a red button on my PowerPoint and explained that I wanted *them* to have the authority to choose what we spent the rest of the lesson talking about, not me, and that they ought to try and come up with something meaty and philosophical enough to fill about half an hour of discussion, with the aim being that we didn't have to hit that red button and reveal my own 'boring teacher's question'. If we ended up doing *my* question, I told them, it would mean the lesson had failed, even though my question was still fairly interesting. It would fail because it would be *my* question we would be asking, and not theirs.

The best thing about that lesson was that in six years of teaching it (and teaching it two or three times each year), I never once had to hit the emergency 'boring teacher's question' button. And every single year the questions the students self-generated were utterly worthy of spending a lesson discussing and far better than my dull inquiry: 'what makes each of these authorities "legitimate"?'. Although their own questions usually aligned with the general philosophical direction of mine, theirs had the extra added element of *ownership*. Their genuine interest in exploring it because it was *theirs*, not mine, always made the lesson come alive.

It is tradition at the end of term to show students a movie in their final lesson, or perhaps spend the session doing a quiz or something else considered 'fun'. Although I have done all of those things too, sometimes I would spend a lesson like that with my classes just chatting with them. A fifty minute, completely improvised and unstructured, whole-class discussion which required no clever resources or techniques of behaviour control. The key was finding out something they wanted to think about and then stimulating their thinking with some good questions they wanted to find out the answers to. I was inspired to do this from my own A-level philosophy teacher, who, as well as fatefully mentioning to me the 'consortium' his daughter trained to be a teacher with, used to hold 'kickabout' lessons with us when we were his students. These lessons took the temperature of the room and, whenever the motivation to do the required A-level work was lacking, involved him simply asking us what we wanted to talk about instead. He'd then find ways of making those topics philosophical and we'd end up spending a productive lesson doing philosophy but thinking we were talking about something else. It was in those 'kickabout' lessons far more than in the planned A-level lessons that philosophy really came alive to me, and when I found myself all those years later teaching GCSE and A-level exam classes of my own I realised my students weren't getting any of that self-directed freedom to explore their own interests because there was just so much exam content we were trying to cram into far too few lessons.

The end of term 'kickabout' chat lessons then evolved into what I called 'Philosophy Unleashed' sessions. Why wait for the end of term to do them when that Friday afternoon period six lesson was always sub-optimal for doing any of the exam stuff? I would take a break from the planned curriculum whenever the time could be spared, or felt needed, and would ask the students what they wanted to spend the lesson talking about, the only guidance being that it couldn't be something on the exam specification.

'Philosophy Unleashed' lessons were a joy, and always led somewhere interesting and philosophically valuable. Although they had nothing to do with either the GCSE or A-level exams, they had everything to do with making my students good philosophers and critical thinkers, and there is no doubt that the development of those skills contributed ultimately to their usually excellent exam results. But the skills were developed non-coercively, through students picking subject matter that genuinely interested them (usually from the week's news) facilitated by me but never dictated. Luckily my childhood fascination with *Ghostbusters, Saturday Night Live*, and *SCTV* also led to a side-hustle in improv comedy. Since my university days I have done improv whenever I had the time, first in my university drama society's show, *Theatre Anarchy*, then in my own groups, *The Fourth Chair, Box of Frogs, The Kneejerks,* and *Fat Penguin.* This meant that in the classroom I was unafraid of running an unscripted and unplanned fifty-minute lesson based entirely from audience suggestions. I had stepped on stages in pubs and theatres empty handed for years, with only 'yes, and…' and my equally unscripted scene-partners to build random words into entire plays before a paying audience's eyes. It was completely undaunting, therefore, to let my students set the agenda and draw on my own years of studying philosophy to help facilitate their self-directed philosophical discussions. They always inspired my own thought too. By April of 2019 I decided to start a blog of the same name – *Philosophy Unleashed* – and write a weekly philosophy essay stirred from both these sorts of sessions and other philosophical discussions I was having with my students between the cracks of the curriculum. Anarchism in action. Informal, non-hierarchical, student-led, and self-directed teaching smuggled into the margins of the otherwise hierarchical, exam-obsessed, and rigidly formal school timetable. However, I was all too aware that there were many students who found these sessions a waste of time precisely because they *weren't* covering exam material. The problem with being critical of the dominant system and trying to offer alternatives from within is that, well, the system is still *dominant*, which means most people either buy into it or have never really questioned it before. It is the perceived normal and natural – correct – way of doing things. If school is about carefully structured learning experiences aimed at getting you top marks in a terminal examination, then these wild moments of improvised, unstructured, and explicitly non-exam focused free-form discussion could be deeply troubling. They flew in the face of the ever-present narrative that every lesson counted, and there was barely enough time in the school year to cover all the content needed for the exam, as well as the increasing standardisation of what a lesson was supposed to be growing in the wake of the 'research-informed' turn in education policy. As the DfE, Ofsted, and various organisations began to hold up the latest developments in cognitive science on memory and making information stick as the guiding principle of what education ought to be, students were increasingly facing a homogenised classroom experience across the curriculum and found approaches to teaching them in more maverick styles like mine uncommon and strange. Those who got it, got it, but more and more students seemed only interested in covering exam material and less concerned with exploring their own ideas. Coercing them into doing unwanted 'Philosophy Unleashed' sessions flew in the face of its non-coercive origins, and in latter years those wonderful breaks from the curriculum became rarer and rarer.

Truly listening to students and letting them take the reigns of their own learning has to mean letting them lead, even if sometimes it leads in directions you personally wish it wouldn't. Good education should be a conversation, rather than a monologue, and in good conversation we are directed by what others say as much as by what we plan on saying ourselves. By experimenting with anarchist pedagogy in the classroom, my students taught me as much as I would teach them. They benefitted from my knowledge of philosophy and religion, but I benefitted from their honest feedback and their own insights about the world. Their personal philosophies and religious beliefs, yes, but also, I learnt the importance of being kinder and more humane than my authoritarian caricature of a teacher was allowing me to be. And when I saw how stuck I was becoming inside the caricature, and how such kindness and humanity was becoming harder to access the more years that went by playing that pantomime role, my students taught me that it was time to take a long, hard look at myself.

When our mother used to take out her frustrations on my sister and me in bouts of abusive anger, we at least knew the cause of her frustrations. What, then, was causing mine?

# INTERLUDE – PHILOSOPHY UNLEASHED EXCERPT - 18/07/22:

## EDUCATED ABOUT EDUCATION - Anarchist Pedagogies and Learning From My Students

I have been thinking - and speaking - a lot this week about the nature of education. As I reach the end of my time at the school I am currently working in, students are understandably asking me what I'm moving on to do. When I tell them I'm taking a break or, more fancy, a *sabbatical,* to undertake some research in Philosophy of Education they inevitably have asked me what I am researching. And when I explain the basic idea, they have further questions I have been more than happy to answer. I have also been interviewed by some scholars working at Stellenbosch University in South Africa about my writing on anarchist pedagogies which gave me lots to think about too. But the main stimulus has been the series of final lessons I have been having with some of my classes. Lessons that began with a simple question I asked a group of fourteen-year-olds I have taught for the last three years: *if I had planned an ideal last lesson for you (an actual lesson aimed at teaching you something new) what would we be doing and how would we be doing it?*

What struck me from their initial answers (watch a movie, do a Kahoot! quiz, go to the computer room so we can pretend to work but actually play Minecraft) was that none of these first offers were actual "lessons". They were ways of avoiding lessons or maybe checking understanding from a previous lesson. But nothing new was being taught.

When I mentioned this to the class someone suggested going on a trip. This was much better, but I did point out that while learning would definitely occur on the trip it was interesting that, so far, the classroom or traditional teaching methods had not been chosen as a desirable possible venue or approach to learning. I asked them if it was meaningful that, given complete freedom, the best *school lesson* they could come up with was either no lesson at all, or to learn somewhere else? Did that mean there was no ideal lesson that could be had in a school?

The students thought about it and then began offering some new suggestions. All of them involved wanting to know more about me as a person. The possible lessons ranged from learning my life story, to a session on the philosophy behind my tattoos, and, of course, because it is a word they have heard associated with me over the years, a lesson on the philosophy of anarchism. Some just wanted to know what I kept in the store-cupboard behind my desk.

I found it interesting that once the emphasis on a *lesson in school* was added to the initial question suggestions became teacher-focused (me telling them something) or subject focused (philosophy) or both. The most seemingly creative topic, not based on me or my interests, was the request to learn "the philosophy of Shrek". But even this stemmed from a previous set of lessons we had done on "pop culture and philosophy" and was following a pattern of lessons I had already given them the blueprint for. However, after several more "philosophy of..." type suggestions were made I pointed out that whatever the topic was no one had really discussed yet how best it would actually be *taught*. For example, I asked, a little tongue-in-cheek given the earlier desire to watch a movie and years of experience watching colleagues search desperately to find a YouTube clip that explained obliquely what they could explain themselves far more easily because they knew students were more likely to pay attention to a video than to their teacher: if I did tell you the story of my life would you rather I did it live, in person, here at the front of the room or if I showed you a video from YouTube of me telling the exact same story at the front of the room a day or two before? (Thankfully, my students said they would rather the live version "because we could ask you questions". However, when I pointed out we could always pause the video for Q&A they couldn't quite articulate why they would rather the live version but still insisted that they did.)

After some thought the class agreed: the best sort of lessons were ones where they could choose what they wanted to learn, and the way they wanted to learn it, so they could learn about something they were genuinely interested in, in a way that worked best for them.

There was some dissent. A few students asked if they were best placed to decide what was and wasn't worth learning because "what if we looked at something we were interested in but missed out something more important"? They thought a teacher making such choices would ensure nothing was left out. However, I pointed out to these students that every decision we teachers make about what we will teach a class means leaving out loads of other things we don't teach. When I choose to teach a class about Islam in our Religious Studies GCSE, then that means I *don't* teach them about Hinduism, or Judaism, of Buddhism, etc. And if I choose to teach them about Islam it means only teaching them those things about Islam contained on the exam specification. Things will be missed out. For example, we do not teach them about Muhammad's Night Journey. There is always something omitted when time is finite. And GCSEs themselves are built on omission: students get to choose some subjects and drop others. The students I was talking to admitted to dropping art, geography, history... all subjects I told them there was lots of interesting things they would be missing out on learning by knocking off their timetable. And I reminded them that there would still be a teacher to offer advice about the projects they chose and help guide those choices to perhaps avoid total calamity.

This led to us considering the role of the teacher in such a class where students are choosing their own focus of learning and method of learning it. Expert knowledge of a general field was one use identified - being able to share, where relevant, pertinent information to help facilitate the student's own work. Facilitation in general was the other key aspect of a teacher's function, they decided. Helping students achieve what they were setting out to achieve. Importantly though, this was an inversely deferential relationship - the learning self-directed by the students themselves, not imposed upon them by a teacher, and the teacher there to help the student achieve a goal rather than tell them the goal they ought to be achieving.

I probed a bit and asked about high-level work and difficult skills. What would stop such self-directed students from just producing the bare minimum or doing work that wasn't particularly difficult? For example, I asked, would you write a detailed and lengthy essay on a particular topic if given the choice not to?

Students said that they would *because it would be an essay about something they were interested in*. And they can see the value in learning how to write a good essay so would want to develop that skill.

I then asked if we could expand the principle beyond a single lesson or project and imagine a whole course run this way? Taking the Philosophy or Religious Studies courses I taught, I said, would they find it better if I carried on as normal, setting specific tasks so specific topics could be learnt in specific ways or if, instead, at the start of the year I simply gave them some parameters: general areas of subjects they could explore and a set of skills they needed to work on. Then they would get to plan how to explore the subjects and develop the skills in a way that resonated with them, using me to help them. The class chose the latter instead of the former. When asked why, they said it gave them more ownership over what they were doing and would keep them *wanting* to learn because they were being led by what interested them.

I was happy to tell them that they had sort of accidentally wandered into learning a bit about anarchism because they were basically describing anarchist pedagogy: horizontal instead of hierarchical, self-directed instead of imposed, a negotiated and consenting collaboration instead of an authoritative and coercive schooling. The conversation moved on, but their thoughts left an impact on me. I had two other classes in the same year group later that week, also with final lessons, but was wary of trying to catch lightning in a bottle twice, let alone three times. Each group is different, with a different dynamic, but I was intrigued to hear their views about learning.

The second class took a different approach. We have spent a lot of time studying ethical theories this year and as soon as I opened my mouth and said "I was thinking about this being your last lesson and what we might do", one student shouted out: "we should have a *utilitarian* vote!"

I asked what that would look like.

"A vote on what would make the most people happy."

But once we agreed that if we really wanted to be happy most of us would want to be doing something outside of school and, unfortunately, we were limited to things we could do in the school, we realised the parameters of school were too restrictive for a truly *utilitarian* vote.

“We should do a *deontological* vote then, sir!” said another.

“What’s a deontological vote?” I asked.

“One that has lots of rules we have a duty to follow.”

The next third of the lesson was spent determining what the rules would be (only two things could be voted for; the thing with the greatest number of votes MUST be done; everyone only has one vote; Student A isn’t allowed to vote; Student B isn’t allowed to vote; the rules excluding students no longer apply; that being so, Student A still can’t vote, etc…) and then we realised we had a problem: what method would determine how we decided which two possibilities ended up in the final *deontological* vote? We needed a prior voting system! So the next third of the lesson was spent establishing how to decide what to vote on (we start with eight possibilities and have to whittle it down to two; Student C cannot be involved in this part of the process; the possibilities have to be realistic; Student D cannot be involved either; etc…) and then the eight possibilities to whittle down until we ended up in the final third of the lesson actually doing the *deontological* vote on what we would do between:

a) playing a game of “heads down/thumbs up”

and

b) discussing and voting on whether or not I was a good teacher

Each student had their vote and overwhelmingly (and surprisingly) elected to play the game rather than assess me. As it was a *deontological* vote, anyone who violated the rules had a serious sanction imposed on them and their vote was not counted. However, when asked how exactly we play "heads down/thumbs up" there was some confusion about exactly how many people would be "it" - three or five - and so another *deontological* vote had to be held on which number we should adopt. This time each vote had to be justified with reasons. Two votes before this exercise in informed-democracy was completed the bell rang and the lesson was over. It being a *deontological* vote, the two remaining students *had* to complete their vote (it was their duty!) and, had we any time left to play, we now knew the winning choice was three, not five. But, alas, democracy.

Still - another class given absolute freedom had chosen games instead of lessons and the self-imposing of rules and restrictions on themselves without any need for teacher coercion (even blocked and barred students A-D had agreed to their disenfranchisement). Interesting. By the time of my third final class in this year-group I decided to home in a bit more:

"What do you think actually makes a good teacher?" I asked them.

This class had been spending the day before lobbying on our Teams page for me to stay on at the school and not leave them. Some of it was tongue-in-cheek but some was sincere. I had asked them whether they would still want me to stay if I did stay but taught every other class in the school and never them, and they had kindly said yes, for the greater good of the school. If they wanted me to stay because they thought I was a good teacher, or were eager for me to leave because they didn't, what was it they wanted in a teacher?

"Someone you can actually learn from" *was* in their list of attributes, but it was the *eleventh* thing they suggested after first listing:

- Someone who is funny and you can talk to and have a good relationship with.

- Someone who lacks hubris. (*They genuinely said this, in those words!*)

- Someone who makes lessons fun and intriguing.

- Someone who can control the class without being too strict.

- Someone who can take a joke.

- Someone (in specific reference to our Teams chat the day before) who won't get angry when they get Rick-rolled (I didn't. It made me laugh a great deal).

- Someone who tells interesting stories about their lives.

- Someone who doesn't set essays every week.

- Someone who lets you sit where you want and doesn't give you detentions for sitting in the wrong seat.

The tenth showed their age, lack of maturity, and lack of understanding of the Equalities Act of 2010, but was the understandable result of feeling let down by too many teachers seemingly "abandoning" them: someone who doesn't keep getting pregnant and leaving you.

After explaining why people need to be free to have children when they want without it compromising their financial security and discussing other Protected Characteristics from the Equalities Act, I asked why it had taken them so long to reach the quality of being "someone you can actually learn from" when that seemed like such an essential aspect of being a good teacher?

"Without those other things you won't be able to learn from them" was the response. If I can't get on with you and have a laugh, if I feel a power imbalance that allows you to act with impunity against me and which I see you freely abuse, if your lessons are dull and I don't care about what we're learning, if the behaviour of the class makes it impossible to learn because you can't control it, if you're free to laugh at me but I'm not free to laugh at you, if we don't know about you and who you are beyond the classroom, if you set us the same work each and every week, if you put controlling where I sit above my enjoyment of the lesson then *I will not be able to learn comfortably in that class.*

Again - interesting. Not only do students feel they learn best when they have choice and autonomy over what they do and how they do it, but the sort of teachers they want are those who treat them like equals rather than like someone subservient and who prioritise nurturing student enjoyment and interest over control and coercion.

We debated and discussed the various merits and demerits of each proposed attribute but we had been late starting the lesson due to a House Economics competition over-running and soon the lesson was over. It had not gone unnoticed by me that all three of these lessons had not only offered great student insight and whole-class participation in interesting philosophical analyses of what a good lesson might be, how to make fair and democratic choices, and what makes a good teacher, but there had been no behaviour issues at all through any of them, even from those students who might usually misbehave in a "normal" lesson. Because it was *their* lesson, and they had been given control of what we did, they were happy to engage. In the *deontological* vote lesson we had even willingly used the school's "behaviour point" system to penalise those who broke the - self-chosen - deontological rules. Each lesson did seem to continue to prove the first group's point.

Today I had the biggest challenge of all. The whole school were out at the cinema for rewards trips for every year group. I was left behind to babysit the students in Year 10 (15 year olds) who's behaviour across the year was deemed so bad they were blocked from going on the trip. The worse behaved students in the year in my little classroom for two whole hours.

I had logged into my Netflix account to show them the movie *V For Vendetta* when I first saw my assignment. I have UCAS reports to write and assorted other jobs to finish before I leave. I'd stick a movie on, leave them to it, and get on with my proper work. Except, as they walked in, we started chatting a bit while I took the register and waited for stragglers. One of them asked the inevitable question about what I'd be doing when I left the school. As I started discussing anarchist pedagogies and the problem with discipline in schools and coercive education, others joined in with their own ideas and experiences of where school discipline had failed to meet their needs and turned them off education. Soon we were all talking about the nature of education, examination, and schools, exploring alternative ways of assessing students and re-imagining some key school routines. All, except those who didn't want to chat, who happily read a book or got on with some other work (in other words: choosing what to do and how to do it). When I spoke to the students about the responses of other groups to the question of the perfect lesson they offered their own ideas - Hide and Seek; WWE wrestling; Build a car and use it to escape the school - and once again we saw no-one advocating any model of actual learning within the framework of a school lesson and all of them equating a "perfect" lesson with the total avoidance of what we do in schools.

At least one of them tried to make Hide and Seek more "academic" when I called them on this.

"It's English revision, sir: Hyde and Seek. Like Jekyll and Hyde. Or RE, sir. Hide and Sikh."

Fair play.

All I know is that I spent a pleasant and thought-provoking two hours with the so-called worst-behaved students in the year having a series of profound conversations about education, bullying, trauma, and school discipline without my having to ever raise my voice, issue a sanction, or make a coercive threat. Motivated by genuine interest and free to express themselves and choose what we did, the whole group worked well together and learnt a lot. *V for Vendetta* was never even mentioned.

I guess the point of this lengthy last essay of the academic year before I take my summer break until September is just to record these wonderful explorations of education with students. It is a reminder to us all that whether we educate people in schools or outside of them, the students - those we intend to do the learning - are always the key people we need to be talking to and working *with*, in collaboration, to determine what ought to go on in any classroom that truly cares about educating and not simply coercing students into forced compliance. That education need not always be hierarchical and imposed but horizontal and self-directed. That schools might not always be the best places in which education happens and that, in fact, some of the norms of the school - perhaps far too many of them - actively get in the way of anything meaningful happening beyond rote memorisation and regurgitation of arbitrary information and that, if we want schools to be sites of authentic education, much work needs to be done to transform the school from what it is today.

I'll certainly be taking some time away from them as I end this particular era of my educational journey and look forward to thinking a lot more about all this as I start my sabbatical. Who knows what the future will bring? There's no external authority telling me what to do with my time or imposing any specific tasks. I just have this general topic in philosophy of education I want to explore and a self-selected and fluid end-goal I want to meet: an article or two? A book? I will be researching it myself, facilitated by those more knowledgeable than myself when I seek them out for help. I will be defining my own success and setting my own timetable. I am eager to start and excited to work hard.

It seems I will be a one-person experiment in the very anarchist pedagogy that first class proposed, bound as I am to the *deontological* decision I made (and, as the second class made clear, am duty-bound to observe), to step away from a successful career as the exact sort of "good teacher" suggested by the third class, and pursue this intrinsic, self-directed goal of educational exploration.

You learn a lot from your students, if you treat them like humans, like *equals,* and listen to them, taking their ideas seriously. I have learned so much over the last eleven years from the students at the school I am now leaving and will take the lessons they taught me into all of my future endeavours. I hope the next classroom I find myself in, wherever it ends up being, is just as educational.

## 4.
## *ATHEIST: Losing Faith in Teaching Faith*

In my last two weeks of teaching at my last school, we were threatened by a parent. They suggested that the school might be picketed to protest a Religious Education lesson that I had planned. As the school is located in Birmingham, the same city famous for the 'No Outsiders' primary school PSHE programme that, shamefully, sparked protests from concerned religious parents because of its LGBTQ+-inclusivity, this was no idle threat. It was intentionally designed to evoke images of the protests at Parkfield Community School a few years before, and had been similarly spurred by a lesson the parent's child had received the day before, involving LGBTQ+ inclusivity and religion. A lesson which suggested that it was possible to be both gay and a Muslim.

Although a good thing to know for any Muslim students at the school struggling with their sexuality, that wasn't the main objective of the lesson by any means. It was actually a lesson in a series of lessons about combatting Islamophobia and other religious prejudices in the UK. Students had to use the things they had learned that term about Islam to combat prejudiced and discriminatory ideas about the religion that had arisen in the decades following 9/11. They had been furnished with lots of data about ongoing Islamophobic attitudes in the UK and had to draw on the actual facts they now knew about Islam to show that Islamophobia – like all prejudices – is based on ignorance about the religion rather than fact. They would then have to do the same regarding antisemitism in the UK, or anti-Christian prejudice around the world, drawing on their prior learning of the other two faiths studied earlier in the year to tackle similar forms of religious intolerance across the Abrahamic religions they'd been learning about to demonstrate their accurate subject knowledge.

As one example of what we wanted, we showed claims made by Islamophobes that Islam might be considered a sexist or homophobic religion and contrasted those claims with examples of female Islamic leaders, or gay Muslims, whose very lives disputed such misconceptions. We wanted to make students aware of the distinction between legitimate *theological* requirements of a religion and arbitrary *cultural* ones. While there might be cultural norms around women and sexuality that could be considered sexist or homophobic within a certain faith *tradition*, we wanted them to see that such prejudices had no essentialism to them. They weren't exclusive to, or inherent to, Islam, even if they might accurately describe current predominant attitudes within that religion locally or historically. Sexism and homophobia could be found in other faiths too, and the existence of women leading mixed prayers at some mosques, or of faithful LGBTQ+ Muslims, immediately puts the lie to the claim that being a Muslim is incompatible with being gay or gender equality. We wanted students to use similar examples to combat the more dominant Islamophobic stereotypes surrounding terrorism and violence. If being a Muslim is really about suicide-bombers trying to violently force everyone to become a Muslim, as many Islamophobic narratives would have you believe, then why does the Qur'an tell us that 'there is no compulsion in religion' and the specific rules of Lesser Jihad, which Muslims use to guide them on when violent struggle is morally justifiable, *explicitly forbid* such indiscriminate murder and destruction?

But this Muslim parent was upset that their child had been told that a Muslim could be gay. In his opinion, this was wrong, both morally and factually. And worse, the teacher who had said this had, in doing so, dared to suggest that the message of the Qur'an – a book the parent believed, and Islam teaches, to be the unchanged revelation of Allah to the Prophet Muhammad – could be open to *interpretation*. That different Muslims might believe different things about what God's message to humanity meant, *even if they agreed that the actual words of the Qur'an had not been changed,* was, to this parent, simply describing the fact that some so-called Muslims were, in his opinion, *wrong*.

Although the teacher in question – not me, although I had planned and taught the same lesson myself the week before and completely endorsed and echoed everything this colleague had said with my own classes – had been talking about specific disputes (like both Sunni and Shi'a Muslims agreeing that the Qur'an tells them to pray five *prayers* a day but Shi'as cashing that out in practice by combining their prayers and praying only three *times* in the day in contrast to the Sunni practice of praying at *five* distinct times a day) as well as the more controversial issues of sexuality and gender equality, what really bothered the parent, it turned out, was that the teacher who had dared teach their child all this stuff was a woman. A *Muslim* woman who went *uncovered.* Therefore, a woman who, in his opinion, because of her lack of hijab, and disagreement with his own interpretation of the religion's clothing requirements, did not really understand Islam and had no authority to speak on it, despite being a Muslim herself.

I had already handed in my notice months before, but hearing our school receptionist recount the angry parent's wrong-minded threat and opinions, and having to grapple with the school's response in terms of both the content of our teaching and our students and members of staff's right to observe their faith in whatever way *they* – not some cantankerous parent – deemed appropriate, I was once again glad that I would be leaving soon and this would all become someone else's problem in September. Because this wasn't the first time the issue of homosexuality and Islam had caused me a headache in my role as Head of Department. The year before, outraged GCSE students, furious I had the temerity to suggest it was ok to be both Muslim and LGBTQ+ and back that claim up with scriptural interpretations, living examples, and references to equalities legislation, had created a parody account of me on Instagram called 'Imam.McKee', questioning my right as a non-Muslim to say things about their faith which ran counter to the ideas they were taught at home or at their local mosque. A time before that, we'd set a past-paper question in a mock exam about homosexuality and religion, as per the exam specification, and I'd had to spend a wretched weekend marking nearly a hundred diatribes about why gay people were an 'abomination' according to the Bible, punishable by death according to Sharia law, better off dead according the students, and how, if they *were* to live, they ought to live their lives loveless and alone because their sexuality was clearly a test from God, or trick of the Devil to make them stray from God's path.

I was as surprised about how common this take on sexuality was across the student body in this supposedly 'woke' decade of the twenty-first century as I was by the fact that most students went on to describe this same miserable God who condemned LGBTQ+ people to death or a life of solitude as 'loving'. My school had a significant problem with homophobia, and most of the problem stemmed from students' religious beliefs. Not just from our Muslim students, although Islam was the majority religion within the single-sex boys' school where I was working and seemed to be the most hard-line in its rejection of same-sex relationships, but from our collective religious demographic of Christians, Hindus, Sikhs, and Muslims, who all mostly seemed to believe being gay was a sin and felt it was appropriate to 'save' their peers from damnation or bad karma by making the possibility of same-sex relationships mocked, reviled, and forbidden at every opportunity. Some went as far as telling LGBTQ+ religious students brave enough to come out that they could no longer be part of their own faith anymore. Others just created a hostile environment for coming out: physically violent bullying, constant verbal harassment, or rolling their eyes and making unhelpful comments any time any LGBTQ+-positive message was attempted, especially in the Religious Studies classroom.

Frequently, LGBTQ+ students would come and find me after experiencing too much of this trolling from their peers. I had made it a point early on in my career of filling an entire section of my large classroom wall with a rainbow-coloured banner bearing the slogan 'RELIGION IS NO EXCUSE FOR HOMOPHOBIA' after getting sick of hearing kids invoking their various gods to make their LGBTQ+ peers feel bad. Students would come and ask me, tears in their eyes, burden on their souls, if they were still able to pray to their God, or attend their place of worship, because so-and-so in their class had told them that they couldn't anymore because of their sexuality or gender-fluidity. They were constantly being fed the message at home, at worship, and elsewhere around the school, that they had to make a choice between their sexuality, or their gender, and their faith and I wanted to make it clear that this was not only *not* the case, and that there were plenty of people of the same faith as them who shared their sexuality or gender-fluidity also, but that those students whose own faith told them being gay was a sin – while entitled to believe whatever they believed – had no right to treat their fellow students badly as a result of those beliefs. Some religions might well have been interpreted as suggesting that being gay is a sin, for example, but homophobia, I pointed out, *prejudice against and discriminatory treatment of gay people*, does not follow from that belief. *If* you believed such things (and throughout their classes, where relevant, they would be shown that in no religion was such a view necessary as there were practicing same-sex attracted members of all faiths, all of whom had found some scriptural basis for reconciling their sexuality with their religious beliefs) then it was between God and the individual gay person how God would judge them, not the gay person and you. Let God punish them, if indeed there is a God, and any punishment needed to be given, but how dare *you* decide to act *for* God and provide that punishment yourself. Did not the same religions which called being gay a sin also preach that we should treat people kindly, compassionately, and with love? I asked them. And that it was blasphemous to put yourself on God's level? Focus on that, and on your own moral actions. Treat people you might personally think are sinners kindly, compassionately, and with love, and let God focus on the rest. It would be a real shame if you were lucky enough *not* to have to struggle with your sexuality, I told them, but ended up in hell anyway because you bullied some poor kid into feeling suicidal because of theirs (something which regularly happened at the school). I also asked them to explore why it was that of all the possible sins which came up in the classroom – theft, murder, lying, abortion, euthanasia, divorce, etc... – it was always homosexuality, and specifically *male* homosexuality, that they felt so strongly about. Often we would pose moral dilemmas about these other so-called sins and devout students frequently showed religious kindness, compassion, and love when it came to, for example, supporting a starving person stealing food out of necessity, the teenager getting an abortion for a pregnancy caused by incestual rape, or the terminal patient in great pain who wanted a lethal injection so they could die a painless death, but found themselves unable to budge on the matter of two men loving each other, or a person born a man wanting to transition to become a woman. I was sick of seeing all this phobic torment and cruelty to our LGBTQ+ students being justified in the name of religious belief, and sicker still of it having a blind eye turned to it institutionally because others in the school didn't want to wade into theological waters they felt insufficiently equipped to swim in. If I could contribute in some small way, through the Religious Education we provided, to making life better for those students, and members of staff, who felt they couldn't openly be themselves at the school or confront repressive religious dogmas and outdated social views, then I would.

I myself am neither LGBT or Q. As far as I know I am not + either. (Although apparently my wife and I making the decision to not have children makes us 'queer' on some people's readings of Queer Theory because it intentionally violates the heteronormative custom of what a family ought to be. And, although I've only ever had heterosexual relationships, and am in a committed and monogamous marriage with a woman, that doesn't mean I've never found someone of the same sex attractive. That Tayce from RuPaul's Drag Race UK season 3, for example, definitely made me feel some *feelings* – and I guess the whole *wrestling* thing is deeply homoerotic…but I digress.) The point is, I had no personal dog in this hunt. I wasn't being oppressed by the bigotry myself or unable to be me. Nor was I trying to convince my homophobic students to *change* any religious beliefs they might hold about sin and sexuality. But after yet another suicide attempt, or another weeping disclosure from another bullied student, I certainly tried to actively convince my students (in line with the school's policy on homophobic, transphobic and bi-phobic bullying, and the 2010 Equality Act) to change how they acted towards others based on whatever beliefs they might hold, as well as rethink how committed they were to holding beliefs in the first place that *they knew* caused such hurt to others.

However, every time the subject came up in lessons and I did so, there would be an inevitable blowback from both students and parents, and every year the blowback seemed to get louder rather than diminish. I was fighting the good fight, but it was extremely fucking exhausting, unendingly depressing, and made me a constant target for some students and their parents. By the time this final threat came into the school, I was at the end of my capacity to carry on fighting. I was feeling totally burnt out.

It wasn't just discussing sexuality that caused the RE curriculum I had designed to come under attack from parents. The angry dad threatening to picket the school that day wasn't even the first angry dad we'd done battle with that academic year. A whole parents' WhatsApp group arose early in September when it was discovered that we were putting 'God on Trial' in one of our GCSE Religious Studies lessons, as we did every year. Sharing outrage and coordinating email messages to the school about the lesson, its alleged blasphemy, and my clear unfitness for my job (joke's on them: I was already thinking of leaving), these parents were furious that their children were being asked to even *consider* the idea that God's ultimate authority and goodness might be questioned.

Not that I was actually asking them to do that, of course, but the facts here didn't matter when outrage was all the evidence they needed. Far from being intentionally blasphemous, God was on trial in my classroom – as God had been tried across our department almost every year since I had started at the school – as a way of exploring that pesky philosophical problem of evil. The one I had been thinking about ever since I was a sweary-mouthed kid writing songs that tried to comedically avoid saying the 'c-word'. The one that had bothered me ever since I saw the thanks of multiple sclerosis, lung cancer, and diabetes that God had given to my most faithful family members for their unwavering worship. The trial was a way of taking the exam specification requirement for us to study the perennial problem in as engaging, fun, and intentionally *non-blasphemous* a way as possible. The name – God on Trial – was a nod to an excellent TV movie of the same name, written by Frank Cottrell-Boyce, inspired by the experiences of Elie Wiesel at Auschwitz, and starring Antony Sher. A film we had shown a clip to students of a few years before when looking at the problem specifically from a Jewish perspective. In the movie, prisoners in Auschwitz put God on trial (as Wiesel claimed they actually did) for breaking the covenant with the Jewish people and allowing the holocaust to happen. In my classroom, we were also putting God on trial regarding the existence of evil, but God here was not being accused of breaking a covenant, as he was in the movie, but of fraud. As God couldn't be all-knowing, all-powerful, all-loving and still allow evil to exist – or so the prosecution team's case went – at least one of those attributes must be lacking. The claim that God possesses all three attributes while evil still exists must mean we have either been mistaken about God's revelation to us, or that someone is intentionally deceiving us about God's true nature. The defence team's job was therefore to use the many philosophical theodicies designed to defend God from the problem of evil to demonstrate that the existence of evil was, in fact, entirely compatible with God possessing all three attributes.

The task came as part of a GCSE topic on the reliability of revelation and other philosophical problems arising from God's existence (a topic whose content was set by the exam boards, not by me). In the past, students had used their creativity to bring the problem to life in our fantasy courtroom in a variety of ways – bringing famous victims of tragedy to the witness stand to testify that God couldn't possibly love them (Job usually made an appearance, Anne Frank too) or putting up well-known scholars or religious figures to testify in God's defence (St. Augustine, Alvin Plantinga, John Hick). Very intentionally, the trial never once questioned the existence of God (for God had to exist if God was to be on trial), only the possibility of God's possession of all three attributes. And God was never allowed to be depicted on the stand to avoid any religious concerns about representing God themselves in the classroom. God was always tried, as God was tried in the concentration camps, in absentia. Although, true, there are some who might find the very questioning of God's attributes and character to be sacrilege, that is unfortunately the nature of the theological problem all students *had* to know for two different components of their GCSE exam (the topic came up again in the Christianity section of the Religious Studies paper too). We would be asking such questions of God, however the topic was approached but, within the context of the courtroom's evidence-based and logically planned back and forth arguments, students would also learn about how to construct a decent evaluative essay on the topic; something they also needed to do for the exam.

Importantly, with all the theodicies available, and the resources we provided, it was never expected that the prosecution team would ever win the case. This was an easy win for any well-prepared defence team as the problem, though a significant one in theology, *did* have many well-known attempts at overcoming it. On the rare occasions when such preparation was absent from God's defence team and the prosecution *did* end up winning over the jury of their student peers, my job as teacher in the debrief would involve showing all the ways in which the defence team should have won the case. Furthermore, no student who felt uncomfortable prosecuting God was ever made to sit on the prosecution team, and I would even explicitly state that it was *me* asking them to do this task so that, if God *did* get offended by what we were doing, for some reason, then *I* would take full responsibility on the Day of Judgment, not them. Being omniscient, I reminded my classes, God would know the offence was mine, not theirs, and punish *me* accordingly.

The trial had been a much-loved lesson because it allowed all this complicated theological discourse to emerge through independent student research, student-led argument, creative exploration, and drama, and was a fun and different way to spend a few weeks on the course. None of this mattered to the parents who emailed the school, however. The trial itself hadn't even happened yet. They'd just seen the title of the project coming up in their children's study packs – GOD ON TRIAL – and jumped to their conclusions. Sadly, even when we explained what we were doing and why, how it related to the GCSE exam specification, and how it had historically helped students achieve highly, we still ended up with several parents choosing to utilise their legal right to withdraw their children from Religious Education and removing their children not only from my classes, but from the subject entirely.

This last year was the first time the trial had led to student withdrawal from RE, but it was not the first time parents had complained about it. Every year we had at least one complaint about the trial and one complaint about that earlier lesson about Judaism and the problem of evil where we showed the clip of the Antony Sher movie. Parents writing to the headteacher and explaining how they didn't want their child to be asked to think about the possibility that God might not exist. This was not something unusual only to our school. When I was in my training year, I remember one of my first ever parents' evenings I attended watching worried parents explain to the teacher who was training me that ever since her lessons on the problem of evil (taught before I had ever set foot in the school) their fifteen-year-old daughter had been asking questions about her faith that they didn't like her asking. Usually, when it happened to us, myself and the headteacher would invite worried parents in to discuss their concerns and show them that I was not the heathen monster they believed me to be; just an open-minded teacher trying to make a difficult and thought-provoking topic fun and informative for their children. Their worries would be assuaged, and the student would continue to study and achieve highly in the subject. In my time as Head of Department I had been accused of every kind of bias and prejudice by parents and students there was to be accused of. I had been told I was trying to indoctrinate students into atheism, as was happening here, but also of trying to indoctrinate them into Christianity, into Judaism, into Buddhism, into Sikhism and into Islam. (Sorry Hinduism – for some reason I was never accused of trying to convert kids to become Hindus. Possibly because I tended to point out that the very concept of Hinduism was a colonial projection attempting to make sense of a wide range of related, but disparate, Indian religions in the first place. That it was better to think of Hindu*isms* than Hinduism as a singular faith?) I had even been accused by one family in my very first year at the school of being the Shaytan himself! The way I and, luckily, my school saw it, was that if you are being accused of trying to indoctrinate people into both atheism *and* theism at the same time, then you're probably not indoctrinating anyone into anything at all. (Unlike the accusing parents, who very much were trying to ensure their impressionable young children were never exposed to any ideas that weren't the parents' own). My approach to teaching religion, and to running a Religious Education and Philosophy department, had always been that I didn't care whether you left my classroom a theist, atheist, or agnostic, so long as when you left it you could explain and defend *why* you believe whatever it is that you believed and didn't just believe it blindly. I had no agenda – in the trial, or in any other lesson – other than exploring ideas and getting students to think critically about both faith and non-faith. Some students had left my subject over the years far more confirmed in their initial beliefs than ever, others had completely lost their faith. Others still, converted from atheism to religion. My classroom was a safe space for free-thinking and intellectual probing of all kinds. If I was trying to bring them all round to my own way of thinking, then I was failing badly. Luckily, I wasn't trying. But over a decade of constantly fighting these battles was taking its toll on my tolerance of intolerance.

Religious Education as part of a young person's compulsory state schooling has always been a controversial idea and, in some countries, there is no such thing. In some places it is, in fact, *illegal* to teach religion in school. Schools are considered by many to not be the appropriate place for discussing matters of personal faith or theological dispute. To do so, so the argument goes, might cause confusion or unwanted intervention in the private religious lives of their students. For the non-religious, such lessons might simply be considered a colossal waste of limited curriculum time. As a dual UK/US citizen who has occasionally dabbled in the idea of maybe one day moving to America, it was odd to think as I became an RE teacher here in the UK that my job doesn't actually exist across the ocean, or even across the Channel, in France. But as an atheist, I didn't necessarily disagree with that stance. My own experience of RE lessons when I was at school myself, was of being bored at endless bible stories I didn't care about and being incredulous that anyone in the room still actually believed any of this nonsense. I would certainly have benefitted from an extra English or Art lesson on my timetable each week, or to have been introduced to *Philosophy* much earlier than I was and to have studied that instead of the interminable Jesus stuff we had crammed down our throats back then.

That said, I learned a lot the day we eschewed the usual bible stuff and visited a Sikh gurdwara. Mainly because, in my small and deeply non-diverse setting where I went to school, there was only one Sikh family who lived in the whole village and until that day at the gurdwara no-one had ever bothered to explain what Sikhism actually was to any of us. Like the few black families and handful of other minority groups in that little backwards village, exclusion and alienation was the only way the new family were welcomed. Likewise, without my grandmother's insistence on teaching my sister and me about our own Jewish heritage, I would have known nothing about the religion that defined one whole half of my family. Judaism only came up in my own school days in the context of the Holocaust and World War II, never in RE lessons. I knew no Jewish people besides us and, had my grandmother not refused each year to send us Christmas gifts and insisted instead that they were for *Hannukah*, grumbled frequently to herself in enthralling Yiddish epithets that compelled us to ask questions, or taken us to the one and only Passover seder we ever attended, it is entirely possible my sister and I would not ever have known that we even *were* Jewish. My mother had long ago distanced herself from the faith of her upbringing, despite the Jewish idea of matrilineal descent meaning that her children became Jewish by birth-right whether she liked it or not. Once my sister and I started asking questions about our Judaism, however, triggered by gran's enthusiastic and ongoing publicity work for the religion, mom couldn't resist lighting the odd menorah candle or breaking out a little Hebrew of her own at times to keep our religious links alive. As she put it: 'if being born from a Jewish mother makes you Jewish enough to be killed by Nazis, I guess you may as well know a little bit about it in case one day you're ever killed for being one.'

When school RE lessons were just about trying to get us to believe in Jesus, I wasn't interested, but when they were about educating us about different faiths and worldviews, I had to concede I found them not only fascinating, but essential. In a pluralistic society, if we are not taught about our differences and similarities, distance grows instead of community. I would have benefitted greatly if we had ever studied Judaism at school. Although the colour of my skin gave me a pass with my peers that the black kids and the Sikh kids didn't get, my connection to Judaism still made me somewhat alien to many of them. Jewish stereotypes and antisemitic language abounded, and I learned to keep quiet about my background and pretend I believed in the same God they did even though I believed in none. Sharing information about different cultural backgrounds and ways of looking at the world is important if we want to be inclusive but, unfortunately, when I was at school, Religious Education wasn't really about that. Stemming from the education system's origins in the Christian church, and the evangelical mission of our historically Christian lawmakers, Religious Education in England was traditionally about sharing the gospel and little else. I left school knowing that Christians believed 'Christ died for our sins' and that we should 'turn the other cheek', but not knowing what those phrases actually meant. Nor did I know what a Buddhist was. A Hindu. A Sikh. Or a Muslim. I remember watching the planes hit the Twin Towers on 9/11, just a week after I had been in New York for my grandmother's funeral (my first time actually stepping foot inside a synagogue) – my mother still there in the city sorting out her mother's estate when they hit – and realising how little I knew about the Islamic faith I was being told by the media was the cause of the atrocity. Amidst the fertile grounds of such religious ignorance, it was easy to see how the seeds of Islamophobia could take root so easily across our uneducated country.

God, and the existence or lack thereof of a deity, is an entirely separate issue from the concrete reality of religion as a real and life-affecting thing. I could see the value of studying the reality of different cultures and beliefs without having to believe that any of them were actually true. Were I an anthropologist trying to explain the behaviour of an ancient civilisation, it would be enough to know that *they* believed killing six rabbits and a fox was necessary to please the 'god of the hunt' before any attempt to gather food, without my having to worry about whether such a deity *actually* existed. That *they* believed, and those beliefs informed their real-life actions, is all that matters. It is therefore both useful and important to know that people we currently co-exist with, in our own experiment in civilisation, might have similarly opaque and esoteric rationales for their actions if we want to both understand why they do what they do, and avoid causing them unnecessary offence or insult. Personally believing the reasons to be flawed, misguided, or utterly stupid – and the actions and beliefs themselves to be absurd – is completely compatible with thinking it still important that we understand, and maybe even respect, those reasons, actions and beliefs held and performed by others *from their perspective*. I might disagree with your rationale for not eating shellfish, but that doesn't mean I don't need to know you won't eat shellfish if I am ever serving you dinner.

At the same time, those other *philosophical* questions are important to ask too. Once we know that people *are* motivated by beliefs they believe are ordained by a transcendent deity, it seems reasonable to ask questions about whether such motivations are sound. And taken in the abstract, as purely theological debate, such questions – if asked seriously – can't help but inform our understanding of the real and lived concrete faiths that people hold. Confessional religious instruction, aimed at converting and inducting students into one particular faith has no place on any right-minded school curriculum, but anthropological religious education, aimed at teaching students about the multitudes of different beliefs and worldviews while offering no single belief or worldview up as THE truth, and giving students the philosophical and intellectual tools to analyse and assess those beliefs for themselves not only has a place, but might be invaluable if we want to truly understand each other as a society. The problem is that such an idea of inclusive understanding has become increasingly at odds with the growing trend towards tribalist isolation and division brought on by, along with other factors, the rise of social media. It is not insignificant that the refusal to allow several students to engage with not only the God on Trial work, but the entire RE curriculum from that point on, came the year the parents finally grouped together on WhatsApp. Gone was the interpersonal dialogue between the parent, the student, myself, and the headteacher, where views could be explained calmly and agreed compromises reached. Instead, we had lines drawn in the sand and feet firmly dug in, unwilling to give any ground.

We rarely listen to reason these days – argument has just become like school debating competitions, themselves modelled on the team-sport approach of parliamentary debates: defend your side and attack your opponent without any intention to actually listen to what they might have to say. My philosophy of what Religious Education should be was based on entirely the opposite assumption: listen to each other and discuss with an open-mind and open-heart so that we may get to know and understand each other more. Develop an awareness of the multitude of different ways of looking at the world and recognise that no one view holds special preference over others unless it can stand up to objective scrutiny. Even those within the same faith fail to agree on all things, and we should recognise that diversity and disagreement is our true commonality. On answers to ultimate questions, we do not yet have the confidence to claim absolute knowledge and must instead defer to the best hypothesis or accept our ignorance and probable biases towards simply accepting the set of beliefs that allow us best to make it through each day.

Believe it or not, I have always wanted to believe. I just couldn't see how you do it given all the unreasonableness and inconsistencies that arise so obviously around religion. A Jewish mother, a Christian father, and both of them actually atheists, or at least agnostics. Being Jewish by birth was great, because the more I learnt about Judaism the more I discovered the phenomena of secular, or cultural, Judaism. That you could still be Jewish without actually engaging in the whole *spiritual* thing. My gran realised she was on a losing battle with me when it came to ritual and regulation, but a winning one when it came to introducing me to Jewish musicians, comedians, and writers, especially ones from in and around her native New York. I rejected Hashem, but fell in love with the Jewish cultural voice; a connection that I still feel deeply to this day as a connection to that side of my family and heritage. Having a Christian minister for a grandfather, meanwhile, and an entire country steeped in the Christian tradition, seemed likely to make me a Christian at some point almost by default. Singing hymns in school, saying the Lord's Prayer at the end of every assembly, eating chocolate eggs every Easter, and performing in the school nativity at Christmas – I just assumed at some point Christianity would beat me down with its sheer omnipresence and win. But, for some reason, the religion just never spoke to me. It always seemed so *boring* compared to the glimpses of Judaism that I got to compare it to. While Christians had parables, Jews had jokes. Where churches echoed with the antiquated Latin of stuffy Public-School classrooms, the Hebrew of Judaism was mysterious and strange to my ears; an ancient unknown language that whispered of an ageless other world. Every Jewish person I met when I visited my grandmother in America was a larger-than-life character, whereas every Christian I knew back home (including my British grandparents, bless them) seemed slightly dull and pedestrian by contrast. I guess I've always liked an underdog. Christians were too establishment – the Queen ran the Church of England for God's sake! And Henry VIII seemed to have just made-up his own version of Christianity so he could get a divorce and piss off the Pope. How could I take seriously what was clearly merely the invention of a murderous and misogynistic madman rather than anything truly divine? Especially when the Catholicism he had rejected had its own indulgences and excommunications that seemed far more about politics and profits than about piety? Jews were a minority, *always* a minority, frequently *killed* for their beliefs. If I was going to be on any team, then it would always be the least mainstream one I could find. The religion of the people, rather than of the powers that be. The religion that encouraged *questions* as much as answers.

The problem was though, the very fact I saw so early that there *were* teams – that religion was ultimately a *choice* – meant its absurdity was always all-too clear for me to ever actually believe. The closest I ever came was a weekend, one holiday in my teens, when my friend and I decided to give Christianity a shot while spending the week in St. Ives, Cornwall. We bought crosses to wear as necklaces, read a bit of the bible, and even came close to going into a church, but by our first Sunday as Christians (about two days into the experiment) we were too struck by the preposterousness of the whole thing to take it any further. If God were real, we reasoned, what did it matter whether we went to a church or not? If God was the sort of thing concerned with whether we were singing God's praises enough, then was God really anything worth singing the praises of? What an ego! Like when the conductor at a classical music concert keeps coming out for a bow at the end of every song, whether you cared for the song or not. Or when the actors in a play demand their standing ovation despite their mediocrity. Give us something to sing your praises for and let it be up to *us* to decide if you are praiseworthy. If this is it, the whole thing we're supposed to be thankful for, a painful life we didn't ask for in a fucked up world that has *always* been fucked up, then colour us unimpressed and don't expect an alleluia. We took off the cross necklaces and started playing punk rock songs instead.

It sounds facetious, and in its childish way it is. But it is also a serious point. *That* there is a God or not is an entirely separate question from whether, *if* there is one, such a God is actually an entity worth worshipping. Even at that age, I had my doubts. Not only the persistent nag of the problem of evil, but this whole business of kneeling and begging for forgiveness for things we seemed designed explicitly to do. Of going through time-consuming rituals simply because *this is what we have always done as this is what has been asked of us*. Of saying empty words by rote about the greatness of something that still didn't strike me as great.

Yes, I wanted to believe. But I wanted to believe in the same way that once as a child I sat and wept while watching the movie, *Forrest Gump*: I wished I were as simple-minded as Forrest was, so that I too could go through life as happily oblivious as he did. But I knew all-too-well that I just *couldn't*. That life for me would always be difficult because I didn't have the simplicity forced on me by learning obstacles that Forrest Gump did. I was too fucking hyper-aware and over-analytic. Too astute and critical to let it all just wash all over me. I would always be asking questions, always be probing holes and looking for answers. Just as I envied Forrest his uncomplicated view of the world, I envied those who were able to believe there was a loving being in the sky looking out for them. Those who believed that when you died you went to heaven and who had a constant companion in God to get them through tough times and be able to speak to in prayer. Those who believed there was a plan for everything written by a being who wanted only the best for them and had the power to make it so, and that all they had to do to receive those blessings and grace was follow a few little rules. Wear this and not that. Pray in a certain way at a certain time. Celebrate this and remember that. Gather together on particular days and utter some specific words when you do. Avoid this and do that. It was a lovely idea. But as well as the impact of already coming from the conflicted heritage of a two-religion family, I had also spent much of my childhood obsessed with the myths and legends of the ancient Greeks. I had read of the gods we no longer were supposed to believe in, who once resided on Mount Olympus, as well as those of the Romans, whose Zeus was called Jupiter, or the Vikings, whose Zeus was called Thor. I had heard from the American side of my family about Wakan Tanka and other Native American spirits now dismissed as superstition instead of faith, and I had seen colourful pictures of weird and wonderful Hindu deities – far older than the Yahweh believed in by my divided grandparents, and far more interesting, yet arbitrarily rejected by them just because they happened to have been born in the West and not the East. It just seemed so obvious to me, as I watched the racism of the myopic small town I grew up in conflate so easily with its religious prejudice, that if God really were an omnipresent being who revealed themselves to humanity surely it wouldn't matter which side of the world your family were from for us all to agree on the nature of the divine? If coming from Asia made you more likely to believe in Hinduism, Islam, Sikhism, or Buddhism, and coming from the UK made you more likely to be a Christian, then wasn't it obvious that these were entirely cultural beliefs invented by humans, rather than supernatural edicts revealed to us by God? The geographic disparity of belief spoke far more of human impediments to travel and communication than they did of an omnipotent supreme being. And those same reasons we explained away the beliefs of the Greeks, Romans, Vikings and all the indigenous peoples whose native religions were replaced through force by missionaries and colonists – that they were primitive people who did not have sophisticated explanation for phenomena and so came up with stories – gods – to explain what they could not otherwise explain – seemed no less fitting for the popular religious beliefs of the day. We may know more about the weather now than we did back then, and not need separate gods to explain away the rain, the sun, or the thunder, but we still fear death and want to tell ourselves comforting stories that might make our demise more bearable. We still lack a satisfactory explanation of why we are here (at least a satisfactory explanation that puts our lives at the centre of its story and gives us a sense of meaning and purpose) and so we live discomforted by the existentialist thought that there is no explanation. That the revelation of the scientists with their big bang and evolutionary theories, that we might just be a giant cosmic accident with no higher purpose than mere survival, could be *true*. So we told ourselves stories of divine wisdom and plans instead. And when we die – a paradise, or punishment for all the terrible injustices that go unnoticed every day.

Considering the human brain can't even look up at the moon without seeing a face that isn't there, or hear a house settle in the night without imagining a footstep, it is not particularly surprising that it generates a similarly organising metaphysics to make sense of the world. We literally have a 'blind spot' in our vision where our brain fills in optic gaps with pure fantasy of what it wants to be there because it can't cope with the nothingness; why wouldn't it do the same with our very existence?

At the same time that all of this was so obvious to me, even as a child the idea of *having faith in spite of all these obvious reasons not to* fascinated me. It couldn't simply be that people were stupid. People demonstrably *weren't* stupid about so much, and many of the religious people I had encountered – my granddad the Reverend, and my Jewish grandmother included – were some of the smartest people I knew. At my school, the most religious teachers I had were all in the science department, a subject I found incredibly difficult and confusing. Maybe the more you knew about the world, the more obvious it became that God existed? Maybe the more you learned the more you realised how little any of us really know? There was no clear correlation between ignorance in other fields and religiosity, and the most unexpectedly open-minded thinker in all kinds of other areas was just as likely to be deeply religious as they were to be an atheist. I wanted to dismiss it all as upbringing and cultural laziness, but maybe there was more? After all, each of my parents had rejected the faith of their childhood. Being raised in a particular religion didn't seem to mean you had to stay in it for your entire life. I was interested in what kept these intelligent people of faith believing. Which is why I was so interested in asking those questions to the youth church leader who came to our school. The ones that first got me into philosophy. And it was why I started out my academic philosophical journey seeking to disprove God's existence once and for all. It wasn't because I wanted to succeed in my proposed mission of concrete atheism, but because part of me wanted to be proved *wrong*.

When the chance to get into teaching Philosophy in schools through the backdoor of Religious Education emerged for me, I therefore did not see Religious Education as a burden. I saw it finally as an opportunity to once again open my mind to the possibility of God, or at least the possibility of a reasoned faith, after years of simply dismissing it. Far from going into teaching RE to convert theists into atheism, I went in with the secret hope that by dedicating my time to these questions of theology I had spent most of my life scorning and then avoiding, by really getting to know the best arguments there were, the ones so good they had been selected to teach to each new generation, I might finally find the holes in my own worldview.

But alas…

Despite the open mind, the continuing theme of my experience as a teacher of RE was the sheer paucity of decent or convincing argument that I could find. The intellectual superficiality of theology compared with the rigor of the ethical and political philosophy I had trained in was something I found truly shocking. A million convoluted versions of that old Lee and Herring sketch that ends in Jesus just saying 'aaaaah' and basking in divine mystery and the voice of the angry disciple saying back to him: 'no, *not* aaaaah', only to be greeted by a second, even smugger, '*yes* aaaaah' as a response. Essentially every inconsistency or inconceivability theology probed was treated as a holy mystery beyond our understanding and attempts to resolve them as a futility born from lack of faith. The faithful apologists wanted to have their cake and eat it too. God was transcendent and beyond our understanding whenever it was convenient, but completely knowable and understood when passing edicts about what we ought to eat, wear, or do. On the problem of evil, we cannot understand God's ways, but on who we should love, or which gender gets more authority than the other, God is apparently crystal clear.

I was disappointed to discover that the arguments in support of the divine remained no more sophisticated than the same empty medieval attempts I had already rejected in my youth. God *has* to exist, the theologians told me, because the world is too perfect to have come about by accident. Except the world *isn't* perfect. Far from it. And the theory of evolution explains the *appearance* of design satisfactorily without resort to God because we are looking at the world at the end of billions of brutal years of arbitrary death, extinction, and obsolescence which makes our current state seem perfect and fine-tuned only because everything unable to survive in it previously is already long dead. And if perfect things can't come about by accident, as the argument claims, then who designed *God*? If you tell me God doesn't need a designer – that God just *is* perfect – then maybe the world doesn't need a designer either? The world is certainly about as perfect as a flawed God who allows evil and suffering to thrive in their so-called perfect world! Maybe the world is the same sort of thing as God? The God who allows evil to test us in our faith, even though they are supposedly omniscient and already know the outcome of any test they have set? The God who chose to give us freewill even though they knew we would abuse it, because they apparently *love* us? Because they knew, in their omniscience, that a world with freedom in it is better for us than a world without freedom? Except, if that's true, then that same supposedly all-powerful God is either unable to create a world in which we could be both free and good, or create a world in which freedom is not needed. Given this same God is supposed to be the cause of everything – creating it *ex nihilo,* out of nothing – then this means it is God's own fault the world requires suffering and evil for it to function, not the free beings God chose to inhabit it. And God *has* to have created everything because that other argument for God's existence is that everything has to have a cause, and without a God at the start of that chain of cause and effect, eternal and standing outside of the chain of cause and effect, then the chain would be infinite, which is impossible. God is the *first cause.* Except *if* God can exist outside of that chain of cause and effect without being, themselves, caused by something then *not everything that exists requires a cause*, so the argument fails. Maybe the universe, too, was outside of that chain in the beginning? A spontaneous quantum event? After all, we already have a cause of everything that doesn't require God anymore: the Big Bang.

It was just a rehash of the same old battles I used to have with the church youth leader at school. The same old sophistry and faith instead of answers. The same old feeling that I would never be Forrest Gump.

The more I taught, the more I learned, and the more difficult I found it to see religious belief as anything more than deep-seated cultural superstitions inherited and elevated through repetition and lack of challenge, generation after generation, until they reached a place of social stature so great that they had transcended to a place beyond questioning. I was right as a teenager when I wrote "*God is the socially acceptable imaginary friend*". As Freud famously suggested, there is no real difference between the rituals of the obsessive compulsive and the rituals of the faithful beyond the perception we have as a community that one is crazy and the other sacred.

Yet my mind remained open to being proved wrong. And each year, class after class, I taught the beliefs of the faithful respectfully, and the arguments of the faithful put forward in defence of those beliefs, in the hope that maybe this would be the year that I would finally see why so many of my students, and colleagues, found them so compelling. At the same time, having not yet been proved wrong, it did make it all the more uncomfortable when I saw these deeply questionable dogmas being used so frequently to justify ugly attitudes towards women and LGBTQ+ people. Knowing that none of the beliefs at the heart of these behaviours were necessary, or even defendable, made someone's decision to commit to them, and choose hate over kindness, discrimination over equality, hard to fathom. Society – and my school's – shoulder-shrug of acceptance for otherwise unacceptable attitudes whenever they stemmed from a place of faith became increasingly difficult to swallow.

As an anarchist, I guess I just find God to be another unnecessary external authority imposed over and above autonomous humanity in order to exert control. The *ultimate* unnecessary authority. My natural inclination is therefore to say no. Rebel. Resist. When you don't even believe in governments, it's pretty difficult to believe in a God. And when you can see so clearly how the very same human authorities you see no need for – authorities which you believe actively damage and corrupt the sort of world we are living in – have used religion historically, interpreting this alleged, and incredibly useful to them, deity's words into laws and norms which happen to benefit the powerful and justify ill-treatment and oppression against their enemies, their competitors, and those weaker than they are, then it becomes very easy to question the veracity of this so-called 'God' and leave a bad taste in your mouth when you see injustices being done in God's name.

I do not have the arrogance to claim I know, absolutely, that there is not a spiritual realm beyond our current comprehension. I can still freak myself out about ghosts I have no rational reason to believe in if I am in a creepy house alone at night after watching a horror movie on Halloween, and I still find myself offering up a prayer if my plane hits a sudden bout of turbulence or someone I love is in hospital. It is *nice* to believe when it is useful. It can be comforting or, in the case of the Halloween scares, it can be fun. But ideas and possibilities are not reality. The idea of God is distinct from the idea of religion, and while the God question might be eternally up in the air due to the impossibility of proving a negative, religion is all-too real even if God might not be. Religions exist. Some bring great comfort to people. But then again, so does junk food. Religion can bring meaning and purpose to many people's lives, but dealing drugs or stealing cars can bring meaning and purpose too. We can find meaning and purpose in many things, and must remember that religion's privileged status as a provider of meaning and purpose comes only from the underlying belief that it is a meaning and purpose ordained by God. But the God that ordained it might not even exist. And the surfeit of religions and their conflicting edicts give firm evidence that, whether or not there is a God, whatever it is that religions are peddling has no guarantee of divine origin, or even of being right. We can just as easily give meaning and purpose to our existence ourselves. And if we do so, we are no longer committed to upholding outdated social and moral norms of and earlier and less evolved time.

Religious Education perhaps has its place within education anthropologically, as a form of intellectual self-defence. A critical and philosophical Religious Education that offers understanding of the shared pluralistic world we inhabit, and protection from superstition and letting our beliefs harm others, no matter how much we may cherish them ourselves. Students should not go to schools and have their deeply held beliefs attacked, but they should also not be able to go through their education without having their beliefs explored. We should all want our beliefs examined and probed, and should never be afraid of changing our minds. I'm happy to hear the arguments against anarchism, against atheism, against anything I believe (I've hoped for years someone can talk me out of my vegetarianism and allow me to enjoy meat again). I've spent over a decade of my life working in an explicitly authoritarian and non-anarchistic institution teaching about the very God I doubt the existence of. I have immersed myself in views counter to my own and been inundated in hierarchy and faith. As this book shows: it hasn't shaken my beliefs, it has only served to strengthen them. At the same time, it has given them nuance and context. It has improved and fine-tuned them; forced them to evolve.

The history of religion, as of all cultural phenomena, is a history of evolution. Ideas develop, ideas clash, good ideas survive, bad ideas fall. What lives only inside our heads eventually hits up against the reality constructed by what lives inside the collective heads of everyone else and, together, we create a shared and ever-changing interpretation and meaning. My main department colleague was a devout evangelical Christian. We left the school at the same time together – me to pursue academic research on anarchism and education, he to take over his church. His faith remains steadfast despite working closely with an atheist like me for over a decade. I am sure I have influenced his thinking on some issues, and I know he and his faith has influenced mine. I can no longer say that every Christian I have met is dull and pedestrian for one thing. And while I might not believe that Jesus Christ was God incarnate, or even that there is such a thing as God, the patience and kindness I have learnt from observing this man who tries to emulate the patience and kindness of his divine role model, has been a very humane gift that I know has made me a better person. It is *healthy* to test your beliefs out against the beliefs of others and see what survives. The worst thing that happens is that you trade in some bad beliefs for beliefs that are better.

Those parents who complained about what we were teaching their children were parents, though apparently religious, who were clearly without faith. To fear your child will stop believing if they ask too many questions about how a loving God might permit evil to exist is to concede that you yourself do not think such questions can be reasonably answered. To admit that your own faith wouldn't be able to withstand such basic scrutiny. They ought to know better, but such fear obviously stems from never having experienced Religious Education this way themselves. Meanwhile, the parents so desperate to keep the possibility of their child being gay at bay that they would rather their child live in suicidal fear of eternal torture and damnation for being who they are than live their lives as a happy, gay, member of their chosen faith are parents who do not deserve to have children.

Some people are gay, as the old Stonewall ad put it, get over it. Your job is to love your children unconditionally, not make their lives miserable. If anyone is going to hell it will be the parents who threaten to disown their LGBTQ+ children or excommunicate them from their religion just for loving who they love and being who they are. And if they're *not* the ones who are hell-bound, then God isn't worth worshipping anyway. If people like that are filling up heaven and being rewarded for their bigotry, then I'll be happy burning with the rebels down in hell.

## INTERLUDE – PHILOSOPHY UNLEASHED POST - 29/03/21:

## OFFENSIVE IMAGES - An Ethic of Kindness

As I write this a teacher in West Yorkshire has been suspended for showing students controversial *Charlie Hebdo* cartoons depicting the Islamic Prophet, Muhammad, in an RE lesson. As an RE teacher myself, who covers the *Charlie Hebdo* issue in class too, and who used to cover the *Jyllands-Posten* Muhammad cartoons controversy too, along with the fatwa put out on author, Salman Rushdie, after the publication of *The Satantic Verses*, back when we taught the old OCR GCSE spec section on Religion and the Media, the story bothered me for a number of reasons.

The first thing I wondered was - did I ever show students those cartoons myself? I know that I have definitely seen them, and that I had Googled the Dutch cartoons while preparing for those initial lessons on Religion and the Media, and the *Charlie Hebdo* ones in the immediate aftermath of the brutal massacre enacted by extremists in response to their publication. Had I ever brought them into the classroom as artefacts to unpack? After all, there is a lot discussed and analysed in the RE classroom which may bristle the pious in any religion. Certainly there has never been a problem looking at a passage of Richard Dawkins' *The God Delusion*, or philosophical examinations of the Problem of Evil, dissecting unsatisfactory theodicies or proposing potential flaws in seemingly solid arguments for the existence of God. For many, even questioning God's existence - as such lessons often do - is an act of heresy or blasphemy worthy of at least protest if not damnation to hell for all eternity, yet those lessons are often the bread and butter of an RE department and tackle important issues in theology. And as David Hume once said "*In matters of religion whatever is different is contrary...every miracle, therefore pretended to have been wrought in any of these religions... destroys the credit of these miracles.*" From some faith perspectives simply teaching the accepted wisdoms of one holy book is a direct attack on the central claims of another. If Christianity is true and Jesus really is the Messiah, then Judaism is undone. Both faiths, however, are undone if Islam is correct and those previous messages passed down through Tenakh and Gospel on which they are based can be rejected as corrupted and replaced with the infallible Qur'an. But the entire Abrahamic conception of God is at odds with that far older conception given to us by Hinduism. A conception itself undermined, or arguably dissolved, by the teachings of the Buddha. Meanwhile Sikhism's Guru Nanak reminds us "there is neither Hindu nor Muslim" - a message given to him after his own meeting with the Divine long after Muhammad was supposed to be the "seal of the prophets". To discuss the pluralism of beliefs and non-beliefs central to the lives of those living in contemporary British society is to accept that one person's heresy is another person's guiding principle. The Muslim who believes alcohol to be haram has to accept the role of wine in the Christian Eucharist or Jewish festival of Purim, and while the Hindu or Buddhist vegetarian may be pleased by the Jewish and Islamic prohibition of certain meats, they may not be too happy with the open menu for other animal flesh considered kosher or halal - or the diets of their non-vegetarian fellow Hindus and Buddhists who exclude edible animals from the principle of ahimsa. RE is a safe space to discuss and explore such differences, including the belief system of the atheist who dismisses the whole thing as superstition and cultural propaganda.

But I haven't brought the *Charlie Hebdo* cartoons into the classroom for the same reason I have not forced a Christian observing Lent to do the thing they have chosen to give up for 40 days or made a faithful member of the Sikh Khalsa take off their turban. Because while *discussion* and *debate* about different beliefs and ideas is our bread and butter in Religious Education, such discussion always needs to be done with the recognition that the views being discussed are deeply held and life-shaping beliefs for all parties and that, while an intellectual kick-around is always a healthy way to check our ideas, or even test our faith, the aim is not to purposefully upset or offend. Nor is it to *coerce* students into doing things which go against their most fundamental beliefs.

So while it might be true that the following argument holds:

1. Some* Muslims believe the depiction of the Prophet Muhammad to be a great sin in itself and hold the related belief that seeing such an image is transgressing bounds established in their religion about shirk and idolatry.

2. However, if you are not a Muslim and do not believe (1), or are a Muslim who does not believe (1)* then a depiction of the Prophet Muhammad is just a drawing like any other. You are therefore free to draw the Prophet as much as you like and look at your own, and other people's, depictions of Muhammad without any spiritual consequence.

3. Therefore it is not wrong *in itself* for a non-Muslim, or Muslim who believes it is not a sin, to depict or see depictions of the Prophet Muhammad and they are therefore free to do so, and Muslims who *do* think that it is wrong are free to ignore or otherwise *not look at* any depictions which may exist.

It is also the case that the following is also true:

4. Muslims who believe (1) will believe any depiction of the Prophet Muhammad to be offensive, disrespectful, and potentially personally damaging to their eternal afterlife. Therefore while a non-believer may maintain the right to draw and see whatever they like they must be aware of the potential to upset others with the images they draw and, if they want to be kind, be sensitive to that. For example, by ensuring the image comes with a warning that prepares the potential viewer or ensuring it is not shown without consent to those who may not wish to see it.

Note - I am not saying a person *has* to be sensitive to the potential offence their image may cause, only that *if they want to be kind* they ought to be. It is an ethical choice: do you care about the impact of your actions on the feelings of others or not? Sometimes, the answer may be a resounding "no"! Coming myself from a background in punk and all of its associated shock tactics, sometimes there may be a good reason to stick a safety-pin through a venerated image (such as the face of the Queen) to make a political point. Certainly there are young Muslim punks who have intentionally shocked the older guardians of their faith by doing things deemed shocking which they want to see transformed, such a Tesnim Sayar's mohawked hijab as a response to demands for female "modesty" in Islam, or Sena Hussain, bravely fronting her band, Secret Trial Five, at a convention of the Islamic Society of North America despite their ban on female lead singers (they subsequently had the plug pulled on her performance). Indeed, were the same Muslim students offended by the inclusion of these images in their RE lessons not also likely to be of the belief that depiction of any living thing is haram, it might have been a funny response to the offending lesson to plaster the school with unflattering caricatures of the teacher who upset them the very next day.

But there seems to me to be a very big difference here between, say, a group of Muslims who decide it should be OK to depict images of the Prophet Muhammad protesting the contested religious restriction by drawing forbidden, yet flattering, images of Muhammad, and an RE teacher showing Muslims images specifically drawn by cartoonists to poke fun at a figure of high esteem in their community to intentionally shock their students. A teacher showing the *historical* Islamic depictions of Muhammad to students to start a conversation about the very idea of such drawings being forbidden within Islam (and with a warning beforehand, and opportunity for students who don't want to see the image to look away) would be a different matter entirely. Indeed, in my own lessons on Religion in the Media back in the day, we used to give students a link on our virtual learning environment to a very good documentary on the Dutch cartoon controversy for those who wanted to research further (albeit, again, with a very clear warning that the doc did contain the offensive images, there was no requirement that they watched it, and advising students who would be offended by it not to watch), just as we would provide extra resources and further learning materials on any subject where we could broaden understanding beyond the meagre 50 minutes we had to cover issues in the classroom. Context and intention are everything. In fact, for some sixth-form students for whom I used to run an enrichment philosophy class, in a lesson on freedom of speech, I remember we discussed the *Charlie Hebdo* cartoons each year and then I asked the class "*I will now show you the cartoons on the next slide of the PowerPoint - who thinks that would be appropriate? After all, we have been talking about free speech...*" There was, of course, no next slide and no cartoons, but the idea of it generated the desired discussion about why there might still be limits on what we do *in practice* even if *in the abstract* we believe we have the freedom to do anything. I did not include the images because I knew doing so would upset many of my students.

Being a teacher, we are warned a lot about the potential to abuse our power in the obvious ways - grooming children, indoctrinating them, etc. But the power to dictate the content of a lesson, and the impact of that content, should not be overlooked. It too can be abused if decisions are made to knowingly upset students without good reason. Which is not to say that sometimes, there may not *be* a good reason. I know plenty of homophobic or transphobic students, for example, who are made to feel uncomfortable every time I show them a same-sex couple or transgender person in an example used in a lesson. Personally I feel it is my job here to represent the diversity of people with which my students share a society - and school - and their discomfort is something which needs to be challenged just as much as I would challenge any discomfort a *racist* student might feel if I used a person of an *ethnicity* they disliked in a video clip or image. There actually *are* some things we need to confront and challenge our students about, whether it makes them feel uncomfortable or not. But gay, trans, or ethnically diverse representation in lesson resources is not making those uncomfortable students do something which goes against their deeply held beliefs, even if it challenges them. Furthermore, it actually makes the classroom *more inclusive* for those students currently under-represented. However, while it might *challenge* my students to discuss responses to depictions of the Prophet Muhammad in cartoons (and the challenge is legitimate. After all - they share a society with people for whom depicting their Prophet *is not a crime and is not a moral wrong*), to *make them see the cartoons* is not merely to challenge them but to actively and knowingly do something to them which *violates* their deeply held personal commitments. Because seeing the image *is* the very thing they think is problematic. It is the equivalent of sneaking meat into a vegetarian's sandwich. Again - you *could* do it, and some cretins actually *do*, but it's not really a morally defendable action.

In my classroom, I don't feel my free-speech is threatened, or my right as a non-Muslim to draw or see images of a Prophet I don't believe in impeded, if I refrain from showing images to my students which I know violates *their* beliefs. It is an act of kindness to them, not an act of repression to me.

At the same time, I do feel deeply uncomfortable with the idea that making a different judgement should lead to a suspension or threat of losing my job. After all, outside of a repressive dictatorship, it remains no crime to show a satirical cartoon of a famous authority figure, even if that cartoon causes outrage and offence. No figure of authority should be off-limits for ridicule, not even God. My decision not to show offensive cartoons of the Prophet Muhammad in my classroom is not in deference to the Prophet and any potential offence shown to *him*, but to my students. If I knew I taught the children of Boris Johnson in my classroom, I wouldn't show offensive satirical cartoons of the Prime Minister either. If the children of a disgraced celebrity were sat before me, I wouldn't intentionally upset them by using the latest tabloid headlines about their parents in my lesson. The respect I am showing is not to the lampooned authority, but to the far less powerful children in my care who don't need to come to school and feel needlessly targeted in my lesson. Ultimately though, if I do make a bad choice and end up upsetting someone (and this happens in RE quite a lot: the lesson on euthanasia we do while one of our students' siblings is on life support; the discussion about abortion vs adoption that stirs up discomfort for an adopted student, or for the student whose historic sexual abuse has already led to an abortion; the chat about disability and karma which essentially tells the student in the wheelchair that their current circumstances are a karmic punishment...etc.) I do have to be accountable to it. But I would favour restorative conversations about what went wrong and why certain decisions were made over knee-jerk disciplinary action and calls for someone to lose their job. Accountability does not always have to mean punishment and retribution. In this case, what makes the protests so frustrating is that the offence and anger felt by those asking for the teacher to be fired and "never teach again" seems to come not from his specific actions - they do not seem interested in his motivations or the rationale behind including the images in his lesson

- but rather from the very existence of the *Charlie Hebdo* images at all. The idea that these images exist and that someone might not find them inherently offensive - may, in fact find them so inoffensive that they include them in an RE lesson - is what has driven them to action; *not* the offence to students in the classroom who may have been upset, but the imagined offence to the Prophet himself. Again - there is no legal or moral wrong committed by a non-Muslim drawing, or looking at, pictures of the Prophet Muhammad for whom there is no belief that such images are forbidden. The only moral wrong is the lack of kindness shown to the children in the classroom for whom there are such beliefs and it is *this* moral wrong which should be the direction of any justified anger in a multicultural and pluralistic society where we understand that we do not all share the same beliefs. Unfortunately, this does not seem to be the focus of the protest at all.

So I guess the story bothered me so much because - despite the media's best efforts to frame the story as another "culture wars"/ us vs them/ pick a side/ freedom of speech vs political correctness gone mad narrative - I don't really side with anyone. The teacher should have known better (or been trained better, as it's basically lesson #1 of RE teacher training to recognise the potential areas our classes which could cause offence to students and minimise the potential for hurt feelings on sensitive issues) and the protestors are missing the point by asking for people to share a theological belief with them which those who do not share their faith have no requirement to believe or act upon. Meanwhile the real issue - the ethic of kindness when dealing with challenging and controversial issues of ideological dispute - has been largely ignored.

**Historically there have been depictions of Muhammad made by Muslims (there is one, for instance, in the British Museum) and scholars suggest the current dominant belief in its prohibition is a more recent historical phenomenon from the last 2-300 years or so, based more in cultural tradition than in scriptural command.*

# 5.
## *PUNK ROCK #1: Angry Man With a Bass*

There had been a point, a few years into working on my PhD, when I realised somewhere along the way I had lost myself. The political annoyances that I would usually put into angry punk rock songs were all becoming wrapped up in my academic research and subsumed into the overall project of philosophically justifying anarchism. I was no longer writing new songs because every interesting thought I had became grist for the academic thesis. It started feeling too time-consuming to drive the two hours from Cardiff to Birmingham (and two hours back again) just to do a ninety-minute band practice for a band very few people even cared about. I'd been in punk bands ever since I was a teenager, but suddenly I wasn't. One grim night at the Flapper and Firkin in Birmingham – the same pub where I had played my first ever proper paying gig in 1998 – we decided to call it quits.

It wasn't just my silent guitar that was making me feel lost. In a bid to buy into the idea that I was becoming an academic, especially once I started teaching undergraduates, I started dressing a bit less punky too. Gone was the infamous (and occasionally bleached) 'pineapple' haircut I'd nurtured throughout my time at university (hair shaved all around the back and sides with a big spiky mound popping up in the middle), replaced with a mundane mop of wavy brown conventional ordinariness. I even stopped wearing my standard uniform since childhood of jeans paired with t-shirts and hoodies of weird bands, or slogans, that I liked, and started wearing the drab attire of academia. Think beige chinos and a fine line in autumnal coloured striped jumpers. At one point I even owned a brown sports jacket that I was wearing entirely unironically.

Thankfully, I also have a wife who loves me. She had noticed the change and, more than that, had noticed there was something missing in my smile. Something gone that was there before. This became especially true once my PhD was complete and we had moved away from Cardiff and back to the Midlands. Without either the thesis *or* the band anymore to pour my political anger into, I rattled around our new home in Birmingham, frustrated at the bad timing (my old bandmate had moved to Sweden a week or so after we returned to the area, preventing the possibility of a reunion). I had no reason to pick up my guitar, no reason to change out of my beige chinos and autumnal jumpers, and no outlet for all the anger I was feeling as the writing on the wall became clear after the 2008 economic crash that the country seemed doomed to revert back to Tory rule and neoliberal austerity after thirteen disappointing, but still *so much better than before*, years of Labour.

Seeing the change in me and knowing the cure, for my twenty-eighth birthday, the January of the year I would eventually become a teacher, my wife presented me with what she called a 'punk box'. It was a simple gift, and, in an instant, it snapped me out of whatever funk I was in and brought me back to being me again. A cardboard shoebox she'd decorated with a handmade collage of all things punk. Ransom-letter magazine cut-out writing and pictures of mohawks, chains, cheap musical instruments, and some of my favourite bands. Inside it was a few punk CDs I'd been wanting to buy, some t-shirts of bands I like, and two new books by Henry Rollins, one of my punk rock heroes, as well as tickets to his upcoming spoken-word show in Wolverhampton.

Rollins, as my wife well knew, was at the epicentre of my initial teenage induction into punk rock. Famously, at least famously to myself and my best friend, Simon, it all started with Green Day. Watching 'Basket Case' and 'Longview' videos on MTV and then going all-in when they released *Insomniac* in 1995. I had bought *Dookie* like everyone else the year before, and liked it a lot, but Simon bought *Insomniac*, and he had a band. Soon, after he and the guitarist heard the songs 'Brain Stew' and 'Jaded', that band became a punk band, and that punk band needed someone to play bass. I did not play bass. I played no musical instruments at all. But the great thing about three-chord pop-punk, my musician friend told me, was that you didn't really need to know much about music to play three chords. And he was right! He taught me to play along to Green Day covers by putting bits of Blu-Tack along the relevant frets of his dad's bass guitar for me to follow with my fingers, and soon I was officially a bassist.

Eventually our investigations of this new thing called 'punk' led us to the second important influence: Jello Biafra, former singer of Dead Kennedys. Despite their classic song 'MTV Get Off the Air', it was MTV (yet again) that actually introduced us to the MTV-hating band. Trying to find out more about this thing we were slowly defining ourselves to be – punk – in 1996, we watched a one-off punk rock special of the *Alternative Nation* show on MTV Europe, presented by Toby Amies. We were disaffected school-kids, just starting out on our GCSEs, so it is unsurprising that amongst all these fascinating clips of old punk bands I had never heard of, my ears pricked up immediately when I heard Biafra's cartoonish voice yell out to a crowd of pogoing teenagers: '*how many of you have been told if you just buckle down, get serious, do your math, do your homework, one day a nice sterile plastic suburban home will be yours? You can have nice plastic suburban kids who will hate you. And if you work hard, make lots of money, you can even afford your psychiatric bills when you wonder what happened?*' When the band then exploded into their song 'Life Sentence', it was like nothing I'd ever heard before. All I knew was that I *had* to buy their music. Doing so the following weekend at Tempest Records in Birmingham spawned a political awakening in both my music and my mindset. I can say with absolute assurance that I would not have studied Politics at university had it not been for hearing *Fresh Fruit for Rotting Vegetables* and *Plastic Surgery Disasters* first and wanting to understand all the lyrics to my growing collection of Dead Kennedys records. Those records made my friend and I realise how little we knew about the world. It made us start reading the newspaper, buying books by people like Noam Chomsky and Howard Zinn, and figuring things out. This, in turn, made us start to write songs about the world we were learning to be seriously fucked-up, instead of our previous juvenilia focusing on how good the

TV show, *The A-Team*, was; not wanting the school nurse to touch our balls during a school medical exam; or the perils of petty criminals we knew from school spending their evenings attempting to rustle sheep. Those songs were fun and foolish, but our government was bombing Iraq every day, spending millions on a stupid 'Millennium Dome' while homeless people starved, and we were relying on journalism that seemed more interested in selling us junk than in keeping us informed. It now seemed far more important to talk about *that*. Soon, after getting a history lesson on 1980s American politics from Jello Biafra, I began to seek understanding too in the lyrics of all the other political bands my love of Dead Kennedys had opened doors to. Subhumans (both Canadian and British), Propagandhi, Crass, Bad Religion… I was forever changed.

But the moment that punk really got so deep into my heart that I became infected for life (not into politics, but into *punk*) wasn't trawling through newspapers trying to make my first pieces of collage-art in the style of Jello Biafra and Winston Smith. Nor was it sitting in my garden shed after school with Simon, a bag of Doritos, and some cans of Coke, listening to Green Day on my little sister's old Fisher Price tape recorder and dreaming of making an album of our own. It wasn't even the first time I dyed my hair green. It was the summer following that MTV special that I spent with my mother and my sister in America. *Get in the Van* was a collection of photographs and tour diaries from the time Henry Rollins spent in the seminal punk band, Black Flag. On the MTV show they had played clips of two Black Flag songs, 'Forever Time' and 'Slip It In'. Rollins had looked wild-eyed and terrifying in the videos, naked but for his black shorts and tattoos. Intense and scary, and the music raw and unrelenting. The image had stuck in my mind and seemed incongruous with the other image of Rollins I'd seen in the later promo for his solo band's song 'Liar'. Thick, studious, black glasses, black t-shirt, and trousers. Of course, then I kept watching and the menacing Rollins of old returned, this time painted red like the devil and screaming in chorus-response to his bespectacled character's spoken-word verses that he was a *liar*.

I liked this guy. He seemed interesting. I saw the book for sale in a Barnes and Noble in New York and as I read *Get in the Van* while we travelled from my grandmother's apartment to my mother's friends in Massachusetts, hearing about Rollins' life on the road, about the bands he played with, the drama, the tragedy, the excitement, the agony of punk rock, I knew that I had finally found my tribe. Rollins was working a dead-end job at a local ice cream store in Washington when the book began and then basically ran off to join the circus, becoming the singer for one of his favourite bands. He never looked back and I was fucking *inspired.* I read every page of that book and spent hours gazing at every single picture. Yet, beyond those quick soundbites on the MTV show, I realised I had never actually heard Black Flag, so as soon as we got to Provincetown, our final destination, I found the one record store they had there and ordered the first Black Flag album Rollins sang on, *Damaged.*

We were staying there long enough for them to get it in for me on special order and once it arrived, I spent the rest of the trip eschewing the pop punk of Lagwagon and No Use For A Name I had been obsessed with previously, and walking between Commercial Street and Bradford Street, or over to Race Point Beach (anywhere my mom or my sister were *not* that day), with my headphones on and Black Flag blaring. The ugliest, angriest music I'd ever heard up to that point. Music that spoke to all the pent-up aggression in my furious adolescent heart. We returned to New York for the flight back home and I returned briefly to the Barnes & Noble, stocking up on as many of Rollins' books as I could find. On the plane home that evening, I didn't sleep; I read.

It might sound weird to punk purists, because Rollins is one of those figures that it isn't very cool to like, but in Henry Rollins I found the essence of the punk rock spirit. You're not supposed to like Henry Rollins. You're supposed to like Black Flag's earlier stuff before Rollins joined. Back when Keith Morris, Ron Reyes, or Dez Cadena was singing. Even *Rollins* prefers that Black Flag. Rollins was considered not only the worst Black Flag singer, but the worst thing that any punk could be: a 'sell out'! Rollins had been a model in a Gap commercial and, as an actor, had 'gone Hollywood' by appearing in actual mainstream movies instead of indie underground DIY stuff. But to me, that just made him even more punk than all the rigid scenesters clinging to their restrictive set of rules of what was and wasn't 'punk'. As far as I could understand it, punk was about DIY – do-it-yourself. It was about rejecting doing things just because that's the way they had always been done and about ploughing your own path, not following anyone else's. I loved the way Rollins had gone out on his own with his spoken word shows, hustling to stay on the road even when Black Flag weren't touring. His self-published poetry and books; the endless journals just as dark and bitter as mine. He had done all this weird and unique stuff because it was what he wanted to do and, reading his tour diaries, although the love of traditional punk music was clear, there was also an open-mindedness to other sounds he had that was similar to my own eclectic tastes. Nick Cave, David Bowie, Iggy Pop, Einstürzende Neubauten, and even *Madonna* were just as likely to pop up in his writing as Misfits or The Ruts. When he started his own band after Black Flag, *Rollins Band*, he didn't just do another Black Flag-like punk re-tread, he gathered together some interesting musicians and fused rock, blues, and jazz to back his trademark speaking and shouting. He picked a sound that didn't sound like anything else that was going on. It wasn't punk, and it wasn't *not* punk. I wasn't even sure if *I* liked it a lot of the time. Just as I didn't actually love all of his books (some of the poetry stuff was just *too* dark at times). But what I did like was that he was out there doing it. Not apologising for it. Not waiting for permission or for trends to fall in his favour. Just getting on the road and *doing it.* 'Don't think about it – do it. Don't talk about it – do it', as his 1987 song yells. Or, as he says in 'Shine' from 1994: 'No such thing as spare time, no such thing as free time, no such thing as down time, all you got is life time'.

His multifaceted renaissance-man approach made him an immediate role model to me - not just doing one thing but doing many. He sang, he wrote, he acted, he did spoken word shows. Following his passions wherever they led and trying his hand at anything that came his way; a DIY attitude that exemplified punk rock to me even if it didn't make the punk purists happy. I read *Get in the Van* that holiday, I read more and more of Rollins' writing and listened to his music, and even though I didn't want to write like him or sing like him, in Henry Rollins I saw exactly what I wanted to be: someone with the freedom to do everything and anything that left them creatively fulfilled and curious about the world. A few months later, when I needed new glasses, the thick pair of black frames I bought and wore throughout the end of my school days were an intentional nod not only to Milo of fellow Black Flag SST label mates, Descendents, but to Henry Rollins in that video for 'Liar'.

My Holy Trinity of Green Day, Jello Biafra, and Henry Rollins baptised me in snotty attitude, acerbic intellect, and dark poetic anger, and saw me born again through the grace of punk rock. There were, of course, other important saints along the way to whom I am also indebted: Bad Religion, for their vocabulary-stretching lyrics of philosophy and theology as well as their unrivalled 'oozin aah' harmonies; NoMeansNo, for the best bass sound I have ever heard, the greatest drumming ever committed to vinyl, and some of the deepest lyrics in my music collection; NOFX for both reminding me to always keep a sense of humour and showing that it really is possible to get progressively better the more you learn how to play your instruments; and the Ramones, the living embodiment that simplicity was king and a handful of chords enough. But Green Day, Biafra, and Rollins must be credited with being the life-changers that led me to all the rest. And when we left the Wulfrun Hall in Wolverhampton that January evening in 2010, after seeing Rollins talk in person for the very first time, it was like waking up out of a daze. I still had my guitar even if I didn't have a band. I still had my writing even if no one wanted to publish it. And I was still *me* even if I had lost myself for a bit. I put away the autumnal coloured clothes and returned to my true punk self.

You wouldn't necessarily know that I was a punk rocker when I first stepped into the classroom. Hair neat and orderly, a suit instead of band t-shirt and jeans, even boring wire-rimmed glasses instead of the Rollins-inspired frames of my youth. But that was my Clark Kent exterior for the punk rock Superman I now knew for sure lived inside. The first time I revealed my true identity to students was at a school fundraising event for Amnesty International. It was a talent show and, amongst the student magicians, singers, and comedians, a few of us teachers had been roped-in to show off our own 'hidden talents'. At some point previously I had mentioned my music around the staff room table and the teacher facilitating the group insisted I enter the competition. I played two songs – just myself, my electric bass guitar, and a lot of angry energy. 'This Is What Democracy Looks Like' and 'Vote For Change'. Not covers the students might actually recognise but my own weird original compositions they would have never heard before; one from my enduring band, *Academy Morticians*', last album, and the other a new one which we would eventually stick on a self-released EP a few years later. The crowd were impressed with my frantic bass-playing and unexpected ability to sing, and I was voted the winner. A few weeks later, some of my A-level students turned up to class with copies of the *Academy Morticians* CD, *What Happened?*, from which the first song was taken, and asked me to sign it. They'd found it for sale on eBay.

About a month later, the Amnesty International Society who had planned the first event decided to up the stakes, keep the momentum going, and put on a full-length concert after school. They invited me to play again. A longer set of three or four songs. Remembering the punk shows my friends and I used to put on at our own school when I was a kid – hiring out the hall as private citizens, much to the chagrin of our teachers, and performing raucous after-hours shows in the same place we held stuffy assemblies during the day – I agreed, imagining our school hall filled with a crowd of equally curious teenagers all keen for rebellious music the same way we had filled our own school hall as kids. I picked a set that, like the two songs I'd done before, were all rabble-rousing anthems of angry dissent (and easy enough to modify the words for to remove any of the school-unfriendly swearing so common to my lyrics). 'March in Line', 'Junk Food News', and 'Retail Therapy'. I wanted the students who saw the performance to have the same epiphany I did when I first heard punk music when I was their age – the freedom, the self-expression, the glimpse of a better world. The urge to pick up instruments of their own and form a band. The beauty of punk was that you didn't even have to be that good to do it – I wasn't, and I was up there on stage anyway.

This was 2012, and the Russian punk activists, Pussy Riot, were in jail. One of Amnesty International's big campaigns at the time was to free them. As a long-time member of Amnesty myself, I had previously bought a 'FREE PUSSY RIOT' t-shirt, and thought it would be cool to make the link between punk and political protest at the show. After all, it was being held to raise money for Amnesty International, so it seemed appropriate. Beneath my standard school suit, I wore the t-shirt – the phrase 'FREE PUSSY RIOT' emblazoned in neon pink above an image of their trademark ski-mask balaclava. The idea was to take off my shirt and tie for the last song of the set and reveal the provocative t-shirt below. But what I – and the student organisers – didn't take into account when planning the event, was that at *this* school most students took the bus in, which meant the vast majority of them all had to leave promptly at 3.35pm in order to get the bus home. I had often wondered why we didn't really have any afterschool clubs at the school (they all took place during lunch break) and that night at the Amnesty International fundraiser I found out: only a handful of students could stay later than the bus. Not having thought about this, the organisers had set the concert for the seemingly reasonable evening start-time of 7pm. Whereas the previous daytime talent show had enjoyed lunchtime footfall, even the kids who didn't bus home had long left the school site by 7pm, and those who lived miles away were not going to journey all the way back into Birmingham again once comfortably ensconced in their homes. So instead of a crowd of politically aware and rebellious teenagers, I found myself walking out on stage to a small audience of mainly the parents of the other performers, the handful of teachers (including the Deputy Head of the school) roped in to supervise, and the smattering of school governors who drew the short-straw and were invited to make up the weak numbers. 'March in line for the London Olympics', I snarled at the parents, colleagues and other invited guests. 'March in line for the Queen's Jubilee. March in line for the coalition government', I spat. 'March in line for the economy.'

The applause was polite. The faces confused. Needless to say, the 'FREE PUSSY RIOT' t-shirt remained covered up beneath my shirt, tie, and bass guitar and, quickly off the stage after my final 'shut up and shop!' was yelled out into the mic, I was followed by a Year 9 boy playing an elegant piano piece far more fitting for the muted occasion. The next day at school, the Head found me to say he'd been told by his Deputy that my set was 'interesting' and he was very sorry to have missed it.

Like much in teaching, it did not go to plan but it still had a lasting impact. As bell hooks once said, 'students leave any classroom with information whether the pedagogy has been engaging or not', and the same appears to be true of charity concerts. Not only did I start feeling freer to reveal the punk side of myself more in the classroom – using Bad Religion lyrics as stimulus to discussions in RE, showing old photographs of my once green hair when talking about outward signs of inward beliefs in Sikhism, or promoting obscure bands like NoMeansNo on the school radio's version of Desert Island Discs – but of the few kids who saw my performance that night, one of them always remembered it, and a few years later asked me to do it again. Well, he actually asked me why I hadn't played again in school since that night, and when I told him that I had just felt a little stupid being a random angry man with a bass amongst all those sincere performances in front of parents, he said: 'but the angry man with a bass was really fun to watch'.

That lit a fire inside me.

Having now taken over co-ordinating the Student Council and finding myself in charge of helping them organise charity fundraising, I decided to take his advice at the earliest opportunity and have some fun again. In 2013 my mother had died of cancer – multiple myeloma – and I had hoped I could convince the students to do some fundraising for a charity that really helped her understand the disease and find some hope, Myeloma UK. Unfortunately, I was still a non-hierarchical anarchist, and insistent that it should be *their* council, not mine. I didn't want to impose my own pet project onto their student democracy and, understandably, the student body had their own stories of personal tragedy and charitable support that informed their decisions about which groups they wanted to raise money for across the years. Lucky for me though, and tragic for the world, cancer is an absolute bitch, and almost everyone has been affected by it. It wasn't before long, therefore, that another charity who had helped mom, Macmillan Cancer Support, were selected by the students for one of our other fundraising days, and so I added my own event to the fundraising itinerary: DR MCKEE – ANGRY MAN WITH A BASS.

My mom had always encouraged my music. It was her old six-string acoustic guitar on which I first learnt to play bass away from Simon and his maps of Blu-Tack, and it was she who, more often than not, drove my band to our early gigs when we were still teenagers unable to drive there ourselves. She always gave us space to practice in the house, encouraging the noise even though she worked from home as a freelance journalist for three days each week and made important phone-calls to editors and celebrities while we roared our noise down the landing, and even when we went away on holidays she would insist I brought my friend along, and our guitars, so we could keep on playing during the break. She bought me my first electric bass and amp, and then again, as we got more serious and started gigging, my second, better, amp and more professional guitar. She even bought me a regular electric guitar one Christmas too, just in case I wanted to learn to play the six-string properly as well, and when she moved to America in later life, she bought me an acoustic bass there too, so I would have something to play when I visited. When Simon and I had written our first few songs that we liked enough to want to properly record, she gave us time at a local recording studio as my birthday present. She *loved* that I loved music. After all, she had strummed us to sleep at night as children, my sister and I, with songs like 'House of the Rising Sun', 'Blowin' in the Wind' and 'Gypsy Davy' rather than conventional lullabies. A hippy folk singer in her younger days, her love of music had never left her, and my own musical awakening coincided with those dark days of her marriage where she was starting to commune with her 'moondancer' drum and Native American mythology. The beat of the drum reminded her of her own musical past, just as the 'punk box' my wife had given me had reminded me of mine. Eventually she would pick up her old guitar again and re-find her own voice, producing folk albums and playing gigs both by herself – Vicky McKee – and with her second husband, Jack, on drums and occasional guitar under the name 'Shore Thing'.

Later, when I learned she was dying, I was teaching.

As I said before, our relationship had become very strained following the death of my dad and arguments about money and our newly discovered secret-sister had led to a near-total severing of our ties. Other than the occasional, perfunctory, phone-call when necessary, we weren't really talking at all, but I had noticed in late 2011 that she had been complaining a lot about a fairly debilitating cold she couldn't quite seem to shake. When we spoke, briefly at Christmas (I was away, visiting my wife's family for the occasion), she sounded very miserable about it all and was finding it hard to eat because, she said, there was this horrible taste in her mouth all the time. Two days later, we picked her up to drive up to my grandmother in Bury for a festive visit. Pretending we were still a happy family together was a game we were all very used to playing, so it's no surprise that even at a time of not speaking to each other the trip still went ahead. But mom shuffled into the car like a zombie and looked really sick. Worryingly so. Almost slipping in and out of consciousness the whole two-hour drive as she tried to rest and ignore the nausea and strange taste she was still experiencing. The sad thing is though, she had always been such a lifelong hypochondriac that for most of our childhood she had *always* thought one thing or another was killing her, and so we had learned very early on to kind of *ignore* her various imagined ailments and not take her too seriously when she complained about something health-related. Genuinely, sometimes we would be sat watching TV as pre-teenage children and she would say to us: 'if I die tonight, please tell the doctor that I had been having a really bad headache' or 'I think my heart is really racing so don't be surprised if I'm dead by morning'. Something I later learned during my teacher training on safeguarding and the signs to watch out for in vulnerable children, was a form of emotional abuse. This was why the previous griping about her nagging illness on the phone had been so easy to shrug off. But after the trip to gran's, my wife, my sister, and I were all worried. I encouraged mom to see her GP and be more pushy with them about taking things further when she revealed she'd been seeing the doctor for months and they had no answers for her.

I got a cold feeling in my stomach when she said that. I had heard a similar story before. One of my lecturers at university who'd had back problems that wouldn't go away. His diagnosis, after months of head-scratching from his own GP, ended up being lymphoma. Happily, he is still with us today after some excellent care, but it was really tough there for a while and he went through gruelling treatment we didn't know if he would survive. I was trying not to catastrophise, but I wanted mom to ensure she left no diagnostic stone unturned as my WebMD mind turned instantly to cancer.

My birthday is in early January. Still not really talking properly, we did chat briefly on the day and when I heard she was *still* sick, I pushed for her to see someone else than her doctor who wasn't really doing much. A few days later mom texted me from hospital. She had managed to get a blood-test privately and when the results came through, she had been told to get to the emergency room immediately. From what they could see she was in complete renal failure and without an urgent blood transfusion was in danger of dropping dead within the week.

My hands were numb as I held the phone and read the message. In the text she told us she was being taken care of and, it being late at night, that visiting hours were long over. Jack was with her, and my sister was on her way. The next day, she said, she was due for a barrage of tests, another transfusion, and wouldn't be able to see me during the morning or afternoon visiting slots, but she asked me to come over to the hospital in the evening when hopefully she was in a better state for visitors.

Writing this now, it seems crazy that I didn't just drop everything and run to her side. Such was the fractured state of our relationship that I did not rush straight to the hospital, and she did not ask me to. I just sat there, read those texts, and then got back to my evening. I even had a Year 8 parents' evening to do the next night before I finally went to see her, chatting merrily about student progress to their parents while one of my own lay seriously ill in the hospital. I feel ashamed that all this felt ok at the time, but to use a hateful phrase: it was what it was.

When I finally arrived, nearly twenty-four hours later, to a hospital which was only fifteen minutes from my house, I remember that she looked so small attached to all those tubes. I can't even remember if she was in the middle of another blood transfusion or if she was starting on the dialysis that would soon became a regular part of her life but, whatever it was, she was hooked up to busy machines and I watched as the blood rushed out of her and raced back in through tubes and, overheated in my work clothes and heavy winter coat after running to her room for fear I'd miss the cut-off for visitors once again, overwhelmed by everything I was seeing, her voice started to fade as she spoke to me about what had happened and black dots danced in front of my eyes. A rushing sound swept through my ears. I could literally feel my blood pressure fall down to my feet and my head grow leaden and heavy, my eyes unable to stay open.

The next thing I knew, I was being wheeled hurriedly in a wheelchair out into the fresh air by a nurse, accompanied by my terrified sister. I was handed a sugary orange drink as I came to in the small courtyard outside, and told to take little sips while I got my breath back. 'Don't worry,' the nurse said, to my sister as much as to me, 'this happens quite often with shock'. And immediately our nerves were settled and we could see the funny side of my blackout. My sister and I laughed at how suddenly I had gone from conscious to un – the first time it had ever happened to me. Turned completely green, then grey, then slumped down in my chair in the middle of mom talking. But, like the nurse had correctly diagnosed, after months of fearing the worst and kicking those thoughts aside, confronted by the stark reality of my mom's severe ill-health, I was in shock. She really looked like she was dying and, perhaps, she actually was?

We didn't know yet for sure though. They were still doing tests. Spinal taps, biopsies, bloodwork. Like I said, I was teaching when I found out for sure that she was dying, not sat laughing in a wheelchair with my sister and a plastic cup of strong orange squash. I was in my classroom the next day and, ironically, it was a Year 10 lesson about the ethics of euthanasia. One of those standard RE teacher things you don't really think much about because they're so par for the course, where you give a class some terrible scenario about someone suffering deeply from a painful terminal disease and ask them if they should be able to ask a doctor to end their life on their own terms, prematurely and as painlessly as possible, instead of dying an agonising natural death. It was a few minutes before the lesson and I got a text from my sister, who had not left mom's side since she got to the hospital. '*Mom's doctor wants the whole family to come to the hospital this evening to explain her diagnosis and what happens next*'.

'*Oh God,*' I replied, relieved we had some sort of information coming in but worried about what it might mean. Why did the whole family need to be there? It didn't occur to me it was for emotional support. My uncontrollable instinct for black humour in a time of crisis kicked in unthinkingly as I continued the text: '*she's going to need a kidney from one of us isn't she? First dad's money and now this!*' accompanied with a smiley face emoji.

But my sister didn't see the humour because she already knew the truth. '*It's not that,*' she messaged back. '*I already know. I was there when he told her. It's this thing called myeloma. But the doctor will explain it all properly later.*'

Myeloma? I could hear my class starting to line up outside but thought I'd quickly Google the word before starting the lesson. As the noise outside grew with chatty fourteen-year-olds all eager to start learning about euthanasia, I read enough to get the picture. Words like 'cancer', 'no cure', 'unpredictable', and 'terminal' jumped out at me. The screen swam before eyes that could no longer properly focus and I took a deep breath as the bell rang – seemingly louder than I had ever heard it before – not wanting to pass out again the way I'd done the previous night. I switched from the Google page to my lesson PowerPoint, tried to shake this latest revelation off, opened the door, took another breath, and let the class inside.

Somehow, I got through the lesson. All I remember about it is thinking that this could be my mom soon: the terminally ill patient in all that pain asking questions about the end of life. That the decision about when, or if, to let her die with dignity might actually one day be a decision we were having to make in real life. And as I realised this, I realised how little I knew about my students each year when I cavalierly covered this and other difficult topics with them. Of course, I had been trained to be sensitive when discussing potentially triggering issues with my classes, but until I found myself being triggered by my own lesson, I hadn't really understood just how awful it might make someone feel to be confronted with the source of their very real and enduring pain as if it were something so trifling and throwaway. Last lesson we did a quiz, the lesson before we gave a presentation, *this* lesson we're talking about the very thing that is happening to your loved one in hospital. I got it *intellectually*, that it might be upsetting, but didn't really *feel* how serious a problem it was. After all, *life* is triggering. You can't tip-toe around every topic for fear someone in any room you might be in will have a bad reaction to it. But, I realised, my heart-breaking with every reminder of my mom's situation as we explored the issue's ethics, that when you know in advance you are going to be covering something that there is a strong likelihood someone in the room might be affected by, you could always be kind. You could at least do the bare minimum to ensure no one *needs* to feel shitty in your classroom and *warn* students about what's coming. Allow them to opt out if that would be better for them. Over the years since that day, although few have actually chosen to skip the lessons, I have had many students with parents, grandparents, or even siblings suffering terrible terminal illnesses who have appreciated the prior warning. Sometimes it is even *the student themselves* who have had the condition that makes such conversations about end-of-life care not merely theoretical. Students who don't know for sure whether they'll still be here at the end of the year to take the GCSE exam, let alone worry about what grade they might ultimately achieve. And you can't speak about euthanasia, or any end-of-life topics, without addressing the related issue of suicide. There has never been a year that I have taught where there hasn't been at least one student in the school who has tried to kill themselves. Usually there are several. The phenomenon isn't new. When I was at school myself, a kid in my younger sister's year hanged himself in his wardrobe with his school tie. Several others tried to kill themselves in other, less dramatic, ways but were unsuccessful. It happens all the time. Of my own students over the last decade, that I know of, one has successfully taken his own life since leaving school and many others attempted to do so while they were still with us; who knows what will happen to them in the future? Two of my students had experienced parents killing themselves too, both being the unfortunate ones who found the bodies. These children are in your classroom, with their mental health struggles, their physical health problems, their complicated family issues, their trauma, and their entire personal history, and if you forget that when you plan a lesson on something that has every possibility of ruining their day, their week, their month, or their year, you forget it at your peril.

And, as my experience with that text from my sister and my pre-lesson Googling taught me, this applies to the teachers in the classroom too. In all my years of teaching I had been trained about sensitivity when teaching emotionally triggering subject content to my students, but never once had anyone ever talked about considering what might be difficult for the teacher to speak about themselves. And not just as an RE teacher delivering lessons about things like euthanasia. In my role as form-tutor to a sixth form class, for example, every year we were given things we had to do Personal, Social, Health and Economic Education (PSHE) lessons on and these included topics such as alcoholism, eating disorders, domestic violence, mental health problems. Not once did anyone ask us if *we* might, ourselves, be recovering alcoholics, or be struggling with eating disorders or other mental health problems. If *we* had been, or currently were, victims of domestic violence. It was just assumed we could spend an hour chatting to our students about this stuff and we would be fine. Just as it was assumed we would all be ok sitting in the hall to hear a talk from a charity seeking stem-cell donors from our students a year after my mom had died. No one thought to ask if watching the emotive videos of people desperate for life-saving stem-cell treatment might remind me of my dead mother, herself promised the potential miracle of that very same stem-cell therapy while she was suffering, but physically unable to get well enough to receive it in time.

One of the problems with the formalism of the professional classroom is the humanity is often forgotten. The teacher becomes a tool of curriculum delivery rather than a living, breathing, human-being. But it is our humanity which makes each of us uniquely placed to deliver that curriculum, from a diversity of different perspectives and backgrounds, and we forget that to our detriment. Just as the way I might deliver a Religious Studies lesson on Hinduism might well differ depending on whether I am teaching it as an atheist, a Muslim, a Buddhist, or a Hindu, and my different experiences will inform my approach, the way I might deliver a lesson on euthanasia or suicide might also be informed by my personal experiences with both, for better *or* for worse. And it might well be appropriate in some circumstances for teachers needing to be able to opt in, or opt out, of teaching certain subjects and for school management to be respectful of the emotional history each teacher is bringing with them into their classroom. That year, for example, maybe I shouldn't have been teaching about euthanasia at that time, or made to sit in that assembly about stem-cell donation so soon after my mother's death. I certainly found it a different experience to talk about suicide with my students in the years following the funeral of my cousin who took her own life than I had done before she killed herself.

*When I was a kid*
*I dreamed I killed myself;*
*A kitchen knife against the throat.*
*Nothing turned black.*
*Everything turned blue;*
*A loving shade*
*Welcoming me into the warmest nothingness.*
*And when I woke up I cried,*
*Because I was still alive.*

*Today, at your funeral, I learned that's exactly what you tried first.*
*Slitting your own throat.*
*Just as I learned we were at the same Green Day concert back in '09.*
*My dad your Godfather,*
*Your name shared with my grandmother;*

*More in common than I ever knew.*
*Except when you woke up your blade was real,*
*And weeping in a hospital bed*
*You soon remedied your tears*
*With your next, more successful, attempt.*

*The priest asked us all to take away*
*Something good from this awful day.*
*Reflect on you and think of a way*
*You've affected the person we are today.*
*Ash to ash, dust to dust.*
*I read from John that Christ was the way*
*Then dropped dirt onto your grave.*
*I watched the hollow faces of those who loved you left behind*
*And in their sorrow, my gift from you I then did find:*
*Gratitude that my great blue childhood hug was just a dream*
*And that I did not listen to that warm, seductive scene.*
*That those who love me*
*Still have me driving home to them tonight*
*And that the only tears I shed now*
*Are tears for your lost life.*

I can understand a teacher, for instance, not wanting to share certain personal things with their students and being worried about addressing domestic violence and eating disorders if they are, themselves, going through those things. At the same time there is also great value in those teachers unafraid to share their experiences, especially if lessons can be learned. Hearing about domestic violence in the abstract might not have much impact, but hearing from a survivor about their experiences, or even from a recovering abuser, would no doubt leave a lasting impression. I learnt more about eating disorders from my sister's own experience with them than I ever did from studying the subject in my A-level psychology classes and was able to use some of her insights to make those sessions I ran far more impactful for my students than they would be without them. And when it comes to mental health, we can't teach our students that it is important to talk about if we don't talk about our own.

After a three-year period in which both my mother and my father died unexpectedly due to sudden, undiagnosed health problems, unsurprisingly, I developed some anxiety around my own health. I had always had mild hypochondriac tendencies inherited from my mother (who had, in turn, inherited them from hers) and since childhood had suffered emetophobia – I was irrationally terrified of vomiting and did everything in my power to avoid the possibility of getting sick in that way. But I had developed strategies over the years to deal with that specific problem. In fact, it was a badge of honour I privately wore that I had ever been able to survive as a teacher considering how scared I had been my entire first few years of catching stomach bugs or of some kid puking in my classroom. And it was a second badge of honour that I had once managed to continue teaching the rest of an entire double GCSE lesson even after a boy *did* upchuck on the floor a few minutes in. After mom and dad though, I started imagining I could hear my heart failing in my chest and having panic attacks I couldn't control, or found myself obsessing about the possibility of an undiagnosed cancer lurking somewhere within me. It was that idea specifically – that something I should have noticed, or a doctor should have noticed, was being overlooked and soon it would be too late – that was impossible to shake. I would leave my wife behind, my sister, and I would die because of medical negligence; my own lack of taking care of myself, or a doctor's inability to diagnose me properly, becoming a death sentence. My background in philosophy didn't help me here at all, as I knew the inherent failing of the sort of inductive reasoning on which medical diagnosis is usually made. Inference to the best explanation not always being an inference to the *right* explanation. This is why the internet diagnoses every set of symptoms as cancer: because it always *could* be cancer. But a trained medical professional knows how to choose the more likely hypothesis for the collective symptoms than the most extreme, though possible, conclusion. However, that doesn't always work as it is playing with probabilities. When my mom presented her symptoms, the doctor had understandably concluded far more likely diagnostics: a cold, a virus. In most cases that would turn out to be true. But not this time. The cancer was missed, and my mom's kidneys were destroyed before the right call was made. My dad had high blood pressure, pains in his chest, but he was too young to worry too much about heart failure they thought, so long as he kept taking his medication. Of course, neither the doctors nor I know if he actually *did* keep up with his meds? Many people don't. Did he? Who knows? But his premature death suggests something in the health-plan went wrong along the way. Medicine is always merely a best guess.

So when I found myself obsessing with my health, unable to sleep as I began to mourn for the years I wouldn't get to spend with my wonderful wife when the inevitable diagnosis arrived, and paying undue attention to every strange twinge and new sensation in my body, convinced they were a death-knell, I knew I needed to get help. I had been so busy learning to be a teacher and dealing with his estate and my grandmother when my dad died, that I never really processed the whole thing. Now mom was gone too and there was another estate to deal with, my grandmother's final year alive too, and her eventual death. All this stuff had been piling up on top of me and I'd been burying it down deep so I could get on with the various tasks at hand. I had anxieties about my health, yes, but I also still had all this grief I had been ignoring for too long and needed to speak to somebody about. So I made an appointment with my GP.

When I started seeing a therapist to talk about what was going on, I never told anyone at work. I arranged it for the afternoon on a day when I had a free period from school and just used to sign out as if I were going home to work, but would instead drive to the Asda carpark in Chelmsley Wood and go to the NHS offices between the Heron Foods and KFC there, hoping nobody would recognise me. I would see a quiet-talking Irishman for fifty minutes who listened to my problems, taught me some mindfulness techniques and other ways of deprogramming bad thinking with cognitive behaviour therapy, and gave me a series of homework tasks to confront both my anxiety and my grief. He didn't cure me. But then he never said that he would. I liked his bluntness. Like the way he told me it was, in a way, perfectly reasonable to be afraid of heart attacks and cancer because, *if we're lucky*, that's the most likely way most of us will die. I had to lose my intolerance of unpredictability, he said, and learn to stop catastrophizing. He told me there was no miracle cure for negative thinking, but that by working on changing patterns of thought, I would develop strategies that should keep the worst of it at bay.

And he was right.

I still have all the anxiety and dread I used to have when I first walked into his office, but these days I know how to acknowledge it and move on rather than let any of it consume me.

Once I saw the benefits of getting help, I no longer wanted to creep around and do it in secret. I was happy to share my experiences and talk about the way I had been feeling before and after. But, again, the idea of professionalism prevented this sharing where it might have helped the most: in the classroom, with my students. I was advised not to reveal that I had a vulnerability or weakness, and not share too much with them. Keep it to myself, even as we told them platitudes about taking mental health as seriously as physical health and that a problem shared is a problem solved.

Which is not to say I always complied with what was advised. In 2020, for example, when Children's Mental Health Week had the theme of 'Find Your Brave', my school's English department held a poetry competition, and I entered so that the following poem could be displayed with all the rest:

*I find my brave as others find their house-keys,*
*Find their shoes and jacket,*

*And walk straight out the door.*
*While they are halfway down the street,*
*I have yet to cross my threshold.*
*Catching my breath,*
*Considering my options,*
*Thinking of excuses,*
*To avoid another encounter*
*With the uncertain world outside.*
*Daily doing battle,*
*With the unseen terrors in my mind,*
*I Sellotape a smile across my trembling lips;*
*Tell myself the story:*
*"You survived this yesterday you will survive it again today."*
*And with vampire's peril I step into the sunlight.*
*Put one foot in front of the other.*
*And pretend it doesn't burn.*

The doctor confirmed that evening at the hospital that mom was dying. The cancer had already destroyed her kidneys and she would be on dialysis for the rest of her life. It was possible she might be able to fight it and push back the myeloma for a bit, he said, even get to a state of near-recovery again at some point and be eligible for a stem-cell treatment that would prolong her life significantly, but this cancer would never fully go away and it *would* kill her eventually. 'Treatable but not curable' was the phrase he kept on using. We can lessen the pain, but not the problem. And after he'd finished speaking, all the rancour of the past few months, all the anger and all the arguments over dad and his money, all the deep-seated scars of childhood, it all just evaporated. She was our mom again, our wonderful, terrified mom. We loved her, she was sick, and she was dying.

The first thing mom did, once all the first tears had been shed, was quit her teaching job. I wrote the email for her myself, typing, as she dictated, the words that ended her second career. She had, at last, actually found a school she was enjoying working at, and she was truly devastated that she was leaving. But she always blamed the horrible schools she'd worked at before since becoming a teacher – the ones that were thankless, demanding, thick with petty politics and cruel with lack of sympathy for a woman in her fifties drastically changing her career into something completely new and unknown – for causing her cancer in the first place. A manifestation of the inner-wound the job had inflicted on her soul after all those happy decades before as a journalist, before marital problems and depression took away her spark and drive. Living in the West Midlands instead of London, mom had always fought to stay relevant with commissioning editors and contacts, knowing that life would be so much easier for her if we all just lived in the capital city instead of the suburban sticks. When dad got his big job at CILIP, she thought her time had finally come. Their main offices were in London and dad would be working there now. But instead of the whole family moving down to London, dad got himself a flat by Euston, where he spent the working week, and refused to give mom a key. That was the last straw – rushing back for the last train home in freezing rain one evening and knowing she was missing out on important career opportunities by not staying late and networking, yet again, she had passed her husband's flat where she knew she wasn't welcome and in that very moment tapped out on her freelance career for good. Fuck him, fuck the London editors who made all their commissions at parties and in bars…fuck 'em all. She never wanted to be a teacher but had enjoyed it enough in the States and needed to make money again. But what joy she had experienced her first few times in the American classrooms was quickly lost in the English state system. Already feeling trapped and miserable, she had fallen at a previous school, rushing to an assembly one morning, and injured her leg. The oncologist said the injury might well have 'activated' the ticking time bomb of myeloma lurking in her blood and set it loose on its deadly journey. That was enough for her to blame teaching for causing it until the day that she died.

But she *did* get out of hospital, eventually. It took several months where we thought it might not happen, a lot of chemo, regular dialysis, and heaps of positive visualisation, but she was kept going by the dream of one day returning to the home she had renovated on Cape Cod following the death of her own mother. The home she had always dreamed of owning, where she could see the sea from her bedroom window. She had visualised spending one more summer there, stepping out into the sea one final time. Mom had been vacationing on Cape Cod since childhood, as well as taking us there for holidays more recently. It was not only where she met Jack, my step-dad, but where they had gotten married in 2008, out amongst the sand-dunes. I had given mom away and hoped she would finally have the happy life she deserved, and which she had never been granted by my father. For several years she did, and the last time she had been happy, she reasoned, before all the illness and pain, had been the summer before on the Cape. In the depths of her sickness, therefore, she was determined to get back there once again. To walk out into the sea and just keep swimming. If she was going to die, she thought, why not do it in style, in her favourite place in the world?

But once she got there, the cancer now at bay and her visualised dream achieved, she didn't want to just swim off into the sunset and die, she wanted to *live.* To keep on living. To fight this cancer as long as she could and not let it beat her and steal her life. And by pure force of will, getting dialysis every three days, relying upon a massive daily cocktail of pharmaceuticals, the support of her husband, and focusing on self-care and whatever made her happy, she managed to not only stay alive, but to *flourish*, for well over a year. We went from barely speaking, to visiting her in hospital every day, to helping her get to America, to visiting her in America and looking after her things back in England, to getting her back to the UK once again to spend one more Christmas with us before getting her back over to the States again for the New Year. We healed our relationship, even if she couldn't ever fully heal her body. And she continued making music and being creative the whole time, even when it hurt her to do so. She took up the new skill of teaching improv comedy, inspired from conversations she'd had about it with me, and was teaching improv comedy – a brand new string to her bow – right up until the morning of the day that she died.

Across the ocean that day, I was at my best friend's wedding. I was his best man. I had given my speech, done away with my nerves, and was enjoying playing some punk rock with him and our fellow bandmate, Tom, on guitar. A celebratory set of cover songs Simon had always liked – Ramones, Dickies, Bad Religion – which we had never played as a band before. It was the first time we'd played together since our *Academy Morticians* reunion gig in 2010, the December after my father died, and both Tom and Simon had played punk songs with me on my wedding day the year before that, in 2009. We had a great time playing the songs and it had been a lovely day seeing Simon and his wonderful wife Helen tie the knot. I was stood basking in the afterglow of performance, watching Simon's dad – he of the bass guitar we had covered in Blu-Tack in our youth – playing a set with his blues band, when my wife came over to me with an uncharacteristically worried face. She'd had a missed phone-call from my stepdad, she said. A *lot* of missed phone-calls. And some from my mom's friends in America too. We knew mom hadn't been doing too well that month. Had been suffering from lots of little mini strokes as the constant dialysis messed up her veins and had been having some radiotherapy that hadn't been working as well as the doctors had wanted. But it was still a shock to sit in the garden of the beautiful Oxford wedding venue that chilly October night, away from all the cheerful noise and dancing, and hear devastating voicemail message after devastating voicemail message from my family across the ocean explaining what had happened. That mom had come home from teaching her improv class that morning with a headache that wouldn't stop. How she'd been sick, lost consciousness, and wouldn't come around. How they'd called an ambulance and she'd been airlifted urgently to Boston. How she was lying there now, but they were saying it was already too late. That the final stroke had left her brain-dead. Mom, it seemed, had become the very example from my lessons: alive only technically, alive because of a machine, and we would have to make the decision soon – *too* soon – of when, not if, we turned the machine off.

As awful as it was to think of her gone, but not gone, in this horrible nether-state three thousand miles away from us all, my sister and I had already said our goodbyes. I had said mine before she was even out of hospital the first time. I was visiting one evening and it had just been just the two of us. The hospital was near my school, and I would go over and visit for a bit most nights after work. We had spent that night chatting and, just before I left for home, I had turned to her and said I was sorry for –

– but she cut me off.

'It's ok.' She had said. 'I'm sorry too, and I love you.'

We had shared a look, an understanding, and as I left the room, I knew we had just said our final goodbye. That if she never left the hospital, it would be OK. We had both forgiven each other for any hurt we had caused and, whenever this cancer took her, this would be the moment we would both remember at the end. Every day since then had been a gift, and the last time I had seen her we had enjoyed the nicest visit together we had ever had. Usually trips to visit mom in America ended abruptly, or with massive arguments. When she had been marrying my stepdad, for example, I had been disinvited from the wedding *twice* before the big day arrived and I gave her away, and one time we had stayed with her and within twenty-four hours had found ourselves booking a hotel room in Boston for a few days of breathing space to break up the strain of a full week under the same roof. That last trip though – like every trip since the diagnosis, but this one in particular – we had valued every moment together. She was in rough shape from the radiotherapy and in a lot of pain, but we had a great time sitting with her and watching old movies like *Citizen Kane*, and going out to some of her favourite places around the Cape. The last time I had spoken to her before she died – just after her birthday – we had talked about how nice that trip had been, and she had thanked me for my thoughtful birthday gift I had sent her a DVD of one of my favourite improv groups – the Upright Citizen Brigade – doing a format – the ASSSSCAT – that I thought she might like to use in one of her classes. But she had also been realistic about those mini strokes and the growing problems stemming from her dialysis. Since September, we had ended every phone-call knowing this might be the last goodbye. I didn't need to go see her shell in a hospital bed and say it again to ears that might not even be able to hear me. It was time to let her go.

When she did go, my stepdad had been with her. He had brought her some sand from the dunes where they had got married and they lay together in the hospital bed as it happened, connected symbolically to her favourite place in the world, hand in hand with her favourite person. Eventually, he would scatter her ashes back at the dunes where they got married, so she could forever be one with the beach.

The memorial was held a week later at the Cotuit Center for the Arts, the place where she taught her improv class and had found so much creative fulfilment that final year of her life. She had shown the place to us excitedly that last visit, clearly in love with it, and we had enjoyed watching the spoken word one-woman show together there, 'Fat Ass Cancer Bitch', and collectively saying a big 'fuck you' to cancer. (As I write this, the self-proclaimed 'Fat Ass Cancer Bitch' is still alive and giving cancer the finger every day with her shows, even if mom is not). Mom had a bumper sticker for the Arts Center on her car that said: 'Do It at Cotuit', and so we did. And at the memorial, after giving my eulogy, I played one of mine and Simon's earliest punk rock songs, 'Nose', on the acoustic bass guitar she had bought me. She had loved that song so much when we were kids that, when we stopped playing it because we felt we had moved on to bigger and better things (political lyrics rather than songs about people getting old and their hair, ears, and nose growing longer) and that it was too derivative of Green Day, she had actually bought the rights to the song from Simon to show us that she believed it, and music in general, had value. That it was something we could make a living out of and shouldn't dismiss. In her last email communication to Simon, a week or so before she died, she actually gave him the rights back because she had never forgotten that stupid song. I hadn't played it since I was in school, but I knew it was her favourite song we ever did and would've made her really happy to hear. Like I said – mom always encouraged and loved my music.

I don't have a copy of the speech I made that day in Cotuit. Unlike the eulogy I gave for my dad, which was meticulously written as a script in advance, and planned down to the last word, every time I sat to write about mom in the days before her memorial, my pen found the task far too big. There was just *so much* I wanted to say. So I decided, instead, to be inspired by her creativity once more and, in the spirit of her improv classes, *improvise* the speech, in the moment, on the day. I can't remember a word I said.

But it turns out we have video.

My stepdad filmed the thing in case mom's friends who couldn't make the journey to Cape Cod ever wanted to see it. He sent me the file and I'm going to transcribe it and watch it again for the first time right now:

*When I was doing improvisation, we used to talk of 'The Great Moose', which was invented by a guy called Keith Johnstone who said that, whatever you do, if you stand up there and improvise, the Great Moose will provide. And mom loved this idea so much that I have about six million things with mooses on them because I once mentioned this idea to her and every time after, when she saw something with a moose on it, she would get it for me – so the Great Moose really did provide. And that was mom all over – she encouraged me and my sister in whatever we were doing, especially creative things.*

*My best friend always remembers something that he said to my mom and my mom always remembered it too. We were children on holiday together and we, on this holiday, brought our guitars with us and just wrote songs and mom let us do that. We were in this lovely seaside town, but we never went to the beach. We just sat in a room playing music. And mom loved that. And we had this imaginary 'club' that we played there – which was basically the dining room of this flat we were in – and we just said that when it was the evening this dining room was now a place called 'Pete's Mackerel'. I don't know why we called it that, but it was a fishing village. But when we told mom this, she didn't blink she just said 'brilliant – what's happening at Pete's Mackerel tonight?' And my friend said: 'I love your mom – she encourages creativity.' And my mom always loved that. There was even an email recently, as it was his wedding and she was communicating with him sorting out a wedding present, and she said to him there would be no finer epitaph for me than: 'Victoria McKee – she encourages creativity'. She was so inspired by him saying that when we were children that she bought him as a wedding present, last week, some Gargoyle-making classes for him and his wife to do. From here in Cape Cod she managed to find out that in the small town they live in in Oxford, there is a Gargoyle making class down the road from where they live and she bought them some sessions there.*

*And she's always done that. When we were children, I liked to draw and I liked to write, and so 'Santa' used to bring me paper. The greatest present you could get. 500 sheets of paper, which I now know is just the standard pack of paper that you buy but I thought at the time was some magical Christmassy Santa number or something. And that used to be there every Christmas so I could write and draw. Then I took writing a bit more seriously and she did everything she could for me. She got me my first computer with a word processing program so I could write little stories and send them off places to start my impressive collection of rejection letters. Then, when I was a kid, I said I liked comedians and comedy and that maybe I could be a comedian instead, and suddenly I started receiving autographs of comedians she met in her work as a journalist. Every time there was a comedian around, she'd come back with a new comedian's autograph for me. When I started writing again a bit more seriously and she knew I liked Stephen King, she therefore did everything in her power to interview Stephen King and take me to meet Stephen King with her, which I did. Basically, any idea that I had, she not only encouraged it, but she then found a way to make me live it, to experience it. Even silly things like wrestling (if you don't know, I like WWE wrestling) and she took us all to Madison Square Garden in 1996 to see Survivor Series because I managed to convince her it was the opportune way to have a thanksgiving with our gran who lived in New York at the time, and she knew it was just about me going to see the wrestling but she did it for us anyway and she even got us off school so we could do it.*

*Anything creative she encouraged. Including my music. When I started writing songs and playing music originally, I was borrowing her and my sister's guitar and so she bought me a bass guitar and amp. She used to take us to gigs across Britain just so we could play them, sat watching us play, take us to recording sessions, help pay for those recording sessions, was our biggest fan and just encouraged all of that. She's always really encouraged creativity in me. In fact, when I finally buckled down and got a real job and became a teacher, it was a point where I kind of thought my parents would be proud that I had put away these silly pipe-dreams of becoming a rock and roll star and was going to get an actual pay cheque, and she was actually disappointed in me. She said 'oh no! You're going to be a teacher! You won't be able to write anymore and play the guitar!' She was more worried that I wasn't going to have the time to do that and be creative and free than she was happy that I was going to have financial stability.*

*She was a very free spirit.*

*That's not to say everything was great. We had a very fiery relationship. We annoyed each other but always knew throughout it that we loved each other. But we had a lot of fights. When it came to her and Jack's wedding, I was disinvited two times the week before the wedding just because we'd always get into these big arguments about things. Including even in improv – we had arguments about improv theory recently – but it was always with love. And one of the things when your mother dies kind of unexpectedly, or at least suddenly, there's always that worry about, you know, did they know that I loved them and did I know that they loved me? And the thing with mom that was always a constant in my life was that I knew that she loved me and my sister. She always would tell us, even when she was shouting at us, five seconds later she would apologise, we would make up, and it was always clear, and it's a nice feeling to know that although I am devastated, I don't have any doubts about that. I know that she knew that I loved her, and even though I didn't get to say goodbye to her recently, when she was first diagnosed in 2012 we had a lovely goodbye in the hospital in Birmingham where we thought that was going to be it the last time. And although it's tragic that she died and it's terrible that she's not here with us today, to me, we had this extra twenty months that we didn't think we were going to get when we first saw her in hospital back in Britain and it was amazing to me that she was able to get back to her dream place when she was in hospital back in Birmingham (not to say that Birmingham isn't a beautiful city). She looked out across the window (which had a view of the university she went to in the UK when she came over) and she knew that she wanted to get back to Onset and have one last summer here, and she managed to get* two *last summers here, which is excellent.*

*She was a big proponent of visualising things and their coming true. Part of the song we heard of hers earlier was about her and Jack, and visualising that relationship working together across the two countries, and she did that. She was able to visualise a whole other life for herself over here and she was originally able to visualise a whole new life for herself in the UK when she was younger and do that too. She was amazing not only in creativity in the arts, but in her own life, at going 'this is what I want to do – how am I going to do it?'. Even her house in Onset is designed exactly the way she visualised it in her mind. And it was amazing to me that she managed to have those two extra summers.*

*When she died, my best friend was there because it was his wedding and he said that she was 'irreplaceable'. He grew up with her as much as I did at our house at the time. 'Irreplaceable' was the word he used and I agreed when I first heard it, but the second word that's more appropriate I think is that she was 'unforgettable' It's impossible to forget my mom. This is obviously a memorial, and we are remembering her here, but we'll never forget my mom because she was such a big character and did so many interesting things in her life. When we were last here this summer, my wife was saying how cool she was as a parent. We visit her parents and have a lovely time, drink lots of tea and talk about the garden and things like that, but when we visited my mom here we came to the Cotuit Centre for the Arts and watched 'Fat Ass Cancer Bitch' and we watched Citizen Kane because we were going off to Hearst Castle and she said it was important that we watched it. We went to cinemas all over the Cape to see all these films she wanted to see, driving all over the place and doing different things. She was a life force. She was unforgettable, and she was a cool mom.*

*Now there's one more thing I need to do before I go, which is play a song which is highly inappropriate for a funeral. It's about an aging philanderer, and I'll play it on the acoustic bass guitar she bought me so that I would have a guitar I could play this side of the ocean.*

And then I played the song about the aging philanderer.

There's something kind of nice about realising that everything you've been writing about the past, even if misremembered, was said and misremembered in pretty much exactly the same way by yourself once before, nearly a decade ago, in an improvised speech you gave at your mother's funeral. That the story I'm telling now, even if distorted by the years, rings even truer because I've told it the same way before.

I played the first ANGRY MAN WITH A BASS show for Macmillan in mom's honour. Just me, a bass guitar, and a setlist of angry songs, played in an empty classroom we'd kitted out with a basic mic and PA system. (Much the same way I had played 'Nose' at mom's memorial).

The room filled quickly as the noise spilled out onto the playground and we raised a good sum of money with the show. I know my mom would have been proud. Macmillan had managed to put her in touch with other myeloma sufferers who had all managed to survive their first round with the disease and get back to living their lives; phone-calls with survivors which had made mom see the possibility for getting back to the Cape. But the best thing about the show for me was that I may well have saved a student's life by doing it because I chose to once again ignore the advice of those who tell teachers not to share themselves with their students and play a song I had written when I was a sixth form student myself. A song about suicide.

*Joey's having a tough time*
*Really is a rough time*
*His life's lost its meaning and he's talking about despair*

*Joey is so depressed*
*His life's in such a mess*
*He feels so alone, like there's no one who cares*

*Joey keeps on crying*
*Talking about dying*
*Now he's dyed his hair the same colour as his heart*

*Joey keeps on drinking*
*To stop himself from thinking*
*He's into self-mutilation: a new phase to start*

*Everybody's been wondering why Joey's changed all his ways?*
*People shrug and dismiss this new sight*
*They say it's probably just a phase...*

*Joey has been cutting*
*His skin up to nothing*
*He quit college today and he wouldn't say why*

*Joey started smoking*
*Haphazardly joking*
*About how everything would be fine if he'd just die*

*Everybody's been wondering why Joey's changed all his ways?*
*People shrug and dismiss this new sight*
*They say it's probably just a phase...*

*Joey has gone missing*
*And now people are wishing*
*That they'd listened to more about what he'd had to say*

*Joey's finally been found*
*But he wouldn't come around*
*Overdosed and died*
*And they said it was just a phase*

*Just a phase*

The song was about my own occasional suicidal thoughts I used to have when I was at school, combined with the story of a friend I was really worried about at college. My own dark thoughts really *were* just a phase, brought on by feeling alienated from my peers and the regular bullying that came from standing out from the crowd in a school that didn't celebrate non-conformity. Once you learn too much about the world, you start to question the sense of staying in it. I had a dream one night when I was fifteen or sixteen where I went down to the kitchen and slit my own throat, and when I did it the whole dream just turned to the most beautiful blue colour I have ever seen and a massive sense of calm washed over me. I woke up feeling serene and wondering if doing it in real life might bring me some peace from all my worries, but then I combatted the urge to find out with stronger logic: if suicide were truly an option I was willing to take, then I had to acknowledge that all other options were suddenly available to me too. Suicide would be the most extreme and final act I could attempt, and so if I was willing to do that, then why not do all the other, far less extreme, though still potentially scary, things that could change my situation instead and keep myself alive? In my case, it just meant standing up to some fears and changing schools at the end of my GCSEs. If I was willing to kill myself, I should at least be willing to give standing up for myself a bit, doing well in my exams, and applying for the sixth form college the next town over a shot. I've never felt suicidal again because that idea has always worked to prevent it. Quit the job, the relationship, the obligation, rather than ever quit the life. If you're willing to *die* to make things better, be willing to go to jail, to live on the streets, or do *absolutely anything else* before going to that suicidal extreme.

So that was my own run-in with potential self-harm. That and a bit of cutting up my arms with razor blades. Not, as most moody teens would do it, '*just so I could feel something*', but because I wanted cool scars like my favourite wrestler, Mick Foley. I learned how wrestlers would cut their foreheads open with small razors to 'get colour' and bleed in their matches. I watched people like Foley fall into barbed wire and thumbtacks during hardcore matches and my friends and I would repeat the brutal stunts in our back gardens. At some point, when I was feeling angry about something, that knowledge, and a high tolerance for pain, collided with something I'd heard about depressed people cutting their arms and I cut up a safety razor and made the tiniest set of incisions along my arms, hoping it might give me cool scars. It hurt, there was no scarring, and when asked about it at school I told people, embarrassed, that my cat had done it. I *dabbled* in dark thoughts, but didn't really live there. The friend at college was a much more severe case. They'd had a bit of a breakdown, legitimate self-harm was involved, and everyone kept saying it was 'just a phase' despite the fact they were clearly in trouble. I kept on thinking about that kid in my sister's year who had hanged himself with his school-tie and how it hadn't just been a phase for him. The college friend, and a few other people around that time, had tried overdosing with pills, luckily all of them unsuccessfully. But I wrote the song because I could see how easy it could be to slip beneath the radar of concern as a kid thinking about ending it all in a world that refused to take you seriously.

Sure enough, one such kid, who had been at the ANGRY MAN show that day at work, came up to me one lunchtime a few weeks later and asked about the song. I told him he could stream it on Spotify, and he did. Eventually, having deciphered the lyrics, he chose to disclose to me his own suicidal thoughts and get some help. For the next few years, he came to my classroom often, and the classrooms of a handful of other friendly teachers, just to unload and seek some kindly ears that cared. He attempted to take his own life only once, but we got him through it. It has been years now since he left school. He's an adult, out in the world on his own. And he's not only still here, he's still here and actually *enjoying* life. I met up with him for coffee, in fact, a few months ago and he's doing really well. I wonder often how much my strange little punk song, written in a few blurred minutes in my childhood bedroom for an upcoming tour of Italy, has to do with that fact? Maybe a little, maybe a lot?

We recorded the song as teenagers in Milan. Another example of my mother's endless support for my music. Young punks at the time, with a self-released demo we'd had reviewed in a few fanzines and our first full-length album on the way, one fanzine writer, who had helped us out a great deal with finding studios and record labels who'd be interested in our stuff, was also drummer in one of the first local punk bands we ever saw, Raggity Anne. His band had fallen apart since we first saw them, but Paul, the drummer and founder of the band, had been sent an invite for Raggity Anne to come and play a tour of Northern Italy. He liked our music and got in touch to see if Simon and I would be interested in joining him to make a new iteration of the band for the tour? Me on bass, Simon on guitar, and Paul on drums. We were seventeen and studying for our A-levels in college and Paul was a much older adult that none of our parents had met. The tour was in November. Term-time. The pre-mock exam late Autumn of Year 13 when every lesson supposedly counted…

But my mom was the same woman who had, two years before, told my secondary school to give me (and Simon) the afternoon off one September day so that we could travel down to London and see our first Green Day show because their music was so important to us. The same mom who had, the November before that, as I said in her eulogy, taken me out of school for a whole week so I could spend one last Thanksgiving with my grandmother in New York, and also see WWE's Survivor Series at Madison Square Garden, for which she used her journalistic influence to get us press tickets. The same mother who, later that year, after Italy, would also pick us up from college and drive us all the way to Leeds so we could not only see Jello Biafra's spoken word show there that night, but meet him too and have dinner with him afterwards. Something she had arranged with the promoter, again using her journalistic hustle. Mom wanted us to enjoy our creativity just as much as she wanted us to do well at school, and not only saw the value in both, but was realistic about the importance of embracing big opportunities when they turned up rather than commit to the dull discipline of rigid rules and regulations. Yes, it was term-time. Yes, we had important exams coming up soon. But when else would we get an all-expenses paid invitation to spend a week in Italy playing punk rock music in a series of theatres, squats, and dive-bars?

In only the most minor nod to safeguarding, she met Paul once before entrusting him with her son and his friend for a week and was sufficiently satisfied he wasn't some monstrous paedophile with malicious intent. Frankly, as soon as she saw all the Bob Dylan and Elvis memorabilia around his house, she was sold. We flew off to Italy and had the time of our young lives. 'Just A Phase' was part of the set as we mixed classic Raggity Anne originals with some new songs of our own, and one night, a few days into the tour, we were given the opportunity to record some of the new stuff by some rich fan of the band. It sounds like a fairy-tale, but it really happened: a son of a millionaire (and millionaire himself) just loved the band, came to all the shows, and paid for us to stay for a few extra days in his mansion in Milan at the end of the tour, paid for a studio, and paid for us to record these songs for *no reason at all other than he wanted to hear them*. It wasn't for a release. He didn't own a label or take any copyright. He gave us the rights to do what we wanted with the finished songs (they were released later on Boss Tuneage) but paid for us to extend our stay, paid for the change in flights, and we had a cool few extra days recording punk rock songs in Milan on this rich kid's generous dime. And when we returned to the UK, I remember no conversations at all with either mom or dad about the schoolwork we missed. I just remember mom loving the new songs, dad remarking on how much better and tighter we played live after the experience of the Italian tour. I remember every magical gig we played that November, all the cool people we met in Italy, and stories it gave us. All the cool bands we played with and great music we were introduced to. And I got As in all my A-levels anyway.

Anyone who tells you school is more important than life experiences, and that every day in the classroom is vital, is someone who is asking you to miss out on living the best parts of life so you can concentrate only on the worst. I am so grateful that my mom, and my dad, never bought into that bullshit, and always encouraged my punk rock spirit rather than squashed it.

I'm also glad, as odd as this sounds, that mom and dad weren't overprotective of me. When I think of the most formative moments of my childhood, many of them involve relationships with adults who were not my parents, or childminders, or parents of my friends, but essentially *strangers* who I was able to freely interact with and be trusted to be ok. Paul is one such example. A random punk rock drummer, artist, and journalist from Scunthorpe who found himself in the Midlands with his band and gave me not only that amazing opportunity to tour Italy, but hooked us up with his band's label to release our first album, *Shallow Permanence*, and gave us the number for Carl Harris' excellent Zoo Studio in which to record it (the same studio mom would use years later to record her folk albums in too – with Carl and her friend Jem Vipond accompanying her and Jack as the band). I'm still in touch with Paul to this day and, after the Raggity Anne stuff, we recorded some more music together under the name The Whining Maggots. It would have been so easy for a parent to treat a man like that with suspicion and just say no to his offer, and I can't imagine any parent allowing it today. Just as I couldn't imagine, as a teacher, inviting a group of students to the pub with me after a lesson to continue chatting about epistemology, yet that is exactly what my A-level philosophy teacher, Dermot, did with us on occasion, so we could continue the discussions from class over a drink and (for him) a cigar. It was Dermot who brought philosophy alive for me, and he is the teacher I still aspire to be, so excellent was he at making complicated ideas comprehensible and balancing rigour with fun in his classroom. If he had not been so encouraging and allowed us to explore ideas in unconventional ways, I would not be doing what I am doing today. And I have always kept in touch with Dermot since leaving his classroom, meeting up every so often when I was back home from university and then, in later years, seeking advice from him about teaching and then, even later still, giving advice to him too. He was definitely a mentor, and it was he who told me that magic word 'consortium' which enabled me to apply to train as a teacher. As with Paul, I am still in touch with him to this day. In fact, I am meeting up with him this coming Monday for a stroll around Baddesley Clinton in Warwickshire and a catch-up coffee. But I know, as a teacher, with today's safeguarding standards, such non-professional relationships, out-of-classroom contact, and certainly bringing alcohol and nicotine into the equation, would be completely forbidden. If Dermot were my teacher today, I would have missed out on some of his most valuable teaching, and that feels like a great shame, even if it is done from the best intentions of eliminating any possibility of putting young people at risk.

And then there is Barry, my old university lecturer, MA supervisor, and another adult mentor who became a friend. Barry came to my wedding, and I would have gone to his son's wedding in return last year had covid not got in the way. Office hours conversations about philosophy and radical politics at Cardiff University slowly graduated downstairs to longer conversations in the humanities coffee shop below, and then to places where we could get a real meal. It was Barry, as head of the Philosophy section at the university at the time, who recommended me for a scholarship so I could complete an MA there, and it was Barry who encouraged me to continue and do a PhD. It was Barry I mentioned earlier, whose unexplained back problems turned out to be cancer. As he had treatment for it, we continued to meet up and chat. And it was then Barry who gave me the opportunity to teach one of his lectures in Black Political Thought while he was out of action, and let me continue taking the lecture in subsequent years even after he had recovered. When I applied for teacher-training, Barry wrote the reference, and when I quit my teaching job at the start of this year, after over a decade of giving it until Christmases, it was Barry who assured me he could still write me a good reference if I wanted to return to academia. Barry – another educator who refused to maintain professional distance and keep things limited to office hours, and another person much older than me who profoundly changed my life by not erecting false barriers around the teacher/student relationship.

Before Barry, before Dermot, before Paul, there was also Graham – that Christian youth minister who started the whole philosophy ball rolling for me by coming to our school and allowing us to ask him theological questions. At some point, our lunchtime conversations weren't long enough to have the sort of discussions we wanted to be having, and we started seeing him one evening a week as well. At least, Simon and I did. Our other friends' parents wouldn't allow it. Who was this weird man from the church who wanted to spend these evenings unsupervised with their children? Buying us takeout and taking us on drives to random places where we could sit and talk about God? We all knew about priests and their predilections. Well, believe it or not, Graham was merely a man hopeful he might spread the good news of Jesus Christ and convert some young heathen hearts. Ultimately, he failed in that mission, but had it not been for those conversations and those weeknight drives, again, I very well might not have become interested in philosophy and be here doing what I'm doing today. To be clear: neither Graham, Paul, Dermot, or Barry had any nefarious intentions and nothing sordid ever happened, or was even suggested. (None of them tried to fuck either me or my friends is what I'm saying). In their own individual ways, they just all played the role of a mentor and provided a valuable bridge to something interesting and life-changing in the mundane existence of a young person with a developing mind.

I can completely appreciate that maybe I was just lucky in that. That other children associating with random adults have very clearly not been so lucky. I did, after all, grow up in the shadow of the Jamie Bulger killing and the Soham murders, not to mention the massacre at Dunblane and Fred and Rose West. But I do wonder, as every year the safeguarding requirements in schools (and other public institutions where young people come into contact with adults) get stricter and stricter, what might be lost in the sacrifices of community and connection that we make for the illusion of safety. Because no one is ever truly safe from possible horror, despite all the rules we've put in place. Terrible abuses still happen, usually with family members and family friends rather than the strangers we have been so trained to fear. My parents were definitely neglectful in the way they raised me. A lot of terrible things could have happened to me when their attention was diverted with their own adult lives. But, luckily, they didn't. And in the cracks allowed by their negligence I was able to have my life profoundly changed and impacted for the better by these other adults in the community who brought different perspectives and knowledge into my life than would have been available through the parochial limits of the family.

## INTERLUDE – PHILOSOPHY UNLEASHED POST - 14/03/22:

## KILLING THE AUTHENTIC SELF - Why Is It So Hard To Be Yourself At Work?

As a member of my workplace's Equality, Diversity, and Inclusion committee I've been thinking a lot about what it means to bring one's "authentic self" to work. A recent survey was published asking for thoughts from across an educational organisation about equality, diversity and inclusion and the key findings summarised a telling dichotomy. One the one hand, the negative, staff had reported an overall lack of diversity where they worked. On the other, the positive, they said that they felt comfortable in the workplace, welcome, and well represented. The results made me laugh. The sense of inclusiveness the non-diverse staff were experiencing seemed, to me, to perhaps explain the lack of diversity. If you didn't fit in to that environment, if you were different, would you want to work there? Probably not. The positive was the cause of the negative, a negative in itself, but it was unclear whether the organisation was aware.

Although not a classic minority group, my own experiences with exclusion started young. A child of an immigrant I was lost frequently at school as my peers drew from shared cultural assumptions that I did not have. Even within my own family, Jewish traditions clashed with Methodist ones, with neither side of the family ever interacting with each other because of an ocean between them, and it felt wrong to pick a side. As a teenager, finding punk rock, I eventually learnt to embrace being an outsider. Fitting in had never been an option anyway, but now I could see that it wasn't even desirable. Conformity was a trap. But I also learnt early that being brave enough to be yourself, in all its confusion and opposition to norms, came at a cost. Even though I loved feeling free enough to be myself, I didn't make life easy for myself as I found more of me - anarchist, punk rock, atheist, straightedge, vegetarian - and lost the ease of just fitting in with a crowd. Life sure would be easier if I just shut up and learnt to blend in. But to do so would to no longer be me.

It wasn't that I couldn't blend in. I blended in whenever it was necessary to do so. Different clothes, a different way of speaking, holding my tongue, laughing off insulting jokes without firing back, going with the flow even as I wanted to swim against the grain. It was just that whenever I did that, I felt phoney. And I always wondered why it was even needed. Why we couldn't just be different from each other - be ourselves - and fit in through our diversity instead of arbitrarily conforming to a standard of "acceptability" usually imposed from above? An exercise of power rather than an expression of our shared and diverse humanity. I have never understood why people are so afraid to see disagreement or clash. It is my belief that such a fear stems not from the inherent awfulness of disagreement, but from its infrequency in our lives and our not being taught how to live with difference. It is, in fact, one of the greatest gifts philosophy brings to its students, I believe, that we learn how to argue about clashing ideas without feeling personally attacked by the objections and with an openness to change our minds if challenged.

These ideas become all the more important when we think about the things that mark us out as "different" which are beyond our control and, in a conformist world, based largely on learning how to fit in, create barriers to success. In a racist and patriarchal, heteronormative world, for example, skin colour, cultural background, gender presentation, and even the person you are in a relationship with can all be things you feel forced to mask in the workplace in order not to rock the boat of institutional acceptability. When we talk about the need for representation in certain roles where such attributes have historically excluded particular groups or individuals, what we are talking about really is breaking down the arbitrary mental criteria we have built in our heads about what is and isn't "acceptable". We are expanding our definition of what it means to "fit in" by recognising that round shapes shouldn't be forced to distort themselves to fit into square holes and that, instead, we should stop setting boundaries that exclude all shapes from entering in the first place. The expectation that a shape *should* be square and not round is the whole problem, and such expectations need to be disrupted and destroyed.

Within my own institution - a school - there are so many cues given to students, big and small, about what they "ought" to do, what is "proper", "appropriate", "acceptable", etc. And these cues are given by staff who, themselves, have internalised so many arbitrary expectations and received wisdoms about what one should and shouldn't do to succeed from their own schooling that have just been accepted and repeated without scrutiny. How can we teach our students to be their authentic selves, be proud of who they are in all their diverse glory, when we also tell them they all have to wear the same uniform, when we monitor the sort of language they use, when we restrict and monitor their behaviour based on standards we can seldom justify independently from an appeal to "the rules"? And more importantly, when we ourselves, as teachers, so rarely get to bring our own authentic selves to work under similar arguments of "appropriateness" or "professionalism" how can our students take us seriously if we tell them to celebrate their uniqueness? We too are expected to dress a certain way, speak a certain way, hold our tongues on certain issues, promote certain values we may not actually hold. Can we really speak of equality, diversity, and inclusion if teachers themselves don't equally represent the rich diversity of the people we share our world with?

It seems obvious, for example, that if an applicant for a teaching job in a school turned up wearing jeans and a hoodie, or with a face tattoo that reads "REBEL", that they would be unlikely to be hired as a teacher. But should it? What has that external appearance actually got to do with the efficacy of their education? Why should we fear rebels teaching our children? A job interview is a stressful time for all involved. Yet how often do we hear about the candidate who gets the job "seeming relaxed" or "feeling like they already belonged"? If we still make our decisions using such biased gut-reasoning we will be forever excluding the anxious, the socially awkward or the neurodiverse. We can take the names and ages off the application data when selecting our shortlists, but as long as we ask for covering-letters we will continue to be wowed by all the same things we seek to be wowed by while perhaps more relevant, but unfamiliar, experiences, or articulation of those experiences, get lost.

Even seemingly obvious professional norms can be questioned. Why should it be obvious, for example, that buying into a certain view of teaching and learning is a reasonable part of the interview process for being a teacher? Isn't it possible that schools thrive best when they have a rich environment of many different approaches to education going on in each classroom? Like a three-ring circus, something to appeal to everyone but not necessarily everything for everyone, can't schools be an intricate tapestry of diverse and interconnecting heterodoxy? Let the maverick teach their way, the traditionalist theirs. Let some teachers run their classrooms with an iron fist and other classrooms be given over to student self-rule. Let experimentation be the guiding principle and let teachers inside the classroom be the human beings that they are outside of it. For if they can't be, then how can they tell the children that they teach that they should embrace who they are and that, whoever they are, they will be included in our rich and diverse world as their true, authentic selves?

I guess what I am saying is there is a vicious circle that needs to be broken. We teach children in schools not only our subjects, but about how success is defined in the world and what is expected of them in order to fit in and do well. And we base that advice on our own experiences, which are riddled with biases and repressions of our true authentic selves, passing down onto those children those same biases and repressions that have been passed down to us and ensuring their perpetual assent. The glass ceilings which need to be broken are fitted first in these schools, by teachers themselves pressed up against the same sharp glass. Until we acknowledge that as a profession and start breaking down those barriers by radically reassessing our expectations of what a teacher should and shouldn't be, efforts at equality, diversity, and inclusion in schools will continue to fall short, and the damaging lessons taught instead will continue to replicate and reproduce far beyond the school gates as our students make their way in the world with the same old biases and repressions internalised once again.

It's time that schools became more diverse, and their staff, at least in the short-term, a little less comfortable.

## 6.
## *PUNK ROCK #2: Inextricably Tied to Punk*

The next time I brought my punk rock self to school, was the following September. The summer before, as with every summer that I had worked there, we broke up with a big final assembly, and at the end of the assembly, we sang the dreary school song. I hated that school song. Not because it was bad (though it *was* pretty bad; incredibly daft lyrics about 'cricket's honest warfare and football's manly strife') but because it had the potential to be quite good. The chorus, especially, I could always imagine being shouted punk rock style in big gang vocals at the end, and I loved how the third verse got very quiet as it sang about all the students who had died over the years – 'sweet voices silent now' – before coming back into another barnstorming rabble-rouser of a finale with a full-vocal roar of life-affirming celebration. However, the song was never sung well enough by a hall full of disinterested pupils and staff all eager for their holidays to begin. I heard it in my head full of crashing drums and buzzing guitars every time I left the building and walked back to my classroom, but the reality was a dainty piano feebly backing the church-hymn mumbling of people who'd rather be doing anything else.

I wanted to do something special to introduce our new fundraising campaign for the academic year. The Student Council had agreed to a year focused on different cancer charities each term instead of tackling different issues each time. We were starting out with Cancer Research, and I had an assembly booked for the first week of term to launch the campaign. With the school song still banging around in my head and years of suffering my imagined arrangement of it, I found myself one August afternoon sat at my computer looking at GarageBand and my guitar. We'd done cake-sales, samosa sales, guess the number of jellybeans, staff vs student football matches, talent shows, non-uniform days, and puzzle rooms, but we'd never done a charity single before. Now that I'd got all my old punk bands' back-catalogues up on the streaming sites, I knew how to make a digital recording available for purchase online and realised that, if I wanted to, I could do the whole thing quite easily from my home. A charity song for Cancer Research. Something the whole school could rally behind.

Punk has always been about doing it yourself. Not asking permission. Acting first and seeing what you can do. What you can get away with. I didn't communicate with anyone at the school and tell them what I was doing, I just picked up my bass and plucked away from memory until I'd figured out the notes for the song. I used the lyrics from an old Speech Night booklet I had kept, and arranged all the parts for bass, guitar, and drums. Then I put it all together and recorded a couple of versions on GarageBand, doing all the vocals myself as well. I told myself I'd only give it one afternoon. My wife was outside doing some gardening and so, I reasoned, if I couldn't get it done by the end of the day, I wouldn't bother doing it at all. But somehow, I did. A punk rock cover pulled directly out of my head and into reality. I designed a quick image to go along with it, invented a band name to credit it to (Dr McKee and the Sweet Voices Silent Now) and I set everything up with my online distributers so it would go on sale everywhere the morning of my launch assembly.

That morning, I stood in front of the whole school, our first week back after the summer, and explained why Cancer Research was important to me and what we were going to be doing that year to support them. Then I showed them a picture of my mom and her guitar. Talked about her myeloma, and also about her music. Explaining that mom had always loved my music too, I then revealed my surprise. I hit play and the punk rock version of the school song began to explode out of the hall speakers while links for where to buy it popped up on the projection screen. When the song ended, the students cheered. The Head came up to me and told me that he should be annoyed and not condone such blasphemy, but he really quite liked it. The song started to be used in assemblies and was played at parents' evenings and promotional events for the school. While it turned out that streaming music isn't a great way of making money, it was a great way of promoting the other money-making events we put on that year. And it still raised a hundred quid (well - I decided to just give the charity a hundred quid from my own pocket once I saw how little streaming actually earned.) My second ANGRY MAN WITH A BASS show a few weeks later raised even more than that, and the crowd went home happy when I did the punk rock version of the school song as my encore. The songs I chose to play that day though, dedicated to both mom and dad, about grief, about loss, about coping with a complicated childhood, mostly taken from the album I wrote to process their deaths – *86* – were designed to speak to the students in attendance who might be struggling with something similar in their lives the hope that it might help.

*The first time I told you I loved you*
*Was in your eulogy*
*We weren't ever that kind of father and son*
*Were we, you and me?*
*More high-fives and the occasional hug*
*Than words such as "love"*
*And all those years of poison didn't help*

*You cheated on her, but never on us*
*But when that voice whispers into your ear*
*Day after day, year after year*
*That you were never here*
*A child finds it easy to believe*

*But if you weren't around*
*When you were fucking around*
*Why are you so frequently found*
*In weekend memories*

*Parents' evenings*
*Teaching me to ride a bike*
*Football matches, cricket games*
*Lakeland walks and mountain hikes*
*Sharing favourite books and music*
*Family holidays, Fish and chips*
*You financed our first album –*
*Shallow Permanence: a Christmas gift*
*It was only when you really were not there*
*That I finally saw how much you had been there*

*Not the best father*
*But the best that you could be*
*And good enough for me*
*Only – by the time that I could see*
*You were gone*

*A Sunday morning*
*A ringing phone*
*In a hotel room in Gothenburg*
*You had died alone*

*Meanwhile mom used the word like a weapon*
*"Love?" with a question mark*
*Emotional blackmail abuser*
*A narcissist at heart*
*Her love always attached with some strings*
*Love that's demanding of proof*
*Love, once pure, corrupted by heartbreak*

*His cheating on her; taken out on us*
*And we were lumbered with all her fears*
*Day after day, year after year*
*That he was never here*
*Fears a child finds easy to believe*

*But when he wasn't around*
*Cuz he was now in the ground*
*Why was it that she was not around?*
*Except whenever*
*money was mentioned*
*Selling 86 and his pension*
*Souring memories; recrimination*
*Making worse the devastation*
*In ancient wounds that had not yet healed*
*Her true character was revealed*
*In earlier years: our primary care*
*But when we needed her most she wasn't there*
*Little did we know she was dying*
*And soon our anger would turn to crying*

*Not the best mother*
*But the best that she could be*
*And good enough for me*
*Only – by the time that I could see*
*She was gone*

*Three years pass by now*
*The phone it rings again*
*My stepdad informs me*
*Cancer wins again*

*They're gone so young*
*And I'm here*

I sang about divorce, tragedy, grief, and pain because I remembered that, for me, that was the real gift punk rock had given me when I was their age, and part of why I found it so easy to resist that beautiful blue dream where I slit my throat in the kitchen and found peace in my slumber: the gift of acknowledging that life *wasn't* perfect, *wouldn't be* perfect, and that it was normal to feel sometimes that life was shit. It felt that way because it probably *was*.

*Privilege can sometimes be*
*A burden of its own*
*We were so lucky but in all the wrong ways*
*Maintaining a façade*
*Could break the bank for some*
*But we had money to throw at our problems*
*Someone to clean the house*
*Someone to mind the kids*
*Someone to deal with all that dirty laundry*
*Someone to organise*
*Someone to buy supplies*
*Someone to do it all so they don't have to*

*We were always so well kept*
*When you outsource care it's not called neglect*

*We had a lot of toys*
*To keep us company*
*Those endless nights when mom was working upstairs*
*We had a lot of books*
*To keep our minds off why*
*Dad never seemed to spend his evenings at home*
*We got used growing up*
*To doing what we'd want*
*Raising ourselves and setting our own boundaries*
*We visited our friends*
*And made our mental notes*
*Of how a real family was meant to function*

*We were always so well kept*
*When you outsource care it's not called neglect*

*How old are you supposed to be*
*The first time you need therapy?*

*We always just assumed*
*That it was natural*
*That everybody had insomnia*
*The same anxiety*
*The same panic attacks*
*The same depression, the same thoughts of suicide*
*We wanted for nothing*
*Except a mom and dad*
*Who actually felt like a mother and a father*
*They gave us everything*
*Except the things we need*
*Just like their own parents had done before them*

*We were always so well kept*
*When you outsource care it's not called neglect*
*It's just the price they paid to pay the prices*
*Of all their cowardice and vices*

Punk acknowledged the gritty reality of flaw and disappointment rather than the fabricated bubble-gum world of my sister's plastic pop music. When I was my students' age, punk had saved my life, and I hoped I might be the lifeline that could pass on that same gift to anyone there that might have needed it.

I'm not sure if that's what happened, but I do know that it wasn't just suicidal students who seemed to seek me out afterwards to talk to about their problems and get some help. It was a variety of kids struggling against those bubble-gum norms of the conventional world. The ones whose families were dysfunctional or violent; the ones finding it hard to make friends from the limited palate of what was available from their classmates; the ones who kept getting in trouble by clashing up against figures of authority in the school; the ones who didn't know quite how to talk to their religious families about their growing lack of faith; and the ones grappling with issues of sexuality and gender that they feared might lose them the love of their families or friends. My raising the punk flag proudly and vocalising my oppositional sympathies against the blindly accepted norms of society was like lighting a beacon which, thankfully, some of those students feeling oppressed by those norms now seemed able to see. Punk as an attitude meant they knew they could talk to me openly – despite my conflictive credentials as one of the strictest teachers in the school – about all the different ways they felt the school, their families, or society, might be limiting who they wanted to be. Stupid rules about hair, about uniform, about where and when they were allowed to study or to go home, about the ways people chose to teach their lessons, about the ways people didn't listen to them, about expectations for what they were supposed to do with their lives. And those who were able to see beyond my superficial persona as a strict disciplinarian witnessed the true me inside as I raised their concerns with the relevant people in charge and frequently took their side against the institutional status quo.

I was the same as a member of staff. One of the few people in the staffroom who didn't merely grumble about issues within the school around the lunch table and fall silent whenever a member of the school leadership team entered the room, but one who wasn't afraid to go straight to the Headteacher, or one of their team, and raise our concerns directly, even if they were in opposition to the Head's own preferred plans or came off as critical of the school. Thanks to the tragedy of both my parents *and* all my remaining grandparents having died since I started teaching, my wife and I had been able to afford to completely pay off our mortgage with the various inheritances that came in over the years. We don't want children, so don't have any, leaving us not only plenty of disposable income to save each month, but if we lost either of our jobs there would also be no hungry mouths depending on us that would starve. Nor would we be in risk of losing our home.

I have never been interested in career or promotion either. I wasn't even sure if I really wanted to be a teacher, after all! I had only become Head of Department because my former Head got promoted to Deputy Head of the school, and it was either *I* step up and do her job going forward, guaranteeing we continue in the philosophy-focused trajectory we were all currently enjoying, or risk a new outsider coming in who might change everything myself and my other colleague loved about our department. He didn't want the job, so it was either me or a stranger. It was self-preservation and a way to keep autonomy over what I did in the classroom that motivated me to the management position, not a desire for a bigger paycheque or a title after my name. Therefore I never really worried about burning any bridges by being seen by management as 'difficult', and knew we could always withstand the financial blow if the school ever got petty enough about potential insubordination to fire me for it. This gave me a kind of fearlessness – reckless and kamikaze-like at times – in my dealings with the senior team that others couldn't access. Recognising the privilege of that position, I often took it upon myself to fight for things my colleagues wanted but were too worried to ever raise, regardless of my own feelings about the issue. If the staffroom was full of grumbling about some silly new policy obligation that meant our workload was raised significantly, I would find myself sending an email or grabbing a quick chat with the Head as I passed them in the corridor and pushing back against it so that concerns were known without anybody more vulnerable than me having to stick their neck out too far. I would do this even if the new policy didn't particularly worry me personally. To me, it was a matter of solidarity. Of ensuring voices were heard. Just as I could afford to live on less money because we didn't have children to worry about, I also had to see that my own perspective on the workload demands of the job came from the context of being happily childless and living with a wife who was also a teacher. We both enjoyed our work and were always understanding of its ridiculous demands on each other if one of us ever had to sacrifice some free time to meet a stupid deadline. As a child of two workaholics, however, who spent too many lonely hours with his dad away at the office and his mom locked upstairs in the home office of her own, I could see why colleagues who had kids would not be so happy to add a couple more hours onto their already full working week. Punk gave me both the 'two fingers up to authority' spirit to not fear talking back when the powers-that-be got something wrong, but also that sense of community and selfless solidarity to want to stand up in defence of those who couldn't defend themselves, whether they were teachers *or* students.

Which wasn't to say I wouldn't also sometimes go into battle entirely for myself, and that sometimes these battles were not utterly futile and foolish. While I can look back proudly at the behind-the-scene conversations I had which reduced the annual number of assessments our students had to take (and we had to mark) each year, which transformed the way that teachers were observed in the performance management process so that discussions were more horizontal and developmental than hierarchical and judgemental, and which ensured protections of gained time and free periods against various encroaching and unnecessary duties, it is frustrating that I would probably be most remembered by all my colleagues for the most visible, yet trivial, battle I waged throughout my time at the school: my apparent war against ties.

I don't actually mind wearing a tie. I have quite an extensive collection of them in fact. When my favourite 'uncle' (a close family friend, not an uncle through blood) and honorary grandfather, Archer King, died, I was proud to receive some of his ties in remembrance. I wear a Roy Lichtenstein pop-art 'BLAM' tie to remember my dad, who had a print of that iconic artwork always hanging in his office, and wear one featuring the New York City skyline/ Statue of Liberty that my American grandmother bought me to remember her too. I never met her husband, my grandad Joe, but I still sometimes wear one of *his* ties I was bequeathed when I was old enough to wear it, and I kept the tie I chose to wear on my wedding day, and gifted a matching tie to my best man and all the ushers, so that they, too, could remember the occasion. I have Christmas ties, a tie for my favourite baseball team, the Red Sox, and even ties for some of my favourite wrestlers. I have ties from museums I have visited and ties that represent different passions of mine, such as books or music. And yes, I have some ties just because they are nice colours or patterns. I do not *hate* ties. But I *do* hate being *told* I have to wear one.

The tie is perhaps the most unnecessary piece of clothing in existence. A flap of fabric that dangles, noose-like, from the neck for no obvious reason. It is not needed to keep the shirt closed, as buttons do that job. It does not tie the neck area to any other part of the outfit, and one can look perfectly fine without wearing one. Many, of course, do, with the tie being seen for what it is by many in modern industry today: an anachronism from a bygone age. I'm a punk rocker – I love a random, unnecessary splash of colour or individual aesthetic flair if given the opportunity. But only if it is one's choice to splash it. If the flair is shared freely and not by force. Too often, the tie is enforced as part of a prescribed uniform and is not the wearer's choice; hence, since childhood, an oppositional relationship has been formed between me and ties. Growing up, a tie became seen as a way for teachers to control us and tell us off. It wasn't tied the right way, or it was missing from our neck entirely, and we would be reprimanded. This pointless strip of fabric became a point of contention rather than a means of self-expression. Uniform stripes of colour that marked students from one school out from those of another. War-colours for school football tournaments and petty local rivalries.

My first memory of wearing a tie was not being able to tie one. I went to my primary school with one of those cheats: the pseudo-ties that were basically elastic bands beneath a shirt collar, holding up an illusion of a knotted tie. I remember being bullied for it – older girls pulling it and letting it snap back viciously into my throat. I remember learning quickly after that how to tie a real one but hating the feeling of constriction around my asthmatic neck. For the rest of my school days, I mastered the art of keeping a top button undone, hidden behind a well-placed knot, and on the last day of term in my final year of secondary school, my best friend and I set our ties on fire as soon as we got home. (Or at least we tried to. It turned out they were made of sterner – more flame retardant – stuff.) Although I was equally unenamoured with the entire notion of school uniform, it was that chokey, dangling, pointless *tie* that sat at the centre of my complaint.

At the same time, I had always understood, growing up in the gendered and heteronormative eighties and nineties, that the world of work would mean, for men, a world of suits. Holding a cigarette lighter uselessly against my school tie that last day of my GCSE exams and watching it fail to set fire could well be an allegory for the futility of believing I would ever truly be rid of them. I knew there were more ties to come in my future and, like I already said, I didn't even mind that so long as it was my choice to wear one. The singed school-tie went straight in the bin, but I had other ties at home I would be happy to put on over the next few years if the mood was right. So when I became a teacher, the tie, I knew, would have to once again become a permanent fixture of my life. I was working at a boys' school, the boys all had to wear ties, every other male member of staff I saw there was wearing a tie; ties here would be inevitable. They even used the ties to communicate important things – ties in different colours to represent the school house you belonged to, branded ties for accomplishments in sports, arts, drama, and music. It didn't even occur to me to not wear one. Work *meant* restriction, work *meant* stupid shit like ties again. I was an adult – this was the real world. This was my life now.

But…

I am also a philosopher. And a punk. And therefore someone who can never let a blind tradition pass him by without at least a little bit of prodding and analysis. One day I noticed a male colleague wasn't wearing one and I asked him if he was worried he'd get into trouble. 'I can't get into trouble', he told me. 'It's not actually staff uniform policy that we have to wear ties. It just says we have to wear "professional dress"'.

A seed in my head was sown. I went straight to the policy.

He was right.

A little further digging and I discovered that this was a consequence of the Equalities Act of 2010, because you couldn't legally specify potentially gender-discriminating dress codes to staff. If *all* staff had to wear ties, that would be fine, but to say a *male* member of staff had to wear a tie and a female one didn't, would be to define and enforce gender stereotypes and possibly lead to some people feeling uncomfortable or unwelcome in the workplace. If, for example, I presented as male but identified as a woman, being forced to wear such an explicitly masculine signifier – the tie – might be considered a barrier. Or, if I were someone who presented as female but identified as male, to *not* be allowed to wear a tie might be equally frustrating and problematic. The phrase 'professional dress' was an intentionally useful one as it allowed flexibility, while also smuggling in conservative gender norms. If most men professionally wore ties and most women didn't, then there would still be a tacit assumption of heteronormative gendered dress-codes, even if they weren't explicitly stated. The problem was, however, at this point in history, men in the professional world don't really wear ties anymore. So the smuggled-in norms were now open to interpretation. I could choose not to wear a tie and still argue I was professionally dressed, despite that not being what the school clearly intended by the phrase.

Which is exactly what I did.

The first day passed without any comment, then the second, and then the third. A few colleagues asked questions, a few students, but no one told me I was doing anything wrong, so I continued, happy and feeling liberated. Then one of the Assistant headteachers came to see me before school one morning. 'You've got to wear a tie, DaN,' they said, as if it were an ineluctable law of nature. 'The boys do, and you need to be a role model.' But that stance was a problem. If you could only be a role model if you were wearing a tie, and only male staff had to wear ties, then we were sending the message that only men should be their role models. Considering the significant problems the school had with sexism in its students, and turnover of female staff as a result of that sexism, this was an attitude that needed to be challenged. Furthermore, there were plenty of other things I was allowed to do as a member of staff that my students weren't – from walking the wrong way down a one-way system in the corridors to drinking a hot cup of coffee in the classroom while I was teaching them. We trusted students to recognise that the adults in the room had different privileges than they did on all these other things, so why not with our uniform too?

'I'm just telling you what the Head wants', he said, before leaving me to it, still tieless, believing the matter to be settled. A few minutes later, however, another Assistant Head came to see me. The bruiser. A teacher famous for shouting at students and, when needed, staff. If they had been cops, the previous guy had been the good cop; I was now looking at bad cop. 'Look, DaN, the Head wants you to wear a tie, so you have to wear a tie, it's as simple as that.' But I wasn't afraid of the bruiser because I'd been working with him for years. Had seen his softer side. I repeated what I'd said to 'good cop' and added that if the Head wanted me to wear a tie, then *he* should come and see me himself because it clearly isn't the policy that I have to wear one and I'd like to hear why he believes that it is.

The bruiser looked bemused. Disappointed I was willing to take it this far. Shook his head and left the room.

I'd now refused the instructions of two of my bosses and asked for direct instruction from the top boss with the complete intention of telling him 'no' too. *And all for something that was totally trivial to me and I didn't really care about.* I had a tie in my bag and had no problem wearing one if told that I really had to. I'd been wearing one for years already, after all. But, as I saw the school was investing the time of *two* members of its senior team to tell me off about this triviality, and learnt from the first that *there had been an actual meeting of the senior leadership team to discuss what to do about me and my tie*, I became curious at how much energy they were really prepared to waste on something so utterly stupid. I was an outstanding teacher – one of the best in the school, I was frequently told. I was well-respected and heavily involved in shaping teaching and learning policy at the place. I was a valued member of the team. Were they really going to threaten me with significant disciplinary action just because I was a male member of staff choosing not to wear a pointless tie?

At the same time – trivial works both ways. I was happy to put the tie back on *if* satisfied there was a good reason for doing so, but the insignificant became significant the more we disagreed. I *wasn't* satisfied the school had a legitimate reason for making me wear one, and now it was becoming a matter of principle.

The Head came to see me at recess. I explained that if the policy was dictating that I, as a man, had to wear a tie *because I was a man*, whereas women did not have to wear ties *because they are women*, then it seemed like the policy was in violation of the Equalities Act. I also showed him a collection of pictures of famous businessmen and male politicians all acting in professional capacity without wearing a tie with their suits. Topping off the presentation was Prime Minister, David Cameron, US President, Barak Obama, and Princes William and Harry *all* engaged in significant matters of state together on a recent visit without a single tie dangling from any of their prestigious necks. To his credit, the Head conceded that I had a point. However, he said, reviewing the staff dress code would take some time, as it would need governor approval *and* approval at the level of the wider foundation of schools of which we were a part to change anything. His intention, he said, was to get it put explicitly, and legally, in writing, that male staff needed to wear ties and clear up any confusion, but maybe he would find out that this couldn't be done. *Then*, he said, I could go tieless. But for now, he asked, while there was some confusion on the issue, could I please keep on wearing a tie until the legal position of the policy was sorted out?

'Sure', I said. Because it really wasn't that important to me. A new policy review might mean in the future ties would become concretely optional and I was happy enough with that. A tie was around my neck before he'd even left the room. However, because it really didn't bother me either way, I didn't think too much about it again. The initial review of the dress code hit a snag when it turned out my suspicions that it didn't pass legal muster were well-founded, but that snag hit at the same time that the entire legal status of our school was changing from 'school' within a 'foundation', to 'academy' within a 'multi-academy trust', and thus policies like staff dress-codes became centralised and lumped in with all sorts of other changing documentation. I had other things to care about than the tie around my neck that I gave very little thought to – however, colleagues continually reminded me of how brave and reckless they thought I had been to not wear one for those few days and it began to irk me how this absolutely minor act was seen as something so bold and transgressive. What kind of fear did these people live in that prevented them from standing up to those in power, even in this pathetic way? Remember – in my mind it wasn't even a transgression: I was only doing what the policy allowed. And if they couldn't even imagine themselves standing up for themselves in such an inconsequential way as choosing not to wear a tie to work one day, would they ever be able to do it for things that actually mattered?

I wrote a small piece about the incident for *The Guardian*'s 'Secret Teacher' column, astounded at how seriously the Head had taken this utterly frivolous bit of non-compliance. The piece was anonymous, but some at school suspected I might be its author. In the piece, I shared my concluding feelings about the experience:

*I felt disappointed more than anything. In a profession that demands more and more every year, were they really going to take this from me too? With our breaks frequently given up to detentions, clubs and interventions; our evenings and weekends consumed with marking, planning, reports and paperwork; our holidays given over to wrapping our heads around new syllabuses and specifications, the sliver of personal autonomy I enjoyed when choosing not to wear a tie was a glimmer of freedom. When professional morale is at an all-time low and people are leaving the profession in droves, is it really worth alienating those of us heroically clinging on?*

*Not a single student had their education affected by the absence of my tie, but for those few glorious days I had one less obstacle in the way of enjoying a job that is more and more difficult to love. Ironically, individual liberty is one of the "fundamental British values" we are required to teach but it seems no one – not students, and least of all teachers – is allowed the liberty to challenge even the most trivial aspect of a school's authority.*

I don't hate ties, but I was starting to hate what that conflict about a tie represented about schools and authority. Still though, I continued to wear one. Never complaining, not even resentful. I even bought new ones. A sparkly new tie with sequins for our fancy school 'Speech Night' and a few new Christmas ties to my growing festive collection. A tie with a pattern from the illustration of the Book of Kells after a trip to Dublin became a talking point in one of my lessons about early Christianity, and in my role as co-ordinator of the Student Council I campaigned with my students and consulted on patterns for a special new school tie for the Council's Chair and Deputy. But, when the COVID-19 pandemic hit and schools re-opened after the lockdown, I told the Head that once again I would not be wearing one, having read guidance from the British Medical Association before the reopening about the added risk of infection brought about by unwashed ties dangling from surface to surface. It was an odd and difficult September that year anyway with all the new protocols to worry about, and no one mentioned the absence of a tie to me at all as we all negotiated our way through the first few weeks of this peculiar new version of school-life. But then, a few weeks in to the 'new normal', despite the email I had written to him in August explaining why I wouldn't be wearing a tie come September, the Head shouted my name as I was walking past him one lunchtime. 'It's not acceptable, DaN. It's non-negotiable and this is getting silly.'

I was already frustrated by much in the school's approach to keeping staff safe since coming back in September. Our protocols were sloppy, with many policies going largely unenforced and infections already sending whole year-groups home every week. As a clinically vulnerable asthmatic, told returning to work was a risk, it was a worrying time. I had been advised in the school's risk-assessment for my return to shower immediately every day after getting back from work, to make sure my clothes were cleaned more frequently than usual and kept separate from other laundry for fear of contamination, and to stay away from other members of staff wherever possible and eat alone, spending my free periods in isolation. Instead of sharing the responsibility between us all, and making the environment safe for everyone, the school's approach had been to let staff be as lax and comfortable as they wanted to be and for the small minority of us who remained worried about infection to basically fend for ourselves. Overly cautious and unnecessary as some of those protocols turned out to be in retrospect, at the time the tie thing was just another one of those small elements of self-preservation I clung to as I moved from classroom to classroom, terrified of catching a deadly virus. I had explained the approach I wanted to take before the start of the year and couldn't see why the school now would be so desperate for me to add this further risk to my working day?

I explained my position to the Head and, heavy with his own months of stress at having to run a school during a chaotic pandemic, he exploded at me, shouting loudly about my 'obsession with ties' and 'need to stand out from the crowd and never do what you're told'. It got fairly ugly and personal pretty quick, but I stayed calm, refusing to call him out on his unprofessionalism as he balled me out in front of the students lining up for lunch and instead be sympathetic to the stress of the situation. Eventually, after daring me to take him to a tribunal, he did calm down, and we reached a negotiation, which he formally emailed to me later that day to clarify:

> *Good evening Dan.*
>
> *Following our conversation earlier today I am writing to confirm that it will be acceptable for you to wear a tie tucked into your shirt. In addition, I recognise that given your asthma, and especially due to current circumstances, it may not to be advisable for you to do up the top button on your shirt. I am supportive of you not having the top button of your shirt fastened as long as this is done as discreetly as possible so as not to draw attention. The bow tie offer still stands.*
>
> *If you are concerned about your clothing and the need to wash items each evening it would be acceptable for you to wear a lab coat or something similar in which to teach so as to reduce the washing load.*
>
> *I am glad that we have been able to find a compromise on this issue.*

The compromise we'd agreed to was that I still wear a regular tie, but wear it weirdly tucked into the buttons of my shirt so that it no longer dangled. Which I did, attracting constant questions and conversations with my students and my colleagues about why I was doing it whereas, before, when I simply wore no tie, no student had ever asked me a thing and life had ticked along smoothly. It was very alienating and frustrating, and for what? The insistence on my wearing a stupid strip of fabric? It was compliance for the sake of compliance, and I resented it bitterly. Still, it was the better of the other equally attention-drawing options. I wasn't going to wear a bowtie, or a lab-coat, and purchase more unnecessary items of clothing just to satisfy this stupidity. And I guess I was grateful that I now, at least, had official permission to continue not doing up the top button on my shirt that I had not done up once in my entire teaching career.

A month and a half later though, the Headteacher was dead. A massive heart attack, completely unexpected. It was the first day of October half term and the first proper break of the post-lockdown return to school. He was cooking dinner for his family and dropped down dead in the kitchen with no prior warning. We were all shocked and saddened by the news, and when I got the terrible email informing us, I kept thinking back to that argument about ties – how stressed he had been about something so trivial. The pandemic was tough for everyone, but as a Headteacher of a school when the government was changing guidance, advice, and expectations every few days – and sometimes several times in the same day – including weekends and holidays, it was a particularly tough time. Many suffered stress-related illnesses. Many others quit the profession completely. It was clear from the way he snapped at me that day that my Head was very much on the edge, and for weeks after the announcement of his passing I wondered how much that stupid decision of mine not to wear a tie might have contributed unnecessarily to his tension? Just one more thing amongst a million of them – but maybe the straw that breaks the camel's back?

It was stupid guilt, even if it was understandable. The day before his death we were joking about movies and discussing the latest election of the school's Student Council. There were no hard feelings evident on his side, and I'd been wearing that silly tucked-in tie ever since our altercation. If that negligible act of utterly minor insubordination really had been enough to cause a man to have a heart-attack, then he was worrying too much about something not worth worrying about, and that's not on me, that's on him. But I carried the burden of feeling like

I contributed in some small way to his death for a long time and couldn't quite shake the feeling. Even now, I sometimes wonder if he might still be alive if I had just worn a tie from the first day of term… but when I do, I remember that if that really were the thing that did it, it would be absolutely fucking *ridiculous*.

Whatever the truth of it, I wore my tie tucked into my shirt the rest of that academic year in his memory. A tie at half-mast in mourning and remembrance of our fallen Head.

Sort of.

Because late in the summer, as a member of the school's committee for Equality, Diversity, and Inclusion, I was doing some training on inclusivity, 'bringing your authentic self to work', dress codes, and the Equalities Act. It was quite specific in the training that male staff couldn't be asked to wear something female staff were not asked to wear (and vice versa) and that gendered dress codes were unadvised. I realised that I'd never actually investigated the outcome of the old Head's tinkering with the academy trust dress code and wondered what had happened with it. I asked the senior leadership team for a copy of the policy and, after a very long back and forth, finally got a copy: 'professional dress' was the phrase that survived. There was no mention of men wearing ties. So, in the summer term of 2021, as the weather got warmer, I just stopped wearing one.

September 2022 saw the new school year begin with a new Headteacher. I didn't wear a tie from the start of the year and, even as I sat through his first eye-rolling assembly to students about being proud of their school tie and ensuring a neat and tidy appearance in their uniform, my neck remained happily bare. As a new school leader, the new Head requested one-on-one chats with all members of staff across his first term to get to know us all and let us get to know him. I was one of the first, and at the end of our very long chat after school that day, he hit the Columbo line on me – 'just one more thing' – and said he wanted to talk to me about ties. 'I've been told you have a problem with them, and I did notice you haven't been wearing one this week…'

For fuck's sake!

Even though it seems obvious at this point, I still sort of couldn't believe ties were, once again, continuing to take up so much of my professional time.

I gave him the short version of the story, and how what had started as personal preference had evolved to something more symbolic now. How it wasn't just that I didn't like being forced to wear them, but that doing so was a barrier to inclusivity and gender-equality at the school. How important I felt it was, especially in a boys' school, to reflect different ideas of masculinity and combat heteronormative ideas that might exclude some of our students. The last two years I had taught my first transgender student and she had opened my eyes to so many daily prejudices and micro-aggressions she had to face just to navigate through the school day. Insistence on ties was just one of them, but I pointed out that there was a reason for the law not allowing the school to dictate that men wear ties, that it was unhelpful to our students for us to do it too, and that, especially as a member of the Equality, Diversity, and Inclusion team, I felt it important to remind students and staff that certain old fashioned norms were becoming obsolete. He feigned sympathy but then went for the classic management tactic: 'can't you just wear a tie until I've clarified the policy position with the governors and the academy trust?' But I'd heard all that before with the last guy. 'No,' I said. 'What I'll do this time is I'll continue to *not* wear a tie until you clarify with the governors and academy trust first whether you can legally tell me that I have to.'

For the rest of the year, until my final day at that school, I only ever wore a tie again if *I* wanted to. Which I did, several times. Because, again, I have never been *against ties*, just against being forced to wear one. Yet the simple attempt to have some minimal autonomy over my appearance and be free to choose when or where I wore one became such an issue, time and time again, it was like a wound I couldn't help but poke at, even though I knew it would sting, and I got a reputation as some kind of anti-tie fanatic that made it seem like all my 'fuck authority' punk rock energy was going into this entirely trivial issue when it wasn't. I was fighting constantly in the background for decolonizing our school curriculum, for LGBTQ+ inclusivity, for better student voice and student democracy, for developing a more challenging, inspiring, and autonomous approach to pedagogy, for questioning the trend of doing everything Ofsted (and rumours about Ofsted) told us to, for more manageable workloads and less box-ticking paperwork, for better communication across the school, for a school diary that actually made sense, for trusting teachers as professionals and not micro-managing them all the time, for trusting *teenagers* more as students and giving them the freedom to develop independently as learners, especially in the sixth form, and I was doing all of this far more than I ever thought about or talked about *ties*. But whether it was making my voice heard about dress codes or making it heard about workload, it was punk rock that gave me my voice and the fearlessness to use it. To question authority, to question policy, to question rules and, importantly, to question myself. To change my mind and be open to doing things differently when it was clear they weren't working. To listen to my students rather than just imposing my will upon them. To apologise to them if I thought I didn't do something particularly well. To have confidence in what I was doing if I thought that it was right, even if those in charge were telling me to do something different. To ask forgiveness if necessary but to never, ever, ask permission first.

It is to the detriment of our profession that there is so little of that punk rock spirit among us. That most of my colleagues would just happily eat whatever shit they were given from their senior leadership team, Ofsted, or the Department for Education, rather than ask any critical questions or dare to say no. Saying no is my punk rock superpower, and I thank Green Day, Jello Biafra, Henry Rollins, and all the rest of my anti-heroes for giving it to me. Not no for the sake of saying no, but no as an option, where needed, to remind the people in charge that they cannot simply ask you to do anything. That there must be *good reasons* for what is asked. That it must *make sense*. And if it doesn't, that you can always refuse. That sometimes those who aren't 'in charge' might have ideas worth hearing too. Ideas that might even be better.

When I look around at teachers, and the different hoops so many agree to jump through or educational fads they buy into wholesale only to drop them in eighteen months' time for the next 'big idea' in education, I think how much better they would be for their students, and for their own wellbeing, if they had the punk rock nerve to just say no to the bullshit that is so frequently imposed upon them and could concentrate more fully on their teaching instead. Sadly though, it is not surprising that a profession built on hierarchical coercion and repressive behaviour policies and regimes of discipline and punishment for its students is one which is itself subject to the same accepted hierarchies of fear and obey in its staff. To be rebellious and also be the teacher in the room is almost conceptually incompatible in a schooling system where hierarchical authority is meant to be absolute and unquestioned. Where the sort of people who choose to be a teacher are, for the most part, the sort of people comfortable enough in that repressive environment during their own childhood to have excelled in it and want to go back.

I remember once watching an episode of Jonathan Ross's old talkshow where Simon Cowell and Marilyn Manson were the guests. Ross asked Cowell how he thought someone like Marilyn Manson would do on his show, The X-Factor, and Cowell astutely pointed out that the genius and popularity of Marilyn Manson is that he's not the sort of person who would ever *go* on The X-Factor. That was what made him Marilyn Manson. Maybe it's like that with punk rock and teaching? The true punk rockers wouldn't go anywhere near a classroom. And those of us who do, will never truly fit in. Either in punk rock circles, where we are now treated with suspicion for siding with the enemy, or in schools, where our personality is crushed. We're too fuck you for the classroom, but too teacherly for the mosh pit. Permanent outsiders. No-one wants us. Like Henry Rollins: we neither fit in where we're supposed to fit in, or where we'd rather be.

*Just as fucked up as I ever was*
*Maybe fucked up a little more*
*The damage of a life lived wide awake*
*While other people close their eyes*
*I cut my hair sometimes to celebrate*
*To mark another minor liberation*
*You join the dots of every scar*
*They come together and they form a mask*
*That's far too easy to slip on*
*I find myself when I refuse*
*When I raise two middle fingers at the world*

*I find myself in my old notebooks*
*Which read the same as this one now*
*And listening back to all those favourite songs*
*Which never fail to make me feel*
*The way I felt listening for the first time*
*I wear myself upon my sleeve*
*In new tattoos and ancient t-shirts*
*I am myself when I am ill at ease*
*Sleepless nights and restless days*
*I am nothing but my patterns*
*Childhood traumas locked in amber*

*We can always disappoint*
*The person we see standing in the mirror*

*But we can also make them proud*
*A lot is lost with every passing year*
*A thousand cuts of compromise*
*But they can never take it all away*
*So hold on tight to what is left*
*I have never been the person that they thought I was*
*Some days I am better*
*Some days I am much worse*
*But I am always somewhere inside even when I'm lost I'm still there clinging on*

*Bursting from the grave*
*I gasp deep at the fresh air*
*A zombie roaming empty streets*
*Finding myself, Piece by piece*
*Just in time for them*
*To bury me alive again*

*My nemesis is the unthinking status quo*
*My secret power is my power to say no*

On my final day at the school, after all the lovely speeches and clapping, they gave me the same parting gift the school has traditionally given to all staff leavers. 'Oh good,' I said, deadpan, looking slowly around the room, holding out the gift in my hands. 'A tie.'

Over a decade of my life given to that place and that was how it ended: in the predictable disappointment of another fucking *tie*.

## INTERLUDE – PHILOSOPHY UNLEASHED POST - 14/02/22:

## QUITTING MY JOB - The Thought Behind Making a Change

I told my form on Friday that this would be my last year at the school. I hadn't been keeping it a secret, but there also hadn't really been a relevant opportunity to bring it up. As we discussed my possible involvement in an upcoming charity football match between staff and students, I had images of old movies flash before my eyes. The cop on their last week before retirement who gets shot before they make it out. I said I'm not breaking my leg with a poorly judged tackle in my last year at the school and the cat was out of the bag. I'm leaving.

Some of the form are also members of my Year 12 Philosophy class. "Can't you wait another year and then leave?" one asked, realising that someone else - someone new - would be finishing up the course with them come September. Someone they might not like as much.

"I've already done that twice" I replied honestly. "There's never a good time to leave."

It was true. I'd first thought about leaving my current job in 2019. I'd started working there in 2011, and 2019 was the year after the cohort who joined in Year 7 with me in 2011 had all left the school and gone on to university. I was on duty in the playground one morning and looked around at all the new faces and thought: maybe I've stayed here too long? Colleagues had come and gone too. In fact, most of the group who joined the school with me in 2011 had long since moved to pastures new. Had I stayed too long in the same place?

As a philosopher the idea that you just should move from job to job after a certain period of time seemed bizarre to me. Why move just for the sake of moving? If I could do what I wanted to do professionally in my current position, what reason was there to do the same thing somewhere else just because it was different? By 2019, however, I realised it wasn't about moving on because of some arbitrary date in the calendar. People moved because even doing something you love in the same place every day for too long can grow a bit stagnant.

By 2019, as Head of my department for seven years, I'd helped develop a curriculum I was really proud of. We tweaked the lessons every year. Changed a few things here or there. But why fix what isn't broken? I'd supervised some amazing student EPQ projects, sent many off to university to study Philosophy, got some of the best GCSE results in the school year after year, and successfully introduced Philosophy at A-level… What I was feeling that day on the playground was not just the loss of the previous year's Year 13s who I had seen through their entire life at the school, but the ennui that came from knowing exactly what the rest of the day, the week, the month, the term, would be like. I could teach these lessons in my sleep. Though each class of students was unique, similar questions would still be raised from whatever new and updated stimulus material we used. Similar responses would come to the questions we posed however we might frame them. It was always different…but it was different on a spectrum rather than anything radically new.

And then there are the institutional things. The things that started to bug me. When you start at a place new, the possibilities of what might happen are endless. You might even, as I did, attempt to be a force for change within the place where you work. By that point, in 2019, I had changed multiple aspects of school policy and even written a policy document or two. But I had also, by that point, seen the limits of potential change. The lines in the sand which would never be crossed. The specific external pressures which would always get in the way of anything too radical. The personalities who would never budge on certain issues. The litany of good ideas which had either died on the vine or withered away with a whimper after an ineffective roll-out or clash with staff morale. I had done a lot of good, but was starting to feel I had done as much good as I could in that particular environment.

I was all too aware of what things would never change, and some of them meant there might always be a certain level of dissatisfaction with what could be achieved there for me. I realised that it wasn't time to think about leaving in 2019 because I'd been there eight years, it was time to think about leaving because in those eight years I'd been there I might have done everything there was that was worth doing and could be done in that particular context. I had enjoyed my time there, but was growing bored of the repetition. I didn't feel intellectually stimulated anymore.

But at the same time - what about my students?

Not the Year 11 or Year 13 students who I would have already done everything I could with to prepare for their eventual exams by the time my term of notice was served, but the Year 12 philosophy group who had just started with me and seemed so eager to learn and the Year 10 classes just beginning to embark properly on their GCSE. And then there was the Year 12 members of my form who I would be abandoning mid-UCAS if I left at the end of the year - a reference half-written and their advice for the future somewhat undercooked?

Whenever a teacher leaves a school there will be students their absence affects. Some, let's be honest, for the good. We may be their least favourite teacher, the scourge of their educational experience, the person whose classroom they dread entering each week and for whom the news of their impending departure will be a cause to celebrate. But for many it will have an impact that's negative. A loss of continuity amidst a two year exam course or sequence of lessons. There's no good time to leave. Give your notice to leave at Christmas and you give your students a false start which then stutters to life again in January and is forced to pivot to a new regime. Leave at Easter and you abandon them just before their final exams. Leave at the end of the year, and those students you would normally take from beginning to end of an exam subject get left high and dry mid-way through their journey. There is no good time to leave.

Some might say we should ignore this. It is, after all, our lives, not theirs, and we must prioritise ourselves over others and do what is best for us. But to be honest you probably don't get into teaching if you're someone who puts themselves first. I haven't lost every weeknight and most of my weekends for over a decade now because I do what's best for me. Perhaps we should prioritise ourselves more, but we can't help it. We do worry about our students. So the impact on them can't be ignored. However, there is some weight to the argument that moral consideration of the impact of our decisions must only be that: consideration. It must be considered, but it can't be the only thing we take account of. And other aspects might take priority or be more compelling. Furthermore, if every possible moment of departure is conceivably bad for a group of students then, it could be argued, that makes the decision to leave more morally permissible at any available time. Unless we are to be in our posts for life - which it is already accepted that we are not - then we simply have to accept that when we choose to leave there will always be some negative outcomes for some students along with any possible positive ones. They are unavoidable and therefore morally neutral so long as they are acknowledged and mitigated for as much as possible. (It is also worth pointing out that those same impacts happen when we stay in our jobs but accept promotions which cut our classroom contact time with students, and few seem to balk too much at doing that). We owe our students something, but not everything.

But all these thoughts became moot when the coronavirus pandemic hit in March of 2020. The week before the first lockdown I was actually looking at other jobs. I had started to think seriously that it might be time to return full-time to academia. Higher education. Philosophy divorced from teaching Religious Studies and time and space to research the things which actually interested me. But then came lockdown and suddenly the old arguments about nothing being new anymore went right out the door. Almost overnight we had to reinvent the entire profession. I had to redesign my entire curriculum for online delivery and reimagine the possibilities of education beyond the structure of the school day and the physical restrictions of geography. The whole period was pretty scary, but professionally it was thrilling as a raft of new possibilities began to show themselves.

I don't think those possibilities ever lived up to their promise, for a variety of reasons, but by the time schools were re-opened in September of 2020 a new consideration of impact was added to my thoughts of leaving. A sense of abandoning ship at a time of crisis. As we returned to the physical classroom, masked and as distanced as we could be, trying to once again transform our approach to lessons to make them "covid safe" it felt like all hands were needed on deck. It also felt like we were lucky to still have a job at a time of such economic uncertainty. If I were to leave then, would there even be a job market to enter?

And then our Headteacher died unexpectedly before Christmas and a further sense of turmoil was added to the equation. Abandoning the ship at a time of plague was bad timing; abandoning it at a time of collective tragedy was just bad taste. Besides, as various lockdowns and isolations were enacted across the school year, that sense of something odd and different persisted. I could no longer say every day was feeling the same. Some days I would come into school not even knowing if my afternoon classes would still be in the building by lunchtime. I would always be on my toes.

The work had become fulfilling, but fulfilling in a different way. Meeting the daily challenge of teaching during covid. Showing up and overcoming whatever obstacles the day hurled at me. But it was not an intellectual fulfilment, and all the talk of "lost learning" and "catching up" for exams that no longer seemed necessary to me was anathema to the new educational horizons that had shown their possibilities in the rubble of a system destroyed by the year before. At home I was doing academic research again. Reading and writing about topics of genuine philosophical interest. Thinking about things that simply felt more important than how best to calculate a teacher-assessed-grade for my exam classes or how we might respond if Ofsted decided to visit the school and ask us about the intent, implementation, and impact of our curriculum. I ended the year feeling much the same way I had that day in the playground in 2019 and spent most of the summer thinking about my future.

September 2021 gave me the perfect opportunity to reassess my thoughts. Despite all evidence to the contrary in the rest of the universe, schools in Britain decided to treat the start of the new term as if the pandemic were over. School was back to as "normal" as possible. We also had a brand new Headteacher, so it was a great opportunity to take stock. See how teaching there felt without the context of the pandemic to distort it, or the aftermath of tragedy to make me feel like leaving the place would be some sort of abdication of duty.

I needed some philosophical clarity to focus my thoughts. Essentially, the problem was this:

1) I have no pressing reason to leave my job. I love teaching, there is no new job lined up to go to, or any people telling me they want me to leave. In fact, I could stay in this job for the rest of my professional life.

2) The job gives financial security. We are still living through a pandemic and it is stupid to give up such security at a time where many don't have that.

3) I have been lucky with this job to find a school where I have been able to teach so much Philosophy alongside the RE that is legally required. Not all schools would be so accommodating and only a handful do what I have managed to do here.

4) I have good colleagues at this job and some really nice classes that I teach. Leaving will possibly leave some of those classes – or

colleagues – in the lurch or put them at a disadvantage.

BUT

5) I am no longer intellectually challenged by the job, and intellectual challenge is important to me.

6) The job, like all jobs, is not perfect. It asks a lot of me and for me to give what it asks of me I have to want to give it. After what is now a decade at the same place, I have perhaps given too much to this particular place without getting everything that was needed back from it. Though other jobs might be equally exploitative it is perhaps part of the dance of exploitation that we cannot be so aware of how much is taken for granted from us? Somewhere new, without the history, I think I could still believe that the trade of time and effort is worth it and hold hope without the expectation of disappointment for my efforts.

7) If I don't explore my options now, when I can afford to do so without any financial dependents or overhanging burdens of debt, when will I explore them?

With that being the context, I started September of 2021 - my tenth year at the school - on a fact-finding mission. Given points 1, 2, 3 and 4, I would need to discover if:

a) it was possible to find the intellectual challenge I felt was lacking,

b) feel motivated to buy-in again fully to the institutional demands I had grown disillusioned with,

and

c) make peace with the idea of staying where I was instead of exploring my options.

With that intention, I began the new academic year in a positive frame of mind, looking for fulfilment, motivation and contentment. By Christmas, however, I realised that none of these three things could be found in a place where I had so much history. Even exciting new developments would feel somehow part of a continuing narrative rather than a departure from the past, and when I got home from work each day it was my academic research that was motivating me far more than another batch of marking the same old assessment pieces I had been marking year after year after year. Paperwork for paperwork's sake, instrumental for keeping some imaginary accountability agency happy rather than having any intrinsic educational worth seemed to be taking up far more of my time than jobs I felt were actually worthwhile. Ultimately the logic was clear: if there were other options available where motivation and fulfilment were possible then why stay on a treadmill that left only discontent, even if it was the safe and comfortable thing to do?

On New Year's Day I made a resolution. I emailed in my resignation and took a leap of faith. Considerate of my classes, and ensuring the school had sufficient time to plan for its future, I agreed to stay until the end of the year, but with no new job lined up to safely move into once my contract comes up and no clear path of what comes next - another school? A university? Stay where I live currently or move somewhere new? - I decided it was time to find my next chapter, whatever that next chapter might be.

Whenever I left there would be students and classes left behind. It is never convenient to move on and it is pretty terrifying to do so when your destination remains unknown. There will, too, probably still be that sense of abandoning ship even though the worst of the pandemic is behind us and the new Head – who I really like – is firmly ensconced and taking the school confidently into the future. I will likely always wonder what might have happened if I'd stayed.

But I would wonder far more what might have happened if I'd left had I stayed.

It's not that the grass is always greener on the other side, but the grass is new grass on the other side. Different grass. A change of grass after sitting in the same field for so long. There is a reason that, be it Buddhist or Hindu notions of samsara, the Nietzschean idea of eternal recurrence, or the Hollywood hell of Groundhog Day - endless repetition is something a diverse array of thinkers agree will eventually motivate us to break free.

Even philosophers can get confused, and grappling with what exactly "the good life" might be has caused many of us sleepless nights. For me though, I now know a little more than Socrates (who, like Operation Ivy, knew only that he knew nothing). I now know, at least, that thinking about those questions - having those sleepless nights - is what I want to do more of going forward, and that I would rather lose a night of sleep thinking about the big issues in Philosophy than worrying about how to make another day in the same old classroom teaching the same old lessons interesting again.

I will miss it dearly when I leave at the end of the year, but I will also be free.

# 7.
## *TEACHER: Learning in Lockdown*

Once again, I had given it until Christmas. But as the chimes of Big Ben rang in the new year on TV and fireworks lit up the night sky outside our window to welcome in 2022, I knew that I had just celebrated my last Christmas as a teacher. In the morning, first thing, as soon as I woke up, I would be emailing my boss my resignation. I had no other job to go to, no real plan of what came next, but the one and only thing that I knew was that I couldn't face another September at that school. Pulling into the same car park for the twelfth year in a row, seeing all the same faces and facing all the same frustrations. I couldn't do it. I was done with the place and, possibly, done with teaching itself. I made a new year's resolution to make a change. Wherever it led me, I would be happy. As long as it was somewhere different.

The Christmas before, I was close to doing something similar. In fact, in many ways I *did* quit my job back then. But I was spared from the consequences of my decision by Prime Minister, Boris Johnson. Not knowing that on January 4th all schools would be shut once again by government edict, I wrote the following email to my school's leadership team on January 1st 2021:

> *Dear XXXXXXXXX,*
>
> *While I am recovering slowly but surely from COVID (still not 100% but hopefully getting there), I unfortunately have to self-isolate a little longer than originally indicated as my wife got a positive test result on December 27th despite our best efforts to keep her healthy. I therefore will not be able to return to work in person until Wednesday January 6th.*
>
> *However, I am writing regarding my concerns with returning to work in general, especially with the new strain of far more*

*transmissible virus. As you are aware I was infected with COVID 19 at the end of term. The second member of staff to get the virus that week. Having gone nowhere else but work and home since October half term, it seems most likely to me that I caught COVID 19 at [school name]. I had been very vocal to XXXXXXXX and XXXXXXXX about continuing holes in [school name]'s COVID-safety since September, and my own personal sense of a lack of safety despite assurances made in my risk-assessment for return to work at the start of the academic year. Mainly the problems I raised came from what I believe to be the continued negligence of the school in enforcing sustained COVID safety or consistency with or for its members of staff. While a lot of effort has gone into thinking about student safety at [school name] since September, staff safety has been unstructured, unenforced, and left far too much up to chance.*

*The staffroom, for example, only finally succumbed to any social distancing markings after October's half term, and these markings were then seldom followed by staff, most of whom still do not wear masks in the shared space, keep the door and windows closed, and gather close around the shared central table to eat communally. But staff themselves are hardly to blame when the school as a whole has made no formal arrangements for staff to ensure their social distancing, and provided no designated plan of which members of staff should be in which safe spaces at any given time to ensure their safety during frees or lunches (i.e. timetabled and measured 2 metre separation in designated offices, mandatory mask wearing/ventilation which is actually enforced, etc.) Besides a handful of notices in online Teams briefings and emailed rule-changes since October (which not only had no follow-up enforcement, but conflicting guidance from [the Senior Leadership Team] when asked about how they ought to be interpreted) it has basically been a free-for-all, relying on the same hope in ad hoc "common sense" which has seen infections soar across the country.*

*While I appreciated XXXXXXXX's attempted solution for me personally (although it enabled him to avoid actually changing the staff approach for all), which was to allow me to eat my lunch and spend my free periods working in the underused Lower School Year Leaders Office instead of the crowded Humanities Office where colleagues continued to work frequently unmasked and without the door open right up to December 18th, even this arrangement has been unreliable. As year leaders still use the office, and there has been no formal plan in place to timetable the shared space, there is no actual guarantee that it is free to use when I need it. As a result, any free period or lunch break I have had has been accompanied by an anxiety of having to potentially once again share the space with someone, as has happened on several occasions last term, or of not being able to use the space at all. Because of staff inconsistency regarding practicing social distance, ventilation and masks, the last time the office was shared with me on the last day of term – a time when I was likely infected with, or being infected by, COVID 19 – the colleague in the room with me for thirty minutes did not wear a mask the whole time and the door remained closed.*

*Although while teaching I have largely been able to ensure all students, and myself, wear masks, and that windows and doors were always open, even here there are issues. For example, of the nineteen classrooms I use, eleven of them have no actual two metre distance between the teacher's desk and students sitting practically sharing the table with me. The week I was infected at school I taught in many of those classrooms where, with students sitting too close to me, I taught a class where at least one student had a positive*

*COVID test that very week. Although that student was not in school the day I taught them, his peers were. The same peers who, when I entered, were maskless, standing close to each other, looking at phones and sharing food, etc.; a habit that seems to have become the established norm for students across all year-groups during the ten-minute turnaround between lessons for which they do not seem to be challenged until I arrive.*

*The most reckless disregard for staff safety, after a term of multiple face-to-face and whole school physical meetings which could have been done remotely, came in the final weeks of term where, despite it being illegal to hold shared dining indoors in a Tier 3 city (which we were at the time) we actually held two staff buffets, sharing indoor seating, masks off, eating together completely unnecessarily and with no "opt out" or alternative suggestions for safety articulated for those who felt uncomfortable. Had I not chosen to be careful myself, and made an objection so that the buffet was held after the speeches instead of, as originally planned, before, the last Friday of term I would have been unsuspectingly giving everyone I ate with the COVID 19 I was likely already infected with.*

*So returning to the point of this email – my own sense of unsafety at [school name] since September, and the school's demonstrable failure to keep me safe from COVID 19 despite my best personal efforts (which have come at great expense being as I basically haven't been able to interact with most of my peers since September and have experienced a fairly lonely and miserable Winter term at [school name] as my caution is seen as anomalous rather than the staff norm) – the fact is what I can do myself can only protect others from getting COVID from me, not – as has been demonstrated – protect me from them. My own safety relies on the compliance of my fellow colleagues and the students we teach to adhere to social distancing, mask wearing, ventilation and proper hand hygiene. Unless there are significant changes and properly planned protocols in place for how staff are to act in a COVID-safe way from January 4th, including active checking of and enforcement of these expectations, I do not feel safe to return to work at [school name] during this pandemic. Nor do I feel the control measures the school was supposed to take for my agreed risk assessment have been met. I was told to "Avoid congregating socially and maintain 2m distance at break and lunchtime" and to "continue to take care to socially distance from other adults including older adolescents" but this remains unguaranteed and often impossible, even with the use of the Year Leaders' Office, as long as the office is used by others at the same time as me who don't adhere to the same rules and the overall placement of staff during free periods remains up to chance instead of having a planned distribution of space and personnel. Likewise, the risk assessment suggested that school should "Review hours of work to enable out of hours work to minimise contact with others and enable social distancing compliance" and yet my timetable gives me fewer afternoons I can leave school early this year than it ever has before, and the school continues to insist we work in school even on days when all our classes are being taught remotely, moving from one potentially dangerous classroom to another when we would be far safer in our homes and with less people in the building. When the national approach is "if you can work from home, you should work from home", that we are not able to do so even when timetable and circumstances allow for it due to self-isolating year groups, etc., feels grossly irresponsible.*

*I was disheartened to see no mention in XXXXXXXX's email this morning of changing staff practices and got no sense that anything different would be done from January on a staff level to make me feel safer or meet the requirements of my risk assessment. The bottom line, therefore, for me is that until assurances can be made that there will be some changes, and that all [school name] staff will be distributed in a planned and well-thought-out way across the site during their free periods and lunch breaks, will comply with mask wearing and social distancing in shared spaces, that all classrooms will have a two-metre distance between the teacher and the students, and that enforcement of these expectations will actually occur this term, I do not feel safe working at [school] right now. I am aware that the introduction of lateral flow testing is going to theoretically make detecting those infected with the virus easier, but a) these particular tests still miss 30% of cases and have been largely condemned by experts, b) an operational plan for the testing still isn't in place due to the DfE guidance remaining incomplete, so mass testing won't be up and running in a meaningful way immediately, and c) I am concerned that the use of these questionable tests will give staff, already lax in their adherence to safety protocols, a false sense of safety that will make them likely to be more relaxed in their behaviours once the testing is introduced rather than more vigilant. While I am happy to continue carrying out my duties and teach remotely from home throughout this time – especially during the first two weeks of term where the bulk of teaching will be done remotely anyway – I do not feel comfortable returning to the physical school site until safety measures for staff are improved.*

*Last term was incredibly taxing mentally, but despite my many concerns raised about [school name]'s safety, I still showed up every day. Ending up getting COVID there anyway, and having to deal as an asthmatic with the fact that luck alone would now determine whether or not my symptoms would be mild or potentially fatal is not a position I intend to be in again. I hope you can either give me the assurances I seek that [school name] will be very different when I am able to leave the house again and return there on January 6th, or will accept that until it is, I will stay working from home.*

*Many thanks,*

*DaN*

I had first started thinking it was time to move on in 2019. I had been at the school too long, I thought, looking around the playground one morning and realising I had seen through my second entire cohort of students from Year 7 to Year 13 and was now facing my third. Colleagues I'd started with had come and gone. Everything was changing except for me. I knew exactly what I'd be doing tomorrow, and the day after that, and I was feeling stuck and unchallenged. Teaching during COVID wasn't the thing which made me want to quit my job, but it certainly helped cement the decision that I should. Like a lot of people, the pandemic had been eye-opening to me, as well as terrifying. A lot had happened to get me to the point at which I felt that email to the leadership team was necessary but, at the same time, I think I was just fed up with the place and looking for an exit.

At the start, when reports started coming in about a deadly virus over in China, I was actually quite proud of myself for the way I was handling it. Considering my past battles with health anxiety, as the reports got grimmer and grimmer, and the virus began to cross borders, with the first cases occurring in the UK, I was strangely fearless about this deadly new disease. Just before the February half term of 2020, a confirmed case in Brighton shut down a school. We were due to be visiting Brighton the next week to see a friend who lives down there and watch Stewart Lee perform. At that point it was the ground zero of UK infections and at no point did we consider changing our plans.

I even remember joking with my form that I would lick a few doorhandles and shake a lot of hands to try and *catch* COVID so they could get a few days off school when I returned. My friend, my wife, and I all laughed about COVID over drinks in a pub after the Lee show, where a man sat coughing violently in the corner table all night. A week or so later, I was visiting family in Pinner for a birthday celebration of my ninety-eight-year-old great Aunt, and we were all amused hearing a story from a guest about a friend who had come back from a trip abroad with a bad cold, all making jokes about it being probably being the dreaded coronavirus. When I got to school again on Monday, we continued making light of this deadly new plague taking up all the headlines. Kids were coughing everywhere and yelling 'ugh – you've got *COVID*', some even purposefully coughing *onto* each other to 'spread the 'rona' around. But then some of them started getting these coughs for real, and more and more guidance came out as the number of cases around the country began to rise dramatically. The jokes stopped and a gloomier mood descended.

Even then, I wasn't particularly worried. Even as an asthmatic, who they were suggesting at the time might be particularly badly affected by the virus. Even as someone who witnessed a friend, the year before, get put on a ventilator after a near-fatal respiratory infection almost killed him after complications with the flu, I just let the potential for panic wash over me. More and more people were getting infected across the country, science-fiction-like hazmat suits were being worn as scary-looking teams investigated each case, and students in my small, cramped, classroom were sick all the time, with coughing becoming the general soundtrack to the term. But wasn't this the case *every* March? And every other month, for that matter? Kids are ill all the time and, as a teacher, getting bad colds and bugs was just par for the course. I was ill with one virus or another every couple of weeks *always* as a teacher – global pandemic or not – and, despite the scary pictures of COVID patients and words like 'quarantine' and 'untreatable' coming out of the news, I was strangely sanguine about the whole thing. I reckoned, despite all my anxieties, that my immune system was pretty robust. Even when the government announced the first spate of self-isolation guidance and my colleague in the department developed a new persistent cough and stayed home, I felt weirdly invincible. We had a trainee teacher with us at the time who I was mentoring too, and she had a mother in hospital. At a time when people were being warned not to go to hospitals unless absolutely necessary, she'd spent all afternoon in one and then come back to school to join me for a parents' evening. She proceeded to cough and splutter right next to me all night, and all I felt was bemused. Earlier in the evening, a day after the government had formally banned any large gatherings from happening across the country, I had asked the Deputy Head why we were going ahead with the event in the first place – essentially a large gathering at a time when such gatherings were forbidden? That same day, every parent in the year had received an email with the latest progress report for their child, so the conversations we would be having with them that night were doomed to be nothing but a rehash of the information they had already received in their inbox. It seemed utterly pointless to meet again in person and say the same thing twice, even if there wasn't the possibility of contracting a deadly virus, but the thought of one hundred and forty pupils, their parents, their teachers, and the occasional accompanying sibling, all sat together in the small school hall when we had just been told such large group events were dangerous, felt deeply negligent. I wasn't impressed with the Deputy Head's answer when she told me we were going ahead with it simply because 'we haven't been told *not* to'. I asked her if we couldn't just unilaterally use our own discretion and call it off, as it clearly wasn't necessary and violated the new rules on mass gatherings? She simply repeated that 'we haven't been told to cancel it,' and then moved off quickly to avoid any further questions.

I guess I had therefore resigned myself to getting COVID at the parents' evening already, so when my trainee called in the next day to say she would be self-isolating as she was displaying further symptoms, I taught my lessons over the next few hours simply assuming I was already infected. There was nothing I could do so, as my therapy had taught me, there was no point worrying.

Soon, new guidance put asthmatics like me in the 'clinically vulnerable' category, and our multi-academy trust told all clinically vulnerable, clinically extremely vulnerable, and pregnant members of staff to stay home, so I did. I still wasn't worried. I spent the time writing and recording a song called 'Social Distance' about communities stepping in where government had failed us, and posted a video of me playing it onto the school staff-room's Facebook page, hoping to lift some spirits.

*I've been self-isolating*
*Since before it was cool*
*But now that I have to*
*What is there to do?*
*There's been social distance*
*Now for far too long*
*Where better than quarantine*
*To write a song?*

*Can we all come together now, alone,*
*And recognise that when we needed help,*
*We always had each other to provide?*
*While the powers that be*
*Wrung their hands.*

*The old way of doing things*
*Falls to the ground*
*No shock to the system*
*Has been more profound*
*We watch the mask slipping*
*Beneath it we find*
*Nothing more was needed*
*Than just being kind*

*Can we all come together now, alone,*
*And recognise that when we needed help,*
*We always had each other to provide?*
*While the powers that be*
*Wrung their hands.*

*There's been social distance*
*Now for far too long*

By the end of the week though, the whole country was in lockdown, and by Monday morning the entire teaching profession had to completely reimagine and reinvent what we did as professionals. An almost overnight transition from a lifetime of being in the classroom to teaching in a whole different way on new online platforms like Teams, Google Classroom, or Zoom. Teaching through a computer screen; our homes now our classrooms, and our students' homes theirs. I still didn't have any symptoms of COVID, and still wasn't letting health anxiety develop too much, but there was a new creeping dread in the fact that all of the most crazy and neurotic stuff I had worked so hard with my therapist to overcome and *not* do anymore was now becoming official government policy. Obsessive handwashing as frequently as possible, avoiding not only anyone currently infected by the illness you don't want to catch, but also *anyone who had recently been in contact with them too* – this was basically the way I had always secretly wished we'd dealt with *all* contagious illnesses, especially stomach bugs, throughout my emetophobic life. Well, be careful what you wish for!

I started writing more poetry as a means of coping with everything that was going on.

*The things that once my therapist*
*Told me that I had to cease,*
*Became global public policy*
*In combatting this disease.*

*We're all now washing hands,*
*'til our skin has turned raw red,*
*And not straying from our house*
*For fear to do so make us dead.*

Although it was chaotic and stressful to try and figure out whole new ways of doing a job that had become so routine, I quite liked that initial wave of online learning. In fact, and this is controversial, I loved that entire early period of the pandemic and consider the first lockdown to be one of the legitimately most fulfilling times of my entire adult life. I say that, of course, in full knowledge that I only got to experience it because a deadly virus was killing hundreds of thousands of people all around the world and that, while I was comfortable enough to have no-one I love *die* of the coronavirus, and a secure job which continued existing – and paying me a full salary – the entire time I was stuck at home, many people lost their jobs, their incomes, their businesses, their loved ones, and the way of life they had hitherto come to depend upon. I know this. And I have to acknowledge, also, how fortunate I was to be in a loving relationship with a woman I actually enjoy spending time with, and living with her in a large house, with a garden, that gave us both enough space when we needed it, and plenty of fresh air and exercise, thanks, also, to the pre-pandemic purchase we had made of a basic home gym of an elliptical and a rowing machine. Others, I know, were not so lucky. My own sister and her partner – a fitness instructor and an actor – rode out the pandemic in a small, hot, London flat with their precariously contracted jobs completely up in the air as gyms and theatres remained closed. When we came back to work once the lockdown was lifted, at least three colleagues I can think of were in the process of divorce, with one being abandoned by her partner on day one of the lockdown as he revealed he had a secret lover he would rather be spending his quarantine with. There was a lot of heartbreak and domestic difficulty as people found themselves trapped, rather than blessed, to be with the people they lived with, and I am not for any moment trying to ignore their suffering simply because my own experience was so fortunate. As I wrote at the time in another poem:

*We held each other closely*
*Knowing we had chosen well*
*While we enjoyed our heaven*
*Other people lived through hell*

There were the terrible reports of domestic abuse, child abuse, and all kinds of awful things that happened for those people forced to stay at home in homes that became prisons for them. Real sites of real horror and desperation. I do not say that I enjoyed the first lockdown in any way to minimise the suffering of those who suffered through it and especially not to make trivial the deaths of those who did not survive it. I am not making the case here that the lockdown was a good thing for everyone, nor that it should have been, I am just speaking frankly for myself and saying that, whereas for others it might have been the toughest thing they ever had to endure, for me, and for my wife, the lockdown came at just the right time for it to be eye-opening, worldview-transforming, and fun. I was in a good place mentally, financially, and emotionally throughout the whole thing, and found myself suddenly getting to spend an unexpected lovely few months with my favourite person in the world, our cat, and having few annoying outside distractions or responsibilities to get in the way of pursuing all of my other interests. What wasn't there to like?

Work, the main time-suck of my existence, finally became manageable, and I realised that much of what I enjoyed doing in my free-time didn't really involve too much dependency on the rest of the world beyond the four walls of my home. As someone who has been straightedge my entire life (a punk rock term for those of us who don't drink alcohol or do drugs), I have never been someone who spends a lot of time in pubs or clubs. My wife and I have always preferred a good night in rather than a sloppy night out and, when we did leave the house, it was usually for a nice meal or a cup of coffee somewhere.

But even then, I had developed a habit over the years of learning how to cook at home a pretty decent version of anything nice we had out. That knack for recreating our favourite meals out at home came in handy during the lockdown, and the same went for home coffee-making. The year before the lockdown we'd started trying to save money by doing better at home what most of the coffee shops in town were offering, and so we rode out the pandemic happily fed and well-caffeinated without missing a beat. More fucking privilege, I know!

*The law required a lockdown*
*All regular life was paused*
*But my life carried on*
*Barely different than before*

We liked to read, to watch TV and movies, to garden (in her case), to play music or write (in mine), to talk, to create. None of this was particularly impeded by having to stay in our homes. Our groceries were already regularly delivered through online shopping systems and that service continued without disruption, our loyalty as long-time customers rewarded with priority slot-booking. While production of *new* film and television had obviously ground to a halt, who has ever managed to watch everything they want to watch? We finally had time to catch up on all the great stuff we *hadn't* had time to see yet from before. The library of books we had collectively been accumulating for years without sufficient time to break the spines on most of them became a similar treasure-trove: like squirrels who had hoarded nuts for the long winter ahead we had a feast of literature and entertainment to dine on as the lockdown stretched out longer than anyone had previously imagined. I had the time to get to grips with home recording technology and develop my skills enough to record a whole new EP and a few singles of my music, while my wife utilised the time off to build an entire garden patio. The global adoption of Zoom allowed us to not only stay in touch with friends and family throughout (we would do regular 'art classes' with my sister and her partner, picking a different artform and setting ourselves the challenge of producing something in that style for an afternoon while chatting and catching up), but actually closed the gap between us and the international or long-distance friends and family we previously spoke to only ever infrequently.

Because of my family's links there, a lot of people we know live in America, and a few others are scattered around Europe. Meanwhile, within the UK, most of our closest friends live several hours away. This had always limited our ability to communicate in normal times. Now, thanks to the pandemic, we could sit and chat together across the miles, and even across oceans. With no one at work anymore, the impact of different time-zones was diminished: almost any time you might call would be a good time to call. Usually too busy during term-time to spend time with friends and spending our school holidays trying to catch up on the previous six to eight weeks of deferred *living*, we had long considered ourselves fairly anti-social people. Trapped at home with all that new free time, we became more social than we had been in years.

As I said: I know all-too well this was not the experience of everyone. I know my lockdown story was one of advantage and luck, and that while I was indulging in Zoom art sessions with my sister, others were losing their lives or worrying if they'd ever work again. But I can only speak honestly about my personal experiences during this terrible time. Like everyone else, lurking behind the privileged holiday from reality was still this horrible fear and terror that we might never leave the house again and that, if we did, we might die a lonely and agonizing death in a quarantined hospital ward somewhere.

Simon, my friend, works in epidemiology when he isn't writing novels under a pseudonym of S. R. Masters, and in the first few days of lockdown, when everyone was talking about it only lasting for a few weeks, he forwarded me some of the academic literature people in his field were reading which, rightly, spoke not about a single, short, lockdown until Easter, but about multiple lengthy lock*downs*, over a number of *years*, and life never being the same for us again. I had read that article and, like Joey in *Friends* putting Stephen King's *The Shining* in the freezer, had put my phone away and politely asked Simon not to send me any more articles like that again. I was scared just like everyone else. But I had been scared of disease my entire life. None of these thoughts bombarding the rest of the world were particularly new to me and, like I said, some of the protocols that seemed so alien to most were things I had already been doing on-and-off for years in my life at different stages of my health anxiety's severity. For me, part of what gave me my pandemic privilege was having had hellish years of dread *my entire life* obsessing and worrying about invisible viruses already. It was like I had been training for this period of quarantine the entire time. This left me more able to focus on the positives of the time than on how scary it was. Scary was my everyday existence – the pandemic just left me as scared as before but with all this wonderful bonus free time.

What gave us all this free time, despite teaching non-stop throughout the lockdown, was the reinvention of teaching now that the job had moved online. Despite the unhelpful media narrative of remote-schooling seeing parents strongarmed into the role of teacher while we lazy professionals sat at home with our feet up, and even in the context of all my preceding waxing about all this incredible new free time, in my experience, and that of my wife, neither of our experiences of teaching online were like that at all. We remained committed and hard-working subject-specialist teachers during work hours throughout the lockdown and never expected, or needed, parents to do any of our teaching for us. We taught lessons, we provided comprehensive resources for independent learning at home without the need for parental assistance, we answered student questions and marked their work. However, what the lockdown did do, was transform the way we delivered our teaching, eliminating much of the unnecessary bullshit that can make the job of a professional teacher stressful and unfulfilling and allowing us to focus more on the *education* of our students than on the frequently counter-educational needs of the *school*.

This important distinction is too often ignored. 'Education' is not the same thing as 'schooling', and it was confusion over this distinction which I think contributed significantly to the negativity surrounding many of the experiences of online learning. *Schools* are merely, in the current social and economic system we happen to have, the mechanism we have collectively chosen as the means to deliver an education. But like any mechanism, there are alternatives we could imagine, and there will be some necessary compromises and difficulties in delivering the intended outcome in this particular way. There will be *costs* it will have been decided are, perhaps, worth it for the overall *benefit* of mass delivery.

Schools enforce rigid structure onto learning, for example, not because it is necessary to do so for *education's* sake, but because it is necessary to do so for the running of the *school* as the chosen mechanism in which to deliver that education. Timetables, assessments, rules, and regulations – these are all accountability and management measures for the institution of a systematised *school,* which education itself, delivered in any other way, does not necessarily require.

Consider two different children – one put through a formal GCSE programme in English Literature and the other teaching themselves the same subject independently, and without final accreditation. Reading books, viewing online lectures, writing their own pieces for their own personal amusement, etc. It is entirely probable that both children might end their two years of very different study 'educated', and that the 'schooled' child's only advantage is not one of education, but of qualification. Both may conceivably be equally knowledgeable about English Literature, perhaps it is even plausible that the autodidact ends up knowing *more*, not being restricted to any specific curriculum. When Bruce Springsteen sang that he 'learned more from a three-minute record, baby, than we ever learned in school', he was probably right. Schooling itself is just about formalizing, assessing, and qualifying on a mass-scale. It has its advantages, but it also has its disadvantages. It is an imperfect, and perhaps even fatally flawed model, and far from the only way a young person might learn. What the pandemic exposed, when physical schools closed their doors for most pupils and the job of *schooling* was now attempted online, was that the model of the *school* in the virtual environment didn't necessarily work best to ensure *education* continued within these new, non-school, environments. But this did not mean that *education* wasn't still possible remotely.

As an analogy, consider this: I have tried to go vegan several times, and each time I have failed. Morally, I believe veganism is right. I have been a vegetarian for nearly a quarter of a century, and the basis for my vegetarianism is the ethical claim that non-human animals matter too, and therefore if I can survive without causing their unnecessary suffering, I ought to. It is an argument which logically extends to a dairy industry impossible to separate from the meat industry and one which, if taken seriously, really *requires* me to go vegan. But every time I have attempted to go fully vegan, I have found myself incredibly miserable and dissatisfied by my meals. I have not eaten meat since I finished my last GCSE in 1998 (the same day I tried to burn my old school tie. I had decided to go vegetarian months before but, desperate to get out of my despised secondary school and meet the entry grade requirements for the local sixth form college, had worried the change of diet might affect my focus and concentration during the important exams. Once freed from those concerns, a beanburger lunch marked the end of both my GCSEs *and* my time as a carnivore.) Becoming a vegetarian, I had found it fairly easy to substitute many of my old meaty favourites with meat-alternatives, even back then. I assumed, therefore, it would be fairly easy to cut out dairy too. But whereas many of my old meat favourites had a 'fake meat' equivalent when I chose to cut out animal flesh (veggie-burger, veggie-dogs, Quorn, Linda McCartney, processed soy and tofu, etc.), it became much more difficult to match like-for-like with a vegan diet. Time and time again I would try to reproduce my favourite veggie meals with non-dairy alternatives and find myself disappointed, eventually deciding life was too short to persevere with such gastronomic misery.

I have learnt since, however, that the problem is not *vegan food* or *veganism*, which has a proven potential to be delicious. The problem was trying to *still eat like a vegetarian* as a vegan. Being vegan and cutting out all those products from my diet should have meant rethinking the menu entirely, not just replicating the old one with new, inferior, ingredients. I would never enjoy a 'creamy' and 'cheesy' vegan pasta sauce as much as one made with real cream and real cheese, but an entirely new sauce, packed with vegetables and its own, different, flavour, can be magic. Scrambled tofu will never be scrambled eggs, but a different breakfast entirely might be capable of taking scrambled eggs' place on my menu if I reimagined what plant-based eating could be.

This is analogous to teaching during the pandemic because, in most cases where the experience was frustrating and difficult, it was because people were trying to replicate *school* instead of embracing the new, different, possibilities for *education* which technology unlocked once liberated from the physical limitations of the classroom.

Again though, I was lucky when we were told we would need to teach online. An early adopter of virtual learning environments, I had been advocating for more innovative incorporation of technology into the classroom for years. *All* of my department's classes were already long inducted into the use of One Note and Teams as we had been uploading lesson resources and extension links, as well as asking them to submit work online, across every new platform the school invested in. By that first Monday of the pandemic, when some colleagues were still trying to figure out how to even create their first class, my students were already logged in and ready.

I recognised fairly quickly that doing a lesson from home in the same way I might do it in class wouldn't work. Most of my students were sharing a single computer with multiple siblings, with some sharing the same device with their parents; all needing to access to wi-fi and do their various disparate pieces of work at the same time. Many of them didn't have microphones on whatever device they were using. Or they had no keypad and *only* had a mic, doing the bulk of their schoolwork on a phone instead of a computer or tablet. You therefore couldn't depend on parity of access or communication for anyone, nor could you use any of the old motivations for work on which the teaching profession in *schools* traditionally depends. Exams were up in the air, with rumours that they would be cancelled, and even those students not sitting exams that year had no idea how long the schools would be closed for, so you could no longer imply the importance of a topic 'for the exam' or even 'for next year'. And gone was any form of sanction or punishment for students not doing their work in class. You could hardly put someone in detention when they were already legally forced to stay in their homes! You couldn't take away their privileges – they had none – and any additional work set because a piece of prior work hadn't been done would continue to be just as ignored as the original assignment had been. I realised that now we were online, everything had changed, and this had to be embraced, not fought against. Therefore, work could only be set that was meaningful, or interesting enough for students to want to engage with it, and work had to be flexible rather than rigid.

Rather than following my old school timetable, I set all students, where possible, a week's worth of work every Monday, laying out all the things I wanted them to do and giving them all the tools to do it, and they then had until Friday to complete it at their own pace. So long as it was submitted online by the end of the school day each Friday, I didn't care if they did it straight away, in the middle of the night, three days later, or right at the last minute, allowing them to negotiate and share devices and workspaces with their fellow family members and take necessary time out for their sanity during those incredibly difficult times.

For some tasks, where it would benefit us to meet up and discuss things as a group, or have me actually teach them something explicitly, I would arrange 'live' sessions for mid-week, or give them a week or so's warning for a future date, giving them time to organise device-sharing at home so they could attend. And, if they couldn't, I would ensure the session was recorded so they could watch it back afterwards. I was able to recognise that the dependency on me as a teacher engrained from years of *schooling* was not always necessary to achieve an *education*, and that the more I gave the students the opportunity to find things out for themselves, the more they flourished without me. Moreover, whenever we finally *did* meet together to discuss their ideas, when done in this way they had all the more to say.

The fifty-minute or hour-long lesson was an invention for co-ordination and organisation of a daily school timetable, not an intractable truth about the length of time necessary to learn something. Much of what a schoolteacher does in their given time is find ways to fill their minutes because they are *there*. No longer bound to structured blocks of arbitrary time-periods, or having to prepare students for over-scrutinized and irrelevant assessment, I found I could do lots of interesting 'flipped learning' with them, where students researched something first themselves so that we could then use our time together to explore it and heighten their understanding through discussion, rather than simply have them be passively told things by me. Topics which might have taken *weeks* in the old fifty-minute sessions could be covered far more quickly when all the pointless, time-wasting, or exam-focused activities were eliminated, and our collective time together could be directed instead on the development of ideas and clarification of misconceptions.

I was still marking work, but only when there were good educational reasons to give feedback on a particular piece in that way, and not merely because it was down in some assessment timetable that I had to satisfy. I could adapt what we were doing to the needs of the students and be far more led by *their* requirements than the requirements of the school's leadership team or distant exam boards. Just as we teachers could no longer coercively punish our students to force their compliance, our bosses could no longer micro-manage and scrutinize the sorts of education delivered by *us* either. And in the cracks away from the professional panopticon, innovation could thrive.

It wasn't all rose-tinted and wonderful, of course. Technology glitched all the time. Sometimes the shared demands on our overburdened internet connections led to a meltdown. The school had decided early on, for safeguarding reasons, that students were not to appear on camera ever, so it could sometimes be fairly demoralising too, holding 'discussions' with a bunch of unmoving icons and not being able to see people's reactions or engagement. Definitely, many of the students 'in attendance' logged on only briefly and then went away playing video games or chatting on Discord servers rather than actively participating in their lessons. Occasionally we would get interlopers from other schools trying to crash into a session and say rude things for a laugh. Other times, the call would come from inside the house, and some disaffected student of our own would do it, attempting to sabotage the classes of their peers. And yes, there were definitely some students who tapped out on education entirely during that time, simply not turning up and not handing in work at all. I am not delusional about the successes of the online experiment any more than I am delusional about the majority of people's experiences of this distressing and difficult period of national lockdown. I can see its many failings despite its opportunities for potential. However, for those who *did* engage, many of my students found this more independent and flexible approach to learning far more prosperous than the old rigidity of the classroom. Some of my best students during the lockdown were those who, back in school, had barely engaged at all.

I also believe that many of the failings of lockdown teaching came not because of teaching online itself, but because of the impact on our students, and their teachers, of a lifelong dependency on the structures and discipline of the *school*. Students and teachers alike had become institutionalised to a particular way of doing things and couldn't operate beyond the now deeply internalised restrictions and procedures embedded within them. If your only prior motivation for work was doing it to avoid getting into trouble for not doing it, it became difficult to find new motivation once the threat of sanction had been taken away. If your psychological association with learning was one of boredom and tedium, then why would you ever willingly continue to subject yourself to that torture again once the opportunity arose so easily to avoid it? And when the bulk of your online teachers refused to embrace the possibilities opened up by the new context and, instead, fruitlessly tried to recreate the stale old norms of their school classroom via Teams, how could you know that a small handful of your *other* teachers were actively trying to do something different within that same virtual space?

It also didn't help that the public narrative from government and media the entire time was that schools were closed (they weren't – the entire lockdown, schools were still physically open to the children of essential 'key workers', even during what would normally be considered holidays and, online, schools operated daily, with a full delivery of education ongoing throughout the lockdown). The media also suggested that unqualified parents were now attempting, and failing, to teach their children instead of professional teachers (they didn't need to be. For secondary students at least, every school I know was supporting their own online teaching and the *teachers* were still doing their job. But I suspect the constant trope of frustrations with parent-led home-schooling and shared videos and social media posts about how difficult it was made parents feel pressured if they *weren't* struggling with complex mathematical equations and long-forgotten scientific formulae around the kitchen table, encouraging them get involved even where they weren't really needed). Nor did it help, once schools were ready to re-open, for either students or teachers to be constantly told by government, or by their bosses, about the 'lost learning' experienced during that time, and for September of 2020 to see most students returning to the classroom treated as if they had learned nothing of value during the entire period of lockdown and were in need of significant 'catching up'.

This undid any good work that *was* achieved at home and discounted months of legitimate *education* by essentially gaslighting an entire generation about their achievements online. A self-fulfilling-prophecy was created whereby the possibilities of online teaching were played down so much, or denigrated from the start, that the virtual classroom was in an uphill battle from day one. Labelled as second-best and inferior, this negative idea was then reinforced by the starting-assumption of its failure once schools returned and teachers were told to re-teach everything to their students as if the months of online lessons hadn't happened. Furthermore, by repeatedly telling students online teaching was ineffective, once it became clear that school infections would still require whole year-groups to return home sporadically for weeks at a time, returning to remote-learning, here education really was poor due to the consistent message they had been given was that there is no good reason to put any effort in to what was done on their computers: it would all be taught to them again later, in person. They were better off playing X-box.

Away from that narrative, however, and in my own experience: where students bought into my remote lessons and I was able to experiment and adapt my teaching in consort with them to achieve mutually agreed educational goals at a flexible pace, while the trappings of the *school* certainly fell away, *education* always blossomed. My A-level Philosophy class, in particular, were a real bright spot during those months of global strangeness. They leapt at the opportunity to do the reading themselves independently and use our time together for informed philosophical discussion, even when that 'discussion' was entirely typed into a Teams chat. When we returned to the physical classroom that September, far from feeling like they had 'lost' any learning, they felt like they hadn't missed a step. If anything, we were further ahead with the course than I usually was at that point in the year. Rather than re-teach and assume failure from our months online, I proceeded moving forward at a similar pace and showed the small minority of students who *had* disengaged during the lockdown where to go to find the important work they had chosen to ignore. Once they realised opting out was no longer an option, they quickly got back on board.

Which brings me back to the experience of newly discovered free time between March and July of 2020 as my classroom became my home office and my school remained physically closed to all but a handful of children of key workers. Without having to stay in my assigned classroom and bodily 'teach' a full timetable of lessons each day, what would usually be a series of repetitive fifty-minute lessons became far fewer actual hours I was spending needing to be in front of my students. Where something *would've* been repetitive, were we in school, such as teaching the same lesson three times to three different classes, repetition could be minimised online by recording myself doing it once, at a time of my convenience, and sending the same presentation to all three groups. Where in the real classroom I would still have to be there as my students quietly got on with their own work, online I could set them off on their task and then end the formal meeting. I was still available to them via email and chat 24/7, but that meant I only needed to respond to students when they had specific needs they needed responding to. I wasn't simply hovering over them in the same room and watching down the clock.

Some weeks, my approach of setting work on Monday to be handed in by Friday meant I didn't even need to actually 'teach' *any* of my classes until all the work was in and I could comment on it. Often, I would give whole group feedback the following week, making this even more efficient, and not have to waste further hours writing the same comments over and over again on individual pieces of work.

Throughout the lockdown my students received a fantastic education, but its delivery was made far more humane now it was removed from examination-style formal assessment, arbitrary deadlines and timetables, and the inflexibility and hierarchical nature of the classroom. With no commute to do either in the morning, or even longer commute through Birmingham's rush-hour traffic to do each evening to get home, I was getting more sleep than I ever had, waking up at seven-thirty instead of five forty-five each morning, and when the school day ended at three-thirty-five each afternoon, so too did my workday. Between nine o'clock and then, despite being theoretically 'on call' and available by email or Teams chat for any students who might need me, most days I would have only one or two 'live' sessions I needed to actually attend with my students. It was quite possible a whole working day might go by, so long as I had planned and marked everything strategically in advance, where I was not needed in person the whole time. Sometimes *several* days passed like this in a row. My students weren't being neglected – far from it. Well-thought-out sequences of self-directed learning and the high-quality resources I created meant they could do far more without me online than they ever could when we were in school. The time I put into doing *that* planning every so often, though significant, would, however, free up many more hours later. And what this meant was that, suddenly, instead of being constantly overworked and over-stressed with all the additional burdens that come with being a teacher, I was left alone finally to *teach*. To experiment and explore. And I had time every single day to do *more than* just teach. To read a book and actually educate myself as well as my students.

You would be surprised just how few teachers actually have time to continue developing their subject knowledge once they become a professional, and how their level of expertise stagnates around the thin pools of learning they swam in during their handful of years as an undergraduate. For many, their specialist field gets stuck in stasis around the same year that they trained as a teacher, and anything new since then passes them by, unseen. There is very little professional development time given over to teachers for simply reading a book in their subject-area because doing so is something that can't easily be monitored and transformed into a tick-box accountability exercise by school management teams and, with the workload pressures most teachers are under, it is far more likely an afternoon off to read a book, if given, will be spent catching up with some marking rather than self-educating. If I can get this pile of essays done during a supposed training session at school, it saves me a job of bringing them back with me to do at home later that night. But as COVID-19 ravaged the planet and my virtual classroom demanded less and less of my time, I suddenly had new hours in the day to pick up a book and *read*. Works of philosophy that had nothing to do with the courses I was teaching but stimulated my mind and made me think beyond the limits of my curriculum properly for the first time in years.

For many around the world, the death of George Floyd that locked-down summer was a significant turning point. A wake-up call that we couldn't continue accepting the same old oppressions and doing nothing about them. It was for me too as I was confronted with my own white-privilege and realised how many blind-spots there were in my own deeply colonised education, even if I thought of myself as someone fairly well-educated about racism. In my entire life, despite giving lectures on Steve Biko and the Black Consciousness Movement of South Africa as part of a series of lectures on Black Political Thought at Cardiff, I had only ever been taught a small handful of black philosophers throughout my time at university. The A-level course I currently taught my students had *no* black philosophers on its reading list at all. While I hadn't set the course, and the fault was with the exam board, I had *known* all this for years but never really had the time to do anything about it. Or, more honestly, had always had the comfort of not having to feel the intensity of the problem myself, as a white male who saw myself frequently represented across the classic philosophical canon.

A few years before, a black student had asked me if there were any black philosophers I could recommend him to read, and I had felt ashamed then that I knew of so few. I had been trying to build up my understanding since that day, but only as one task among many. A curiosity more than a priority. Now, however, I had the time and I no longer had the excuses. As some braved the virus to march together and proclaim that 'Black Lives Matter', I showed my own solitary form of solidarity by educating myself further and reading books by W.E.B Du Bois, Tommie Shelby, Marcus Garvey, Charles W Mills, Lewis Gordon, Kehinde Andrews, Angela Davis, and Frantz Fanon. I read about black British history in the work of David Olusoga, Afua Hirsch, and Jeffrey Boakye, and I worked furiously on diversifying our Religious Studies and Philosophy curriculum as much as I could within the limits imposed by the exam boards.

I also worked with our students, who were finally being vocal about the many micro (and not so micro) aggressions they had experienced around race, sexuality, and gender across the school, and helped them voice their concerns to the Head and wider Foundation body, eventually forming a Black Lives Matter student committee before it was ultimately neutered into the far less radical 'Equality, Diversity, and Inclusion' committee once the more revolutionary students graduated at the end of the next academic year.

I wasn't only reading about race and racism though. Just before the pandemic, a publisher had discovered the weekly philosophy blog I was writing and contacted me to see if I was the same DaN McKee who had written his PhD thesis about anarchism. When I revealed that I was that very same anarchist, he asked if we could work together on turning the thesis into a book. I had spent the autumn and winter of 2019 editing down the thesis and turning it into what would become *Authentic Democracy: An Ethical Justification of Anarchism.* We were planning to release it on May Day of 2020. When the lockdown hit, undeterred by a global pandemic, Paul, the publisher, managed to find us someone to turn it quickly into an e-book so we could at least release *something* if the physical production proved difficult. Being a small publisher though, his printer was a one-person operation and therefore still able to work, alone and safely, during the lockdown. The e-book came out as planned on May 1st, and the paperback, miraculously, followed very soon after, albeit with very little ability for us to do much publicity for it in a closed-down world.

Revisiting my academic work, I had been reminded of how much I enjoyed writing 'proper' philosophy as well as my more throwaway weekly blog articles for *Philosophy Unleashed*, and I began to wonder if I still had what it took to be an academic philosopher. In my time as an academic, I had spoken at conferences but had never actually tried to get an academic paper published. I was more interested in making my thesis as good as it could be than thinking about what would look good on a CV and had ignored my supervisor's advice to focus more on writing a series of chapters, which could each be turned into a journal paper, and wrote a monograph instead. When I left academia, therefore, the fact that I hadn't got anything published was a bit of a white whale for me. Was I actually any good, or was the PhD a total fluke? My original supervisor, Andrew Belsey, had unexpectedly retired a year into my PhD and his replacement had never been particularly sympathetic with my work. From the moment he took me on he filled me with self-doubt and insecurity and made me feel as if what I was doing wasn't proper philosophy just because it dealt with real world politics and wasn't steeped in the abstract Frankfurt School of critical theory that he happened to think important. I had experienced something similar when I finally learned to drive – a fantastic teacher started me off when I was at home during the summer between my first and second years of university. He was incredibly encouraging and said I was ready to book in for my test immediately once I got back to Cardiff. But after one terrible first lesson with my new instructor in Wales, who did nothing but criticise me the whole time we were in the vehicle together and make me very nervous, I had my confidence completely knocked. Instead of listening to his negativity though, I clung to the words of my original teacher and booked in for my test anyway, completely against the new instructor's advice. The entire period before the date of the test the new guy nit-picked and criticised everything I did. Driving me to the test centre on the day of the test, he told me that, although I'd definitely fail, it would still be a good learning experience for the next time I tried. Fuelled by spite and self-belief, I passed. A really strong and non-negotiable pass too – only two minors. When I got back to his car and told him afterwards, he looked shocked. When he dropped me off back home, I told him I hoped I'd never see him again. It was the same with the PhD thesis. Against the advice of my supervisor, I held my nerve with what I had written, ignored much of what he suggested, got second and third opinions from others in the department, and demanded he book me in for my viva voce and final submission even though he thought I wasn't ready. Again, fuelled by spite and self-belief, I passed comfortably, with only minor corrections. When I told him he could now call me 'doctor', he smiled and gave me his congratulations, but I could see in his eyes that he hadn't been expecting it, and we haven't spoken since.

That doubt had gnawed at me a little as I moved on in my life, away from academia. Having been told my work was no good by my supervisor for so long and never having had anything published that was peer-reviewed, were my PhD referees just giving me an easy ride that day? Were the letters of recommendation and good references I'd amassed in case I decided to go back just a professional nicety rather than honest accounts of my abilities? After all – even the negative supervisor himself had written me a glowing one. Maybe they were completely meaningless? Had I gotten away with something, or did I actually deserve my philosophical credentials?

We all suffer a little imposter-syndrome, no matter what we do, but when you have to fight against so much countervailing criticism and claw your way to success against the tide, it is even easier to feel like a fraud when you get there. Before the PhD, I had been one of the golden children of the university – I won all the prizes going in the Politics Department, a scholarship from the Philosophy department to do my MA, and then won a grant from the Arts and Humanities Research Council to do the PhD. I was a well-liked teacher to the undergraduates, I stepped in to lecture when Barry was off sick, and I was clearly being groomed by the Head of Department for the job market as I started writing papers and doing conferences. But my decision to walk away from it all and reject all that help, I think, on top of my battles with my supervisor as I completed the thesis, put that tiny seed of doubt in my mind that, somehow, I had ultimately failed at academia rather than making it my choice to leave it. My confidence now boosted by the impending publication of the book, and my growing dismay building around the state of state education in England, I used some of the free-time I gained during the lockdown to try my hand at finally writing a proper academic paper, just to see if I could.

In 2019, Ofsted had included a new expectation in their inspection framework that teachers in state schools attempt to teach 'character' to their students, using an idea of character education informed by Aristotelian virtue ethics and work on character education such as that done at Birmingham University's Jubilee Centre for Character and Virtues. Having worked as a professional teacher since 2010, it was my view that the sort of character required to succeed professionally within the English school system was one riddled mostly with vice, making teachers uniquely *unsuitable* as role models of virtue to their students. I decided to put this idea together as an academic paper from an anarchist perspective and submit it to the journal, *Anarchist Studies*. In May of 2020 I heard back and was told the piece had promise, but still needed a little work. With time to do that working during the ongoing lockdown, by August, after several rounds of revisions, it was accepted for publication.

The *Anarchist Studies* paper coinciding with the interesting and reflective experiences of online teaching made me read around philosophy of education in general, especially on the possibilities of education outside of and beyond the classroom. As I was reading up on structural racism, and expanding that reading to learn about structural sexism and heteronormativity too, I was also reading about education outside of such problematic structures – liberatory and transformative alternative visions of education – and starting to read about substitute approaches to coercive behaviour management in schools, such as restorative and transformative justice. As I read about the connections between racism and systems of prison and policing, I noted the role of carceral logic in the everyday running of the school, and the more that I was reading and thinking about all this stuff, and enjoying the experience of teaching outside of that repressive school framework, as well as the intellectual stimulation found in returning to the world of research, the more I started to ask myself questions about what I really wanted to be doing with my life.

I realised further that what I was choosing to immerse myself in during these weeks of freedom was specifically *philosophy*, not religion. In fact, I read nothing at all about faith, God, or religious belief during the entire lockdown, yet it was religion I was spending the majority of my professional life teaching, even now that we were online. Religion which was the word that came first in my job title, *before* Philosophy. Philosophy was something I really only taught properly at A-level, to a small handful of students. The rest of the time it was something I had to smuggle into my Religious Studies lessons and see if I could get away with. Something which, ultimately, the Religious Studies discipline undermined with its far looser approach to rigorous thinking and openness to superstition, mystery, and magic.

Religion bored me if I were being honest, whereas philosophy made me feel alive. And taking a step back and looking at my life, I could see that I wasn't teaching enough of it.

And then there was teaching itself. The stuff about character education in the Ofsted framework was just one questionable new trend. Far worse was the constant push to make uniform the practice of teaching itself. A new ideological certainty had invaded the profession, based in misapplied research from cognitive science about how 'learning' works, which was basically making a push to concentrate all pedagogy on the process of memorisation and the building of mental schemata. While useful for examination recall and behaviour management, it was an impoverished view of the true potential for education and yet it had gained the ascendency at a policy level. Unquestioning and uncritical acceptance of a self-supporting echo-chamber of #edutwitter, John Catt published, and ResearchED-endorsed tracts of repeated regimes of 'evidence' and 'research' saw the profession fawn over selective publications by people like Barak Rosenshine, Daniel Willingham, John Hattie, Doug Lemov, and Daisy Christodoulou, and transformed conversations about education into conversations about a one-size-fits-all pseudo-scientific approach to the classroom. Year after year, conversations around school improvement and teaching and learning were becoming increasingly conversations about formalising our teaching into neat little packages of information to be introduced by scripted direct instruction and then regurgitated by our students to an agreed formula. Part of what I was enjoying again about teaching online was how much it flipped those scripts and made us have to think on our feet once more about what we were doing; be creative and try new things. As someone who actually engaged in research *as a researcher* and didn't just get my pedagogical information from the Department for Education or Twitter, I was all-too aware that the cognitive science approach to learning was only one way to think about education and its needs, and that 'research-led' or 'evidence-informed' were nice-sounding labels which intentionally masked the fact that *other* research and *other* evidence had alternative things to say. That it depended on what you saw the purpose of education to be: passing exams and learning information by rote so it can be recalled on command later, or developing knowledgeable, resourceful, critically thinking, and intellectually independent democratic citizens of tomorrow? Different ends of education led to different conclusions about 'efficacy', and different 'research' or 'evidence' could be prioritised or ignored depending on your agenda. I was dismayed more and more with the recognition of how spineless my school – and any school – seemed to be in the face of all these passing fads and blatant ideologies. That whatever new hoop the DfE or Ofsted threw at them, they never seemed to question them or fight back. They just shrugged their shoulders and obeyed.

The obsession with exams was a particular disappointment. A lot of lip-service was given to going beyond the curriculum and not just teaching to the test, but in practice the bulk of what was being done in the classroom was being done because it was on an exam specification, and this entire dominant 'research-led' approach to pedagogy was based around the needs of these stupid summative assessments at the end of each stage of schooling rather than the needs of *education* itself.

Frequently I would flag up to students that exams were an unrealistic and unnecessary way of assessing your learning and watch their presumptions explode. 'Imagine,' I asked them, 'that you were a scientist working on a cure for cancer but you decided the best way of getting to a cure would be to deny yourself access to any of your books or papers, lock all your research and resources away, and depend entirely on your own memory to do the job, refusing to speak to anyone else or let them help you, and setting yourself an arbitrary time-limit to achieve your goal. Would you be a good scientist, likely to find a cure, or a terrible one?' It's the same for anything else – a philosopher, a historian, a mathematician, a geographer. In none of these disciplines are you expected to commit the entire domain of knowledge to memory and in all of them collaboration and knowledge-sharing is key to good practice, not isolation and individualism. Right answers in all fields take as long as it takes to get them and can't be done to order or against a clock.

I would make the analogy to television reality shows like *The Great British Bake Off* or *The Apprentice*. In each of these competitive shows we have people who can bake, or people who have a history of being successful at business, yet as we watch them compete, suddenly, great bakers and business-people *fail* and find themselves eliminated from the show. Why? Because they haven't been asked to bake a cake properly, they have been asked to bake a cake, in a tent, to a certain specification, within an unrealistic time-frame. Or they have been asked to make a profit in a task they have little experience in, limited resources for, combative and counter-incentivised team members, within, again, an arbitrary and unhelpful period of time. Because the *point* of those shows is not for *everyone* to bake a great cake or make the same profit, it is to make winners and losers so that a single champion can be crowned and make great television. It is the same with exams. We do not examine students to check their learning, we do it to arbitrarily categorise and separate them for an equally unfair job market. We manufacture an inherently inequitable assessment process *precisely* so that at the end of each year only *some* students will come out on top, and others will fail by design.

I could just as easily sit my philosophy class together and ask them some questions about a topic, listen to their responses, give them access to resources that might help and see where the conversation goes and how they use or don't use the resources to check their understanding, and I would get a far better idea of their actual ability as *philosophers* than I do from sitting them in silence, setting a timer, and telling them to write an essay without checking any notes. And if some of them struggled, I could offer them further help to see if they might do better with some additional support. If they failed despite all this, there is no good *educational* reason not to give them a second opportunity, or a third, or a fourth, to try and do better next time *if what I cared about was their reaching the end goal of being educated about something.* The idea that you have one chance, and one chance only, to do well in a terminal exam is all you need to know about how seriously examination of this type is interested in universally educated outcomes. That exams are so self-evidently problematic and contrary to any meaningful goal we might have for education, yet are the major end to which all schools seem currently directed made me increasingly disheartened by the entire institutions of *schools*. The lockdown was re-energising me as a *teacher*, but had given me the space to see so many of the flaws in the system of *schooling* if my desire was to *educate* my students and not simply get them to pass some unjust exams.

This became especially true following the second, far less enjoyable, lockdown of January 2021. While the first lockdown was liberating, fears of what that liberation had allowed and the narrative of 'lost learning' meant that, when schools closed again the following Winter in the wake of a new covid variant, we were put on a far stricter regiment for what we had to do online. The school-day was essentially replicated virtually, with every timetabled lesson being done live on Teams whether it was useful to do it that way or not. Students were spending from 9am to 3.30pm staring at a computer all day and teachers were tied to their desks too, even at home, attempting the impossible and self-defeating task of making their vegan versions of a vegetarian meal taste as good.

It was a pretty miserable experience for all, made all the more miserable once schools returned to the physical classroom by the edict that priority in school now had to be given to our exam classes, who would be being assessed internally now instead of by the exam boards. *However*, we were not allowed to teach those exam classes any new content. Instead, we had to revise what had been taught to them so far so that they would be ready for the terminal assessments we would be administering.

After being off school for months and forced to sit through questionable online lessons they had already been told couldn't teach them anything and were as good as not being in school at all, once back in the classroom these students were then taught *nothing new* for the rest of the year, just drilled on the content they already knew so that they could be tested on that same content in a series of teacher assessments designed to get them a final grade.

While my GCSE classes were doomed to this dispiriting approach due to the sheer quantity of assessments I had been made to administer to them by the school (despite my many objections), my A-level class were in a far better position. They had excelled throughout the pandemic in their online learning and we had already sat them through various robust tests on most of the topics on the course earlier in the year. With only one more significant essay they needed to write for me, I asked the class directly if they wanted to spend the next few weeks revising or if they would rather take responsibility for their own revision at home and spend all of our remaining timetabled lessons together *just doing some philosophy*? No agenda, no specification, *nothing to do with the exams,* just exploring any issues they were interested in as a group.

They all opted for just doing some philosophy and so, until the end of their time at school, we did no exam preparation at all, ignored the exam specification completely, and explored their own philosophical questions. The sessions became so enjoyable that they started bringing in guests who were free and bored of their own tedious revision in other classes. We talked about existentialism, institutional prejudice, anarchism, the monarchy, free-will, free-speech, class, and all sorts of other interesting topics. We actually *learnt* new things together and, more importantly, we *enjoyed* ourselves while doing it. When the final exam arrived, the quality of their individual work was fantastic, and we got the best results we had ever achieved. Not because we marked the work ourselves, but because our class became better *philosophers* for having spent their time doing actual philosophy instead of preparing to jump through pointless hoops.

The point of all this is that, like many people suddenly ripped off the daily treadmill of their previous lives when the pandemic struck, I had time to take a step back and reflect on what the fuck I was doing with my life. I was enjoying doing more philosophy and being able to teach more creatively. I was enjoying spending quality time with my wife and getting to indulge in our hobbies and passions without always being bogged down with the demands of a job which, now the job had changed, had been exposed as being *completely unnecessary*. I was enjoying feeling rested in the mornings instead of stressed and anxious. I was enjoying learning and writing. I was enjoying fresh air and exercise. I was enjoying playing music. I was enjoying *not* being able to use strict punishments and disciplinary tactics to get work from my students and having to use reason, dialogue, compassion, and self-motivation with them instead. I was enjoying feeling more connected to the wider world in ways I never had before now that the wider world had opened itself up to online engagement. I was attending academic conferences, lectures, and even gigs, plays, and comedy online that I would never normally have been able to see or be a part of in the physical world. I was immersed in ideas and innovations and quite enjoying the little bubble of potential and possibilities that came with our collective isolation, all grasping for solutions to make connections and progress at the same time.

It was almost as if the mask of the world had slipped. We saw in an instant that the old narratives had just been myths: we didn't need to commute into an office every day to get things done. We didn't need to consume as much as we did before, to *pollute*. We didn't even need to work – while our government's furlough scheme paid some people a percentage of their old wages for doing nothing, better ideas of a universal basic income which had been bubbling around before started to get amplified, their wisdom lain bare. Rents froze, or could even be ignored completely. The homeless were given places to stay and keep safe. Paywalls crashed down and previously private goods became public. The most valued people in our communities became who they should have been all along: the nurses and doctors, the supermarket workers, the bin collectors, the cleaners, and, yes, the teachers, as we clapped for carers and stopped worshipping at the feet of bankers, landlords, and CEOs. Jobs formally dismissed as menial became essential, and those generously compensated and considered important were exposed for what they really were. We remembered to care for each other as spontaneous mutual aid groups popped up to check on neighbours and bring supplies to the elderly or vulnerable. And we put on masks and kept our distance, not to protect ourselves from a potentially deadly virus, but to protect those around us with whom we shared space. A small act of love and community to acknowledge our ineluctable connection to each other.

In those early days of the pandemic, we saw a glimpse of another world, and despite all the fear and terror, that world was arguably *better*, in some respects, than the one we had left behind.

Sadly, a glimpse was all it turned out to be. A new drive to get 'back to normal' was pushed as early as possible from our government, and as those in charge undermined our collective solidarity by breaking the rules as the rest of us made sacrifices for safety, a new virus of *whataboutism* and erosion started to spread with equal virulence. If Dominic Cummings was allowed to break the rules and visit family, *what about me*? If these people were allowed to work still, *what about me*? If people were allowed to take to the streets and march in the cause of black lives, what about taking to the streets to march to end the lockdown and reopen the pubs?

Rather than taking that step back and reconsidering how things were, taking the opportunity to reassess and rethink how we might do things differently going forward, building on the lessons learnt and innovations made during the lockdown, a sort of basic nostalgia for the way things used to be took over and as soon as people were able, they embraced the old normal again in place of the possible new.

I get it. The past has a strong pull for all of us, and what is familiar and comforting will always appeal more than something strange and different, even if different might have been objectively better. But for some of us that glimpse of an altered world was difficult to ignore and impossible to forget. As the anarchists had always said: another world is possible. In some ways we had now actually *seen* it. Had seen our entire old world transformed overnight. If we could do it for COVID-19, why couldn't we do it for the climate crisis? Or to address mass economic inequalities or other structural obstacles and prejudices to living a flourishing human life? To simply go back to the way things were and pretend this was the way things simply *had* to be would be dishonest now we had seen the reality of our potential for change as soon as the collective will was there. But as the government advice changed from 'stay home' to 'stay alert', I could see the writing on the wall.

*Stay alert*
*Stay alert*
*Their incompetence is coming for our life*

*Stay alert*
*Stay alert*
*To how they're making us a sacrifice*

*Stay alert to their propaganda*
*Bold faced lies told with fake candour*
*In the name of ideology*

*Stay alert to manipulation*
*Distortion of the situation*
*Put us at risk for their economy*

*Stay alert*
*Stay alert*
*To how the world transformed so easily*

*Stay alert*
*Stay alert*
*To all the things they don't want us to see*

*Stay alert to the latest branding*
*Designed to twist our understanding*
*Repeat their slogan in our Twitter feed*

*Stay alert their green and yellow warning*
*Suddenly the truth is dawning*
*They don't give a shit about you or me*

*Stay alert*

As an anarchist, I am used to my idealism being the minority opinion. I seldom find myself knowing the comfort of fitting in with the views of the crowd. While I wasn't surprised at how quickly English society at large raced to return to old ways, I *was* surprised that within the slightly smaller sphere of *education*, where supposedly intelligent and forward-thinking people worked, there was so little appetite for doing anything differently and building on the lessons of lockdown. Whereas, for me, the disruption had exposed the many failings of the old system and created cracks in which to experiment with something exciting and new, for my colleagues, and teachers around the country, the only lessons they'd seemed to have learned was that remote teaching was terrible, and the sooner we got back to doing exactly what we'd been doing before, the better.

I think it was this, as much as anything, that made me so furious when we returned to work. A fury that quickly became transferred onto how little anyone was taking any of the COVID safety protocols seriously. We could either be a world that cared about each other, I reasoned, or one that didn't. That counted for COVID guidelines as much as it did about education. The clear, socially-conscious, rules in place around wearing masks and social distancing being immediately ignored by so many members of staff from day one, choosing to put not only themselves, but their students *and their students' families*, in jeopardy of catching the virus, seemed to me to be symbolic of the whole ugly problem. Supposedly educated educators ignoring the widely available science of infection and choosing instead to follow the much-criticised guidance from a Department for Education more concerned with getting children's parents back to work than they were with community safety in schools.

I returned to school that September not only disappointed that we seemed to not be capitalising on any of the radical potential for change of the last few months, but disappointed that people seemed so unwilling to look after one another in even these most minimal ways. I didn't like wearing a mask while teaching either, but I got used to it quickly. It was marginally uncomfortable, but not impossible to do. I didn't like minimizing contact with colleagues I would have once socialised with, but if they weren't going to do those basic things like wear a mask or keep a little distance when we spoke, then I was left with very little choice given that, at that time, asthmatics like me were still considered as being more vulnerable to COVID complications and the possibility of dying from the virus.

Already falling out of love with my work, I wasn't willing to die for it. But I think it was the fact I was falling out of love with it – or *had fallen* out of love with it – that amplified the annoyance. Already thinking I was wasting my life in that place, doing things that did not bring me joy and which got in the way of the things that did, it was easy to feel like the place was actively trying to kill me. In truth, my colleagues were all just trying to survive their own experience of the pandemic. While I had enjoyed my time stuck at home in my own wonderful little bubble with my wife, many of them had struggled. Being back at school gave them a chance to feel normal again. Re-connecting with people and getting back to what they used to do before COVID-19 was all part of the way they were coping.

As an anarchist, I have never really thought too much about the law. I don't do things because the law tells me to, or prevent myself from doing them because the law tells me not to. When I was following the rules around COVID-19, it was because I believed they made sense *independent of any law*. I wasn't waiting for permission to ignore them because, autonomous from the enforcement of the rules, I actually *wanted* to do what I could to protect others and myself. I thought wearing a mask and keeping our distance made sense: a logical compromise to still interact while keeping each other and our community safe. Most people, I came to realise, aren't like that. For most people, it seems, the rules were impositions enforced from on high, and as soon as it was discovered that you could break those rules and get away with it, you would.

Just as anarchists find cracks in the rules and regulations of normal society in which to experiment with their freedoms and prefigure alternative ways of living, those who are not anarchists, and find themselves oppressed by rules and regulations, do their own experimentation in the cracks when the authorities are no longer looking too. Of course they do – why wouldn't they?

I can therefore see why both the staff and the students might have rebelled against the COVID protocols they felt were being forced upon them, even if I question the intelligence of their doing it when we still knew so little about the virus and all we *did* know was that our carelessness could very easily cost someone in our community their life. But my active and very visible opposition to the general view around COVID protocols at the school was, I think, to use Gwyneth Paltrow's memorable phrase, a convenient way to start a 'conscious uncoupling' with the place I had been working at for nearly a decade and knew now I needed to leave. By isolating myself to avoid unnecessary social contact, by keeping my mask on even when I was the only person still doing it, all served as a convenient excuse to separate me from the people I had been working with for far too long and knew I needed to eventually leave behind.

Yes, I didn't want to catch COVID, or give it to anybody else, but I also didn't want to be working there anymore. It was easier to criticise my colleague's approach to COVID-safety than it was to question their most fundamental professional beliefs about what education and teaching was meant to be.

Another lesson from wrestling: sometimes a character gets stale and needs to move territories to somewhere where they can reinvent themselves afresh. I had come back from the lockdown with all these new ideas about what teaching could and should be, and yet once back in the same old school with the same old people it was not only all-too easy to fall back into old behaviours, it was expected of me. For the entire duration of the 2020/2021 academic year, I didn't put a single student into detention or tell them off if they hadn't done their work, yet nobody noticed. My reputation for being a strict teacher remained. While my A-level class were enjoying the freedoms of a more participatory education, COVID-restrictions on group-work and sharing resources, combined with a well-trodden and deeply embedded curriculum plan, made it hard to break too radically free of what was already in motion in the lower school. There was plenty I wanted to do differently, but there didn't seem to be the appetite in either my students, or my colleagues in the department, for doing it. It was like being a wrestler who had spent the last six years performing a certain well-known series of moves wanting to come to the ring one night and suddenly throw all the old trademarks away and wrestle their match with a brand-new gimmick: the fans can only see your history and won't accept you if you don't honour it. However, leave the promotion and turn up somewhere new where you *have no history,* and you can be whatever new character you want to be.

Here, I would always be *that* Dr. McKee. The one you'd heard about. The one who taught your older brother. The one who did that thing that pissed you off. I couldn't escape it. Maybe somewhere else I could be myself again and not the caricature I realised during lockdown that I had become?

*I exist behind a guise*
*Crushed beneath professional hair*
*Cannot breathe inside this suit*
*The one I swore I'd never wear*
*They were the worst days of my life*
*Yet I'm back inside in that cell*
*The one I thought I had escaped*
*The one that I always called hell*

*The things we do to pay the bills*
*Can make us strangers to ourselves*
*If only I could see me now*

*But I have become someone else*

*In my bathroom there's a mirror*
*But staring back at me*
*Unrecognizable reflection*
*Pseudo identity*
*I plaster on my daily smile*
*The one the world expects*
*I turn away and close the door*
*My tie a noose around my neck*

*I hear the words fall from my throat*
*Saying things I don't believe*
*Same old stories I was told*
*The ones from which I had been freed*
*Until I had masters to please*
*Bosses I'm forced to obey*
*The evil's always so banal*
*When normalised as just another day*

*The things we do to pay the bills*
*Would make our younger selves blush red*
*If only I could see me now*
*But the me I was is dead*

*In my bathroom there's a mirror*
*But staring back at me*
*Unrecognizable reflection*
*Pseudo identity*
*I plaster on my daily smile*
*The one the world expects*
*I turn away and close the door*
*My tie a noose around my neck*

*Life –*

*binding me,*
*hiding me,*
*holding me prisoner,*
*entwining me*

*Now I need,*
*to break free,*
*now I need to begin finding me*

**INTERLUDE – TEACHING MYSELF EXCERPT - 01/09/21:**

*Teaching Myself was a short-lived and ill-fated mini-blog on my personal website www.everythingdanmckee.com, focused on my disaffection with teaching, that I tried to start writing in April of 2021 and stopped bothering with when I quit my job in January 2022.*

## NOTES FOR SELF-IMPROVEMENT

- There's no such thing as a stupid question is one of the more important principles your best teachers endorsed. Don't let frustration, speed, or inconvenience allow you to undermine that principle in your own classroom.

- If teaching is making you unpleasant, terse, jaded, then either quit teaching or do it better. Don't lose yourself because it's easier to manage behaviour through fear than through kindness.

- Kindness is always better. Always.

- Remember what you hated as a student yourself. Don't do that. Even if there are justifications and rationales for being awful in the classroom, remember what it feels like from a student perspective and what impression will last.

- Note down the good things pupils do. Acknowledge them. To yourself. To them. To their families.

- No more behaviour or achievement points. They are a false currency.

- No more endless detentions. Brief discussions on what went wrong are ok, immediately following the incident. Two mins is more effective than an hour two days later.

- No rules - just clear expectations. Flexibly interpreted but consistently reinforced.

## 8.

## ***Just When I Thought I Was Out...***

Who was the real me? Was I a teacher, or was I an academic? Some very lovely reviews of my book and the *Anarchist Studies* journal paper acceptance had made me realise how much I enjoyed doing philosophical research and that I still had contributions to make in the field. I had been accepted to write a whole chapter for a book on Anarchism and Punk off the back of an abstract and was relishing the work whenever I found the time to do it in between my teaching. I wanted to do more of that sort of thing, not less, and I was starting to get my teeth into a growing new research interest as my political theory and philosophy of education work combined with much of the reading on race I had been doing during the lockdown: the connection between regimes of punishment in schools and the persistence of prisons despite their self-evident failing as a means of tackling crime and continuing contribution to racial injustice, especially in what was known as the 'school-to-prison pipeline'. I would love to do some proper research on the ideological underpinnings of that issue, and the faulty retributive logic which supports it, but couldn't see the time I would ever be able to do it as the old treadmill of being a teacher creaked into action once again.

Yes, there were long holidays, but if I spent all my holidays locked in my office doing academic research, I wouldn't be spending them with my wife, doing all the other things we loved to do and never had the time for during the working weeks. If I had an *academic* job, I reasoned, instead of a teaching job at a secondary school, then doing such research would finally be *part of the job*. Rather than having to find stolen moments between my work responsibilities, the research would *become* the responsibility.

It was an interesting thought.

But there were equally interesting challenges in returning to physical schooling during a pandemic, despite the fear and stress. Myself and my department had spent many years developing a fun and interactive curriculum, heavily involving discussion and group work. Now we had been instructed by government guidelines, questionable though they were, to put all desks in rows, rather than tables grouped together. Students had to face the front of the room, in a minor nod towards avoiding transmission of the virus, and were not supposed to turn and talk to each other anymore. The sharing of resources was to be minimised to prevent cross-contamination. My background in improv put me in a good position to adapt to the new restrictions. Like a scene done once and then asked by an audience member to be repeated, only this time without using the letter 'S', or with no hand movements and in half the time, teaching that year required constant concentration and the ability to pivot and reimagine tasks for the supposedly 'COVID-safe' classroom.

We moved as much writing and resourcing online as we could and devised new ways of delivering old lessons without eliminating all of the fun. My favourite example was getting a class of Year 8 students to produce a 'COVID-safe' mini-play of various aspects of Sikh founder, Guru Nanak's, life. Each row produced the best dramatic interpretations that they could of various chapters in the Guru's life, all while facing the front and never leaving their desks – and their creativity and innovation blossomed as they rose to meet the challenge and performed a range of interesting and diverse scenes entirely from their seats and without looking at one another. So the schoolwork I was engaged in was intellectually challenging *enough*, but I would find myself in my spare moments and evenings thinking more about research projects and books I wanted to read than about my next lessons. Those nuts and bolts tasks of teaching – the endless admin and the unnecessary accountability paperwork that I had previously sucked up as just being 'part of the job' – now seemed like an impediment to the real work of teaching, and to the stuff outside of the job that would actually fulfil me as a human being. Since being freed from them briefly during the lockdown they were now back with a vengeance, and I began to resent them more and more.

As I started to work on the punk and anarchism chapter for the book, as I began to make notes on the issues around prisons and regimes of school punishment, *this* was the stuff that consumed me each evening rather than whether my curriculum mapping and lesson sequencing was compliant with the latest demands of Ofsted and if I had a plan to tackle the so-called 'lost learning' of my classes.

The 'conscious decoupling' I was engaged in was helped not only by the distance I was forced to keep from my colleagues during this time, but by the wearing of masks around the school. Although mask-use was sloppy at the best of times, and their compulsory wearing was only ever enforced in fits and starts, for much of the year many of my classes were just rows of faceless eyes and hair staring back at me, hard to distinguish from each other and easy to conflate and get confused. Students have always been my main driving force as a teacher. While some teachers retreat to the staff room each break to bitch and moan about the young people they are trying to educate, my sympathies have always lain more with my students than they ever did with my colleagues. Nine times out of ten, I would take the students' side over that of the staff, which was why I was so good at my Student Council role, and I would always much rather spend my lunch breaks or recesses running a club or helping a student with a problem than spending it kvetching with my peers over a sandwich. I still harboured my own childish sentiments that teachers were somehow *the enemy* and, I guess, psychologically, saw myself still on the side of the 'people' rather than with their 'oppressors'. I wanted desperately to be the teacher I had always wished had been there during my own school days, even though, more realistically, with my stupid approach to behaviour management, I had become exactly the sort of teacher I had despised.

If my ill-advised character-work as a disciplinarian hadn't soured my relationship with many in my classes already, then the anonymity of the COVID masks – and frequent absences as year groups shifted online for two weeks at a time whenever a new confirmed outbreak of the virus occurred in their year-bubble – managed to keep the majority of new students at a further distance. It was hard to put a name to half a face, especially as the bubble system meant I was going to *their* classroom rather than them coming to mine, leaving seating plans up to the unpredictable fate of fellow colleagues rather than being able to control where people sat and having, at least, *that* in front of me as an *aide mémoire* for who sat where.

Much as I would love to tell you my love for my students made it easy to remember names, I struggle with names at the best of times, and teaching over three hundred different students a year it was always a difficult task to cement new names to new faces. In my own classroom, I used certain tricks to help commit new names to memory. For instance, if I noticed more than two new students with the same first name across different classes, then I would put them all in the same seat as each other so I could reinforce the idea in my head: whoever sat in that chair was likely to be called *NAME X*. Eventually, that first element sorted, the surname and other specifics would come later. You always remembered the names of the loud ones, the disruptive ones, the really clever ones, but quiet students who kept themselves to themselves were often harder to remember. However, even here, seating plans could help: they were *The Quiet One*, yes, but *The* specific *Quiet One* on the same table with *A, B,* and *C*.

In the new COVID context though, everyone was just a pair of peering eyes above masks at various levels of secure: over the nose, under the nose, around the chin, in the pocket. With teachers told to stay at the front, two metres away from them, and not interact and move around the room anymore, those elements of personality so important for making connections became limited. And when masks were removed, and interactions allowed again, it was against global public health advice while other countries were still keeping their physical schools shut. I became known as the insane stickler still wearing his mask and staying at the front of the room even when none of the other teachers were doing it. My once-subversive act which had gained me a reputation as someone who stuck to all the rules rigidly was once more working against me and hoisting me by my own misjudged petard. Now that there were rules I actually thought important, and their disregard problematic, I had become the teacher who cried wolf.

To the students, understandably, even though I was no longer disciplining them for any of the stupid school rules based on coercion and control, no longer giving out detentions or any other sanctions, my frequent lectures about being kind, wearing masks, keeping distance, and looking out for each other *even when authorities told us we didn't have to,* was just another stupid thing Dr. McKee was trying to do that no-one else seemed to care about in the school. Just as I had trained them to do, they ignored my pretence of authority and did what they knew to be right, even if the people in charge were telling them they were wrong.

School was a battle I didn't want to be fighting anymore. A battle against COVID, a battle against entrenched ideas about who I was, a battle against colleagues and students who didn't seem interested in doing even the bare minimum of requirements to keep us all safe, and a battle to even teach in a way that felt worthwhile. Without the interactions, the fun, the joyful learning environment, and with so much reduced to what was *necessary* rather than all of the far more interesting *unnecessary* stuff I had always embedded into my curriculum, the task of figuring out how to teach that curriculum in this hostile new context was intellectually stimulating, but not particularly pleasant. It was interesting, but I did not look forward to my days at work. In fact, I was rarely sleeping a full night through during the weekdays and found myself yearning to get to Friday from the moment Monday's hateful alarm clock rung out and startled my already open eyes.

I would go to work and count-down the hours I had to be there. Break up the timetable into manageable baby-steps I could survive, just like Richard Dreyfuss told Bill Murray's character to do in *What About Bob?* If I could get from morning registration to break-time, period one to period two, it would then be only two more lessons until lunch. If I could make it to lunch, I could make it to the end of the day. The whole time, with COVID still running rampant and, in those early days of the 2020/21 term, still no vaccine, I became obsessed with a singular thought: this place I hated going to but *had* to go to because of capitalism, because of the need for an income, this place which was prematurely open and putting us all at risk just so that others – parents – could be equally exploited and sent back to their own unsafe workplaces quicker than it was wise to do so, was going to kill me. I would catch the dreaded virus here and end my life as one of those depressing historical statistics looked at by future generations: *During the COVID-19 pandemic, the catastrophic mistake was made in September of 2020 to send people back into schools. We now know that this decision cost the lives of many thousands of teachers, students, and their families...*

One of the terrible things about being an anarchist, or anyone who has really studied the history of states and the appalling things states and other authorities have allowed in the name of their own self-sustenance and continued control, is that you cannot trust the seeming benevolence or wisdom of such authorities. Whereas others might find comfort from being told by the government that everything was OK, I could treat such proclamations only ever with suspicion. I would think of chemical ingredients allowed for years so that someone could make a profit while blind eyes were turned, even as the death toll went up; of wars fought illegitimately and the soldiers sacrificed on the basis of another venal myth; of factory disasters that forced changes in legislation only once the visibility of the tragedy meant the danger could no longer be swept under the rug; of Aberfan, of Grenfell, of warnings ignored until it was too late; of the injustice of the prison, and the entire mechanism of the police, in a criminal justice system that had entrenched the mass suffering and abuse of so many rather than alleviate it; of the poverty that remained a choice, not a necessity, and which cost so many their lives every day; of the racism, the sexism, the homophobia, the transphobia, the colonialism and brutal genocide and enslavement of whole nations that still went unapologised for and ignored. To get the economy moving, schools had to be open. That was the only logic that mattered to government. They would be opened whether it was safe to do so or not. The guidance around COVID protection completely ignored what the science was saying and was purely about the goal of economic growth. To *know* this and have no agency to do anything about it felt like nothing else I have ever experienced: an unwilling *fait accompli* where I felt I could see the car-crash coming but had no ability to take the wheel and steer myself to safety. Like all illegitimate and unjust wars, it was wrapped up in jingoistic notions of sacrifice and the greater good: we had to be back in schools because of all that 'lost learning' suffered when the schools were closed. But I didn't believe the learning had to have been lost. Education *could* be transformed and done well from home. I had been pressganged into fighting a war I didn't even believe in and all I could think about was how angry I would be, after all the years of health anxiety, after all the years of trying to look after myself and make sure I didn't drop down dead, if this stupid *job* killed me by infecting me with a virus we had every means to mitigate against but had simply *chosen not to*.

So when I did, indeed, get the virus at the end of that first term, precisely because the school had foolishly decided to lower its safety protocols in the final weeks before Christmas, I felt both vindicated and also terrified. Christmas, despite my atheism, has always been my favourite time of year. Something about the twinkling lights against the darkness, the generosity and sense of charity in the air, the warmth against the cold, and probably the fact that, despite all my parents' marital problems, we seemed to always be together and at least *attempting* happiness from Christmas Eve to Boxing Day each year. In many ways the so-called 'spirit of Christmas' is the spirit of anarchism: selflessness and love for all people, expanding the circle of community as far as you can and thinking of our connectedness for a change instead of thinking individually. 'You are now in Bedford Falls' is tattooed across my arm, and my wife and I watch *It's A Wonderful Life* every Christmas Eve. A movie where a lonely attempted suicide is overcome by the love of a community and the recognition and support of our collective interconnectedness. As I had been breaking up the interminable first COVID term into baby-steps of chunked time as a coping mechanism, I was so looking forward after that longest, darkest, few months (including the death of our Headteacher) to reach the reprieve of the Christmas break. To have two weeks away from masks, away from alienation, away from stress and sorrow, and have two weeks back at home with my wife and our *real life* again.

At first I thought I was just shattered from the most exhausting term of my career. A friend of ours, a fellow teacher, had once described spending the first days of their own Christmas holiday doing nothing but lying on the sofa, napping, and watching the dumbest TV they could find. That seemed ideal, but with every nap I took my fatigue didn't seem to drop. I didn't have any of the classic symptoms we'd been asked to look for, but by the next day I had quite the headache on top of my tiredness, and by Sunday I was having that woozy feeling of leaving my head behind every time I turned it. I felt terrible, but I didn't want to believe I had succumbed to the dreaded plague. I knew the number of days of isolation that would be required. Saw how close we were to Christmas and did the maths. I remembered key events in my past – completing my university exams, completing my GCSEs – when similar symptoms had arisen and been my body's way of dealing with months of pent-up stress and worry. That was surely all this was: my anxiety from September to December finding a release valve through a hideous migraine? But after a mad, sweaty, sleepless night, semi-deliriously believing myself to be on a boat with Michael Palin after watching one of his documentaries just before bed, I got up the next morning and found it almost impossible to walk to the bathroom without losing my bearings. I stumbled downstairs and put batteries into the new thermometer we had bought when the lockdown first began but hadn't yet had cause to use. My fever was significant, and I was hot to the touch. I crawled back upstairs, and my wife put a cold compress on my head and booked us both in for a PCR test later that morning.

Although paracetamol and sleep seemed to get the fever under control, I felt terrible all day and stayed isolated in our bedroom just in case. When I woke up the next morning, I had been texted my results. As predicted: I was positive for COVID-19.

Amazingly, despite spending the last two days with me and sharing a bed until that night, my wife's test was still negative, meaning that not only did I have the plague for Christmas, but I would have to stay isolated from the person I love the whole time to protect her from catching it too. The person I needed the most to talk me down as I saw my future ahead and imagined my inevitable demise. My GP called me and did not help calm me as he implied the fact I had such a high fever was a very bad sign, and I remembered interviews I'd heard on the radio with people throughout the pandemic who'd lost loved ones. How they had been left in their isolated rooms at home to die, delirious, scared, and alone.

I noticed at lunch that my taste was off too. A salad my wife had prepared me had no flavour anymore but for the vinegar, which I could smell far too intensely to enjoy. I wondered how the neighbour's chimneys were being so potent for a good few hours before I realised that the smoky smell of burning I couldn't shake was coming entirely from me, and not the air around me. I could no longer trust my own senses – imaginary smells and invisible tastes. Christmas was ruined – all the wonderful food and drink I had ordered us online all those months ago, setting an alarm for midnight to get the coveted Christmas Eve slot, it would all taste like nothing and we couldn't celebrate together anyway even if it did. Christmas was ruined and I was probably going to die, exactly as I had feared all term.

And through the walls, from downstairs, I could hear my wife was starting to cough...

Strangely, I never had a cough with COVID. But as Christmas headed towards Boxing Day, my wife was now coughing with some persistence. She booked herself in for a second PCR test and, sure enough, got her own positive result the next day.

Now the horror narrative in my mind had changed. My fever had broken after a few sweaty nights, no cough was developing, and I was even feeling healthy enough to run a few miles on the elliptical each morning again. But what if my school didn't kill me, but killed my wife instead? What if *that* was the awful finale to this terrible tale? A Shyamalan twist: to lose *her* rather than be lost myself?

Again, there were some rough days of worry between then and New Year, and every cough felt like a portent of certain narrative doom. Happily though, my anxiety and catastrophising was that alone: a fiction in my mind. She pulled through too, although not without suffering from the after-effects of long-COVID. Both of us took *weeks* to get our taste back, and neither of us can say we have fully recovered our original sense of smell, even now. My wife still suffers from long-COVID to this day. I wrote that email to my school on New Year's Day because, despite our surviving it – and being grateful that we had survived when so many other people had not – our survival had been entirely down to luck rather than anything else.

Going back the following week with no further guarantee for our safety seemed like suicide, and not the fun Jimmy Stewart and Clarence the angel kind in Bedford Falls. Now that I'd actually experienced the virus, I could say for certain it was like nothing I had ever had before and was not something I'd wish on anyone else. Until we changed our approach, I wasn't going back to catch it again or help spread it through the community. I was also, frankly, pissed off that I would be going back having not had a proper break. Instead of relaxing and enjoying the festive period, I had shivered and suffered in bed alone and then spent the rest of the time weak and recovering or looking after my wife. I had been cheated of a break and still intended to have one.

Of course, we all ended up having a break – a very extended one – as the government announced that second full lockdown (not soon enough: they allowed schools to be open for one incredibly unsafe day of mixing and transmission on January 4th before making the announcement. Luckily, our schools had both planned an INSET training day, which it did online, and we were both required to stay at home in quarantine until January 6th anyway, so the government's ineptitude did not negatively impact our particular school community *that* time). As discussed, this second lockdown had none of the charm or benefits of the first, but my wife and I were thankful for the additional time to recover from COVID, napping in between lessons and expending far less energy at our desks than we would have done in the physical classroom. Had we been forced back into the workplace without it, I have no idea if our health would have held out. It still took a while to get back to full energy. Without the vaccines, which came out later, I would not have returned to work. I was quite prepared to quit rather than be forced back if nothing was going to change.

The following year, still mildly traumatised by what had happened, I wrote this song:

*Last Christmas I had COVID 19*
*And the very next day I still had COVID 19*
*Because it turns out that motherfucker stays for a while*
*This Christmas as the tree lights shine*
*And Cliff Richard sings of Mistletoe and Wine*
*I can't help thinking 'bout the Christmas that I could have died*

*It's been nearly two years since this virus first arrived*
*And it's easy to forget we've been lucky to survive*
*So far*
*So far*

*Last Christmas there was no vaccine*
*And very few treatments waiting under the tree*
*So I'll raise a glass that my white cells did their job*
*This Christmas I'm at least double-vaxxed*
*But the variants are coming out thick and fast*
*And I can't help thinking 'bout the Christmas that I could have died*

*Because all around me at this special time of year*
*Masks start to slip to sing a song of Christmas cheer*
*Too close*
*Too fucking close*

*Last Christmas I had COVID 19*
*And the very next year there is still lots to fear*
*But you wouldn't know it from the tinsel on the street*
*This Christmas I'd love to let go*
*But the daily infection numbers grow*
*And I can't help thinking 'bout the Christmas that I could have died*

*Trying to eat a mince pie with no smell or taste*
*Hoping I wouldn't be the next they'd ventilate*
*Too many Christmas dinners have less mouths to feed*
*This year*

*But we've survived*

*So far*

By the time the lockdown lifted though, vaccinated and feeling less raw, I decided to go back to work with everyone else. Like George

Costanza showing up the next day after he had quit and pretending nothing had happened, I just never mentioned the email and got on with the job at hand. When summer finally rolled around, I had to acknowledge that 2020/21 had been an incredibly abnormal academic year. Not just the COVID stuff, but the death of our Headteacher that first half-term too. When I had first started thinking about tapping out on teaching during that initial few weeks after lockdown, his death forced me to stick around out of a sense of duty to cope with the fallout. Just as my mother's cancer diagnosis led to immediate forgiveness and a transformation of our relationship, in that moment of pulling together to ensure we survived the loss of our boss, even with all my frustrations around COVID and general disillusionment with the place, I didn't want the school to crumble under the weight of its grief. Nor did I want to add any further problems to its caseload. With the focus on whole-school-leadership changes, not only would the school needing to find a new Head of RE and Philosophy be an additional burden it didn't need at that time, but I couldn't trust it would be a burden they would do a good job with under the circumstances. Despite all my misgivings about the place and my role there, I remained proud of what we'd done in our department and didn't want it to all amount to nothing with a successor who wasn't up to scratch. I also knew I needed a clearer head with which to make any big decisions about my future.

When I finally did send my resignation email, therefore, it had been a long-time coming. I knew even before midnight hit and we welcomed in January 1st of 2022 that I needed to do it, but I had first given the school a fair-hearing by working there as open-mindedly and open-heartedly as possible since September. I treated it as if it were a fresh start rather than just another year in the same place. New Head, new year, new attitude. No more COVID-restrictions (beyond the – largely just symbolic at this point – mask that myself, one other colleague, and a few students still doggedly wore) and lessons that were essentially back-to-normal. I could see the school in the best possible light and see if I felt I were capable of ever being happy there again.

It would be so easy, after all, to be able to just stay where I was without disrupting our lives or jeopardizing the security of long-term stable employment. If I could convince myself I could stay, things would be so simple…

But I felt like a ghost, shuffling through the halls of a place where once I had been alive. Everything felt stale, even in its relative newness, and those things which were new seemed to be cementing only those worse aspects of the profession I was growing increasingly oppositional about. The uniform cognitive science approach to pedagogical strategies, professionalism as a mechanism for homogeneity, box-ticking managerialism under the auspices of 'school improvement'. All around me people were worrying about things I just couldn't find important, and the things I found to be important were things no one else seemed to care about. Meanwhile, at home, I still found more joy in my bookshelves, my research, and my writing, than I was finding in the classroom. Not *every* classroom, to be fair. I loved my A-level philosophy lessons, and the weekly Philosophy Club I had started on a Monday lunchtime where students set the agenda and we could discuss *anything*. I enjoyed my Year 9 lessons too, where we were doing 'non-religious philosophy' to introduce them to the world beyond theology we hoped to get them interested in as future recruitment for the A-level, and there were lots of lovely individual moments with individual classes that reminded me why I had stayed there for so long. Basically, if I was teaching philosophy, I was happy, but when I was trudging through all the compulsory *RE* stuff I found dull and dated, and having to take seriously all this arcane and meaningless *bullshit*, I realised all-too frequently that life was too short. I had been there *too* long. The world was a big place, and I was eager to know what else was out there.

My decision to resign as a New Year's resolution on January 1st was not mere dramatic symbolism, it was done that early in the year because I also knew that my department colleague would be leaving at the end of the year too, to take on his church work fulltime. The school would therefore not only have to replace me, but him too, someone who had been working at the place even longer than I had. As philosophers, we were familiar with the ship of Theseus – the ship that goes out each year, gets banged up a bit, and gets a few repairs until, after a hundred-or-so seasons, every single piece of the ship has been replaced. We ask students every year if Theseus is still Theseus once none of its original materials remain and, often, I used schools as another analogy. Once students noted that changing small bits gradually over a hundred years might be OK, but if everything on Theseus had been replaced all in one go it wouldn't be, I pointed out that every year the school said goodbye to last year's Year 13, and some of Year 11, but welcomed in a whole new Year 7 and Year 12. Some teachers left, or retired, and other new teachers joined the school. But we still called it the same school, and when former students returned each year for the annual reunion dinner held in November, they recognised the place as their own *even though none of the students and very few of the staff were the same*. However, I said, if next September they fired all the staff and replaced them, including the Head, *and* kicked out all the students and gave new places to different children in every year-group, then something important would be lost, even though the school had the same name and geographic location. In some very real sense, it would no longer be the same school. The change would be too big and too sudden.

I worried that taking *both* myself and my colleague out of the department at the same time might be a change too radical for it to retain any of its former self. After working so hard to give the department a distinctly *philosophical* identity, it would be far too easy for us both to leave and, within a year, see it return to the simplistic 'pin the tail on the church' approach to RE we had worked very to avoid, with children colouring-in and labelling unchallenging diagrams of places of worship and researching the basics of different religious festivals and rites of passage. Neither of us wanted to see that. By giving the school plenty of warning, and time to find good replacements, I hoped we could maximise the likelihood that at least *some* of Theseus might survive our departure.

Luckily those years with Graham, with Dermot, with Paul, and with Barry paid off. Because of those formative relationships, I have never really minded students wanting to stay in touch with me after they left school. Occasionally, sixth form leavers would pop back for a visit the Christmas, Easter, or Summer of university, and a few would keep in touch for longer. Some would follow me on social media, or just keep popping into school and keep me abreast of their life. Philosophy students usually, or occasionally members of my old form groups. One such student had always wanted to be a teacher and, after finishing his philosophy degree, asked if he could come in and do some work experience with us in the department. He did, and he was also invited back when he was studying for his Masters degree in philosophy as a special guest for our annual House Philosophy competition we ran at the school. We had the odd coffee here and there as he got onto a teacher training programme, and I had kept in touch over the years as he started his career as an RE teacher. He messaged me one night in February, as I had told him to look out for the ads that would be appearing for mine and my colleague's jobs. I knew he was unhappy at his current school and looking to make a change. 'Do you think I should apply for your Head of Department job?' He asked. 'Or should I wait for the normal teacher one instead?' I thought of my own ascent to Head of Department less than a year into my teaching career and told him that, despite it being early into his career, I thought he may as well go for it. The worst that could happen is they might tell him he's inexperienced and still keep him in mind for the other job, so why not give it a shot?

I had no say in the hiring process for my replacement other than being one of the two observers during the teaching section of the day-long interview process. I had no say on who did or didn't get shortlisted for interview, and no say in the final decisions on who got the job. My former student, however, was selected for interview, taught an amazing lesson and, without any help from me, got the job. It was wonderfully poetic, to be leaving my department in the hands of a former student and felt like the passing of a torch.

I had also chosen to resign in January to free me up to apply for academic jobs. My plan, as I wrote the email, was to see what was out there and hopefully find myself a position for September at a university somewhere. My wife loved her job at a nearby school and didn't want to leave particularly, however, we had both agreed that if an amazing opportunity came up somewhere else in the country, then we would be prepared to move if necessary. She could teach English anywhere if needed, so if a philosophy job came up in a university in, say, Scotland, or down South by the coast, or even in Ireland (where I am also a citizen), she encouraged me to apply. We loved our home and the life we lived in it, but the actual area in which we lived, although it is the town where both of us were born, had never really been our first choice of address. A bland suburb on the outskirts of a city neither of us really spent much time in, it had simply always been convenient for work. We would rather be living in the vibrancy of somewhere like London, or in the beauty of the middle of the country. Where we currently were was neither fish nor foul – not beautiful enough to step out the door and go on long walks, but not vibrant enough either to indulge in our hobbies and interests without getting on a train to someplace else. It was fine, and in great commuting distance to pretty much anywhere else we wanted to be, but we would be happy to move if a reason to do so came knocking. At the same time, for all its faults, it was still *home*, and we were happy here. It would have to be a *really good* reason to give it all up. The town might be unexceptional, but it was still home, and had become part of our heart. In a perfect world, we would reach September and I would have a job at one of the many local universities in Birmingham, Coventry, Leicester, or Warwick, and we could stay here, she in her job and me in my new one. But we were also realistic about limiting my possibilities to only the arbitrary handful of places nearby, so as well as applying locally, as and when academic jobs came up, I also applied for positions in Bristol, in Dublin, in Glasgow, in Leeds, and in London too.

However…now that I was seriously considering pursuing a career in academia I started spending more time with academics, going to academic events, and reading academic articles, and the more I did this, the more I was reminded of why I had chosen *not* to go into academia in the first place. While I enjoyed the intellectual challenge of whipping a paper into shape for publication based on the feedback from referees, the more I started paying attention to the field of academic philosophy *as a profession and not as a hobby*, the more I saw how utterly arbitrary much of this feedback was, based on the whims and research-interests of the academics co-opted into doing the review rather than anything profound or objective. Just as my experience with two different PhD supervisors saw one person's view of academic excellence become completely eviscerated by the perspective of another, schizophrenic reports from different reviewers appeared to be the norm, with one person saying your work was an important contribution to the field and the other saying it was utter dogshit. More than this though, was the reminder of how pedantic academic philosophy was when it comes to anything applied and practical. Whereas I have always been interested in thinking about ideas in relation to their impact on the actual world, most professional philosophers prefer to deal in abstract definitions and distinctions. Whereas I wanted to make bold claims and tear down entire edifices, academic thinkers were content with making minor, nuanced, adjustments to mere words. Writing papers is the means to secure grants, promotions, and permanent employment for professional academics rather than the means by which meaningful ideas are shared to change the world. The journals they are published in are seldom even opened, let alone read. One only had to look at the *speed* of publication to see the total lack of urgency in the work. The article of mine accepted for publication in the August of 2020 finally came to print in the October of 2021. As I write this now, the chapter written and submitted for the book on punk and anarchism in early 2021 is still awaiting publication as we near the end of 2022. Meanwhile, another paper I have written on punishment in schools was recommended for publication after some revisions earlier this Spring, but since the revisions were submitted in the early Summer I have yet to hear anything back. Several papers I wrote waited nearly a year to be rejected, and I found far more joy publishing them myself on my personal website than waiting another year to place them, or fail to place them, elsewhere. At least on the website people can actually read them. Meanwhile, I was attending seminars and conferences and once again finding myself bewildered and bored by the interest so many people had in tweaking irrelevant minutiae while having so little interest in thinking about anything important.

None of this thinking was new, even if I had spent the last decade or so forgetting it. The month I was finishing my PhD I had written this article for an online postgraduate journal and I could have written an identical piece again as I saw the calendar count down the days on my departure from my school:

> *I started studying philosophy as an academic subject at A-level. During our GCSEs, my best friend and I had enjoyed terrorizing the local church youth leader with our doubts about God every time he visited our school, but countless hours spent in detention for continually questioning the various wisdoms of our elders had caused us to seek a more nurturing environment for enquiry than was currently on offer in our rather parochial classrooms. When we discovered then, that the rival sixth form college ran a course in philosophy, seeing both an opportunity to question received truths without getting into trouble, and a chance to escape the clutches of our small-town education, we both jumped at the chance.*
>
> *A decade later, a successful philosophy B.A., and M.A. under my belt, and just a few months to go before the completion of*

*a Ph.D., it seems hard to believe then, recalling how eagerly I ran to the subject all those years ago, that I am now planning, post-thesis, to walk, just as eagerly, away.*

*If you talked to me twelve months ago, I would have told you the same thing that I told anybody else asking about my life-plans: I am going to be an academic. Once the doctorate was in the bag, I would find a job in whatever department would have me, and there I would spend the rest of my days, philosophizing, teaching students, and experimenting with facial hair. Hell, I had even gone out and bought elbow-patches for all of my jackets!*

*But philosophy is nothing if not self-reflective, and soon, as the major work of my dissertation was done and my mind found itself finally free to think on things other than the ethical justifications for political power, I began to at last address the nagging doubts about my chosen profession that had been growing increasingly vocal inside my preoccupied head.*

*Is this really what I wanted to do with my life?*

*As an undergraduate, and even at M.A. level, philosophy had been a means to questioning the world in which I lived, for engaging with, and making sense of, our complicated existence; not as an academic, but as a person. Philosophy allowed me to better understand answers to questions both profound and pressing: what do I believe to be true? Is the war on terror just? Can we ever know right from wrong? What makes a government legitimate? Is there a God?*

*But as I began my doctoral work, I started to notice the subtle difference between being merely a student of philosophy, and training to become a professional in the field: after years of absolute intellectual freedom in the subject, there was now suddenly a 'right' way, and a wrong way to do things; a 'right' way that I was finding increasingly limiting.*

*Each time my rewrites got a new seal of approval, I noticed that there was less and less of myself, and the original intentions of my work, appearing within their pages as, slowly but surely, the demands of my supervisor and department steered my research further and further away from answering the questions that had brought me to philosophy in the first place, and more towards fitting my thoughts neatly into some pre-existing discourse within the field. The originality and uniqueness of my work which had gained me first class grades, grants and scholarships pre-doctorate, was now becoming a hindrance, as my writing became labelled as 'controversial'.*

*'Cut out X and Y', people would say, 'and concentrate more on Z'; but their advice bored me. Inevitably X and Y would be, to my mind, the most interesting things about the research, with Z simply being a concession to some earlier criticism, put in only to appease. The more I stopped to think, the more I realized that whilst I still loved philosophy's potential for enquiry, and the multiple ways in which my own way of looking at the world had been forever changed by the subject; and whilst I still loved teaching philosophy to the first year students I tutored in order that they could then have the intellectual tools with which to broaden their own views of the world; as a profession, academic philosophy seemed all too often to eat itself; myopically stripping the subject of its engagement with the real world and reducing it merely to private, jargon-heavy, conversations, held only between specialists.*

*Where this revelation leaves me regarding a post-Ph.D. career, I'm not entirely sure; and it is a fairly frightening*

*prospect to realize that you've dedicated ten years of your life in training for a job you no longer want! That said, as any good philosopher knows: life is not always about the answers one finds, as much as it is about asking the right sorts of questions, and sometimes it is as useful to know what an answer is not, as it is to know what an answer is.*
*For that small solace then, I thank ten stimulating years spent studying philosophy. It is only because of the subject's strengths, that I became able to see its weaknesses, and gain the courage and confidence to reject it and embrace the uncertainties of a life now unplanned.*

I had *definitely* been here before. Did I really want to try this all again?

Not that I was having to worry too much about getting trapped in another life I didn't want. No-one seemed too interested in hiring me. Application after application got sent out, and despite the book, the growing research profile, and the years of teaching experience in schools, no one even wanted to give me an interview.

Part of the problem was that I was only ever applying for permanent positions, rather than the far more precarious temporary posts designed for early-career academics which would mean having to pack my bags and go live somewhere random for eight to twelve months with no guarantee of a permanent job. As I said, I wasn't prepared to totally blow up our lives, make my wife quit a job she loved, sell our house, and move across the country, just for an eight-month promise, but nor was I prepared at the age of forty to commit to sabotaging our marriage by agreeing to something faraway and long-distance: me living in another city five days a week to make it in a career I was increasingly unsure that I actually wanted. I happen to love my wife, and love spending time with her. I am not in my twenties, unattached, and eager to jump from job to job, city to city, to chase a dream which maybe isn't even a dream. Work is not my raison d'être; real life is. My marriage is my real life – we work so we can afford to live it in a world where the obscenity of *earning a living* has been imposed upon us. I did not choose to leave a job that made me unhappy so I could live a life that would make me unhappier still.

Unfortunately though, any permanent position that came up was looking for established, world-leading, candidates in the field, and my decade-plus career break from academia, research specialism in a marginal field, and relatively small list of publications simply couldn't compete. Meanwhile, long-term fellowships explicitly designed for 'early career' researchers seemed to all exclude people like me who, although only starting out now on an academic career, had actually acquired our PhD more than a decade ago. I was too experienced to be 'early career', but not accomplished enough to be considered experienced. From an HR perspective, I was DOA. I never reached a shortlist.

As the summer holidays bore closer, my final weeks at work racing towards their conclusion, I had no new job lined up for September, not even a taste of an interview, and a growing realisation that I didn't particularly want what I thought I had wanted anyway. Reading books like Peter Fleming's eye-opening, *Dark Academia*, seeing people whose work I respected and admired complaining so frequently on Twitter about the grind of academic work, the pointlessness, the precariousness of the job market, and *the same tedious demands on time and energy that existed in teaching*, and talking freely with people I met working in the sector who were either, themselves, desperate to get out or depressed about what the job had become, I felt a job as an academic philosopher might be jumping out of the mild discomfort of a slightly simmering frying pan and into a raging inferno.

'*You*?' asked one leading academic I spoke to in the field of Philosophy of Education. 'There are loads of *really good* philosophers struggling to get a job right now. You'd have no chance. Better off trying to work in an Education department because at least there your teaching experience is actually an advantage rather than an irrelevance.'

Teach more teachers? Maybe not a bad idea. But even that wouldn't be easy he continued: 'of course the problem there is that permanent jobs, even in Education departments, are still like gold-dust. And I'm not sure how high up the list of hiring priorities an *anarchist* educator would be?'

He wasn't being rude, he was being honest. It is a fringe field of expertise and the word 'anarchism' is still deeply misunderstood, even academically. Many see it and immediately think it means throwing bombs and causing disruption. I wasn't only inexperienced and lacking a good CV of publications, I was an *anarchist* to boot. An anarchist who got most excited every time that he wrote one of his applications about the possibilities of *teaching* philosophy if he got any of these jobs than he did about anything else the jobs were offering. After all, I had been doing research and writing on the side of my full-time teaching duties for the last few years anyway. Yes, there had been the lockdown, but I'd put my book together and started *Philosophy Unleashed* long before the lockdown and had continued producing research papers, and my weekly blog posts, since the lockdown had ended. I didn't actually need to be a professional academic to be given permission to write this stuff and explore issues I cared about. If anything, the more I tried to focus my thinking into avenues I thought would improve an academic CV, the more the work got away from what I actually wanted to be writing about, and the style I wanted to write it in. And while I did get excited thinking about the possibilities for teaching new and interesting things in the different environment of higher education, it would be equally new and exciting to teach in a *different* secondary environment too. Somewhere that wasn't the same place I had been treading water in for the last decade. In fact, in higher education, I was quickly learning – or re-learning (after all, why had I been doing so much teaching back when *I* was a postgraduate student?) – teaching held very little interest to many professional academics. Classes were a hindrance to them; an obstacle in the way of their research, better to be farmed out to postgraduates or teaching assistants than be taken very seriously. Thoughts about pedagogy, even from academics who taught about education, tended not to translate into anything particularly radical in the classroom. And when they did, in one experience I had with an academic who had contacted me to discuss their experiments in anarchist pedagogy, it could cost them dearly on a professional level. They had lost their job after dabbling just for one year with some radical teaching. Another, as I discussed the possibilities of the classroom for bringing students into a Deweyian 'community' of learners and the potential for collaborative research at the university level, dismissed the very idea that a *student* had anything of value they could teach a *teacher*.

By the time my last day of term rolled around, I had stopped talking about trying to find a job in academia and started to tell people who asked me what I'd be moving onto that I was just taking a 'sabbatical'. A sabbatical to do some academic research and writing. Which then evolved into me saying I was just taking a sabbatical to do some research and writing. If I wanted people to actually *read* what I ended up writing, and wasn't simply doing it to build up a CV for a career I no longer wanted, why would I write something in a dry academic style when I could have the freedom now to make it as accessible as possible? As we finished the final assembly of the year, and of my time at the school, with the traditional and distinctly *non-punk-rock* version of the school song (sung particularly badly that year, almost as if to remind me exactly why I was leaving), I think I already knew that I wanted to get back into a classroom again rather than leave it for good. I had no doubt that education had far more possibilities than the rather limited and compromised version that goes on in our schools, and that there were far more interesting ways of teaching than the dominant approaches favoured by Ofsted and the DfE, fit mainly for examination than for intellectual growth. But at the same time, within that flawed framework, there were still some cracks where experiments with alternative approaches could take place. Sites of resistance and refuge. I had experimented a lot myself already over the years, and there was far more I wanted to try before giving up entirely. While the system of schooling remained the prevailing approach to education in the country, the choice was to either find a way within that terrible system to do some good, or walk away entirely and do no good at all. Just as my anarchism recognised that the idealism to which I aspired was unlikely to take place in my lifetime, and that the job of today therefore becomes prefiguring the kind of world I want to see exist once I'm gone, my idealism around the better possibilities of education that might exist in the future should not preclude me from doing the best I could within the current confines of today.

Never let the perfect become the enemy of the good.

Yes, I could seek out alternative educational spaces already attempting to transform what education could be, but in a way those spaces were less interesting to me because the sort of people using them have already accepted that there is a problem with the dominant system. I was more interested, as always, in trying to wake people up from their ideological slumbers from the inside, than in simply preaching to the already converted. Yes, schools were a problem, but so was academia; maybe even more so? At least schools provided an opportunity to get people thinking about things *before* they became too entrenched, and the job was student-centred, rather than students simply being an annoying by-product necessary to generate tuition fees and subsidise research.

My specific ennui was not coming from the problem of schools in general, but the problems of *this particular school*, just as it had been *that particular school* that first Christmas of my first year of teaching that had almost caused me to quit the profession the first time. Back then, I had been prepared to storm into my trainer's office and tap-out on the whole thing only to find that a few hours in a different institution made all the difference and I wanted to stay. I knew for sure that I was done with *this* particular place, and that for a million different reasons (not any of them an indictment on the school itself, simply with *my* individual relationship with the school, after a decade of working there; a product of our particular history together rather than any objective fact about the place) I would be happy not to work there anymore and that it was time to move on.

But I was no longer so sure of where I was moving on to.

It probably *wasn't* to the lecture halls of a university, but it probably wasn't some other career entirely. Much as I tried to embrace the possibility of such freedom, I couldn't actually see myself walking away from teaching entirely. Applying for a job at a local Starbucks, or with the Council, or getting into business, or learning a new trade. None of those alternative futures appealed, even if they would potentially be a breath of fresh air. A job where I didn't have the massive responsibility of opening up young minds and producing critical thinkers, where I didn't have to fight against the latest idiotic government policies and big ideas, where I could clock out at the end of the day and leave my work *at work* instead of taking it home with me and letting it dominate my evenings and weekends sounded nice. But it also sounded like it would lack those vital ingredients of interacting with students, sharing my passion for philosophy, and helping young people come to ask big questions and think for themselves.

As the weeks ran down on my final term, I felt like someone visiting a loved-one in a hospice. I knew that we were on borrowed time and that death was inevitable, but I still couldn't help wishing for more. I would think about all the good times we'd had together and ignore all the bad moments in our past. Teaching my classes, I came close to tears several times as I thought about the fact that I wouldn't be there next year to see how it all ended for them, or, indeed, to teach anyone at all. September would come and go with no new form to get to know, no new names on the registers to learn, no new ideas to try. I thought about all the lives I knew I had changed for the better during my time at the school, the students who had got in touch after to say thank you, the ones doing amazing things with their lives now because of something I had opened their eyes to or helped them to achieve, and the ones who I had just been there for as a friendly ear or person to chat with. I thought about what fun the classroom could be, and how I had lost sight of that somewhere along the way as I associated mine with all the stress and disappointment of the school itself, rather than its role as a site of great potential. I thought about how nice it would be to start again somewhere else, in a different classroom, with none of the history, none of the entanglements, and none of the baggage.

I would miss this place, I would miss the kids and the opportunity to explore weird and wonderful ideas with them, I would even miss some of my colleagues, even if I had never really – to my eternal regret – taken enough time to properly befriend many of them. Even before the 'conscious decoupling', my wanting to get out of the building as soon as possible each day, even from the start, as I struggled against the idea of full-time employment and battled for a work/life balance with an ingrained suspicion of exploitation and healthy dose of punk rock mistrust, I had kept most people from work at arm's length. Anything that might mean staying longer than necessary at the end of the day, such as going to the pub on a Friday evening, meant missing out on what I considered to be 'real' quality time at home. It became something I foolishly avoided as I put up walls around me and made a distinction in my mind between *work* acquaintances and *actual* friends. I barely had enough time to see my real friends scattered around the country and the globe; why would I spend what limited scraps of free-time I had as a teacher during term-time with people who were merely acquaintances? Hold onto that attitude too long and it becomes incredibly hard to break the pattern or change the relationships even if, later, you realise its flaws. The walls remain assumed even when you try to show people there is now a door. I was good for a laugh at lunchtime, good for a grumble in a meeting, good to send off to say what everyone else was afraid of saying to the boss, but after too many years of rejecting invitations and olive branches beyond the staff room, I wasn't anything more than that. I wasn't part of anyone's *life*.

While others I worked with got married to each other, had children together, shared holidays, went to football matches to support the same team, and spent weekends in each other's company, I, by misguided design, kept myself to myself. When I left the school, I realised I had more friends who were former students than I did former colleagues there, and I am not particularly proud of that fact. Alongside the 'conscious decoupling' of what few relationships I did have in those final years, although I know I had impacted the school, its students, and its staff for the better during my time there (although I know I wasn't actively *disliked),* when I left, I did not have much faith that I would be particularly missed.

Wherever I ended up working next, I vowed, whether it was a university, a school, or anywhere else, I would make myself more available to my colleagues and keep counter-productive barriers *down.*

*Wherever I ended up working next*?

I drove away from the end-of-term barbecue, my goodbye tie a kick in the teeth on the passenger seat next to me, a wrestling podcast on the stereo, and I felt incredibly confused. I had been waiting for this moment to come since January, since *before* January, since that morning on the playground in 2019 when I first felt the world had moved on without me and knew I had to start getting out, and yet I wasn't driving away full of joy and liberation, I was driving away feeling like I was leaving something imperfect behind, but something that, imperfect though it was, perhaps had still been better than nothing? Had been something I might *miss.*

My wife had been brilliant about my leaving the whole time. Had been encouraging me to do it for as long as she had been watching me come home angry and ranting about the latest stupid thing the school was doing that I thought was a terrible mistake. She'd seen too many years of me banging my head against a wall. We owned our house outright, she earned a decent salary, and we had some savings without any dependents to spend them on. She was happy to support me for as long as was needed. For me to live off the savings we had previously hoped one day might fund some exciting travel, or at least a new kitchen. For me to be a 'house husband' for a while and just focus on the book I wanted to write, even if it wasn't going to get me an academic job. She just wanted me to be happy. I was about to be given that gift of absolute freedom and indulgence – and yet… Without a group of students in front of me to kick about some ideas with, such freedom and indulgence felt empty.

I hadn't quit my job in January for freedom and indulgence, I had quit it to change from the secondary school classroom to the university seminar room.

Yes, I had wanted to focus on my research interests and give that more time than I could give it as a hobby, but only as part of a package that involved me teaching philosophy too. I had imagined a university philosophy department, free from the requirements to teach RE, free from the national curriculum and stultifying exam specifications, and free to teach exciting new topics. I had big plans for my research into prisons, school punishment, and ideology, but I didn't just want to sit alone in a room and *write* about such things by myself, I wanted to *talk* about them, to *teach* around it. My work was a conversation, not a monologue. I wanted push-back and people to ask me questions. Never in my life had I sat with a class of students who'd given any of my wacky ideas a free ride. I would talk about the possibilities of a world without government, and they would tell me all the ways in which they thought I was wrong. I would tell them that I thought schools were a terrible place to learn anything important, and they would point out that, if that was true, then their learning that important truth in a school would also make it false. Even my antipathy towards God and religion, after so many years of having to teach topics I considered turgid, had been enjoyable *precisely* because the continuing faith of my students. *Their* belief that this stuff was important, despite all my concerns, became a constant dialogue with my atheism. I didn't want to write a book for the sake of writing a book, I wanted to communicate an idea, and like any good idea, it was only worth communicating to a larger audience once it had proven its worth through prior conversations with smaller ones.

As I drove home that July afternoon, instead of celebrating my freedom, I felt like I was mourning a loss.

I'd made a vow, however, that I wouldn't deny myself the joy of potentially the last school summer holiday I would ever have by worrying about my future. Nor did I want to sour the break for my wife, who needed it, as every teacher does, to feel human enough again to get back on the treadmill re-energised and ready for the start of her new term in September. We'd booked a three-week road-trip around Scotland, a trip to London to visit my sister, and a range of other little enjoyments to make the most of the valuable time off and, like the proverbial ostrich with its head stuck firmly in the sand, I was graciously able to avoid the loom of September's impending unemployment by simply ignoring it.

By the start of the new school year, I was even excited about finally being able to sit down and work on my research project properly after six weeks of letting it all percolate in my head. I'd worked out a little routine for my days to give them some structure: research project in the morning until a late lunch around one, then do some household chores before spending the afternoon either doing further research or tinkering with *this* book, which I was also thinking it might be a good opportunity to finally complete after starting to write it in June.

I also had a post for my *Philosophy Unleashed* website to write each week and decided, in a moment of punk-rock-inspired hubris, to also document the Sabbatical at the end of each week on my personal blog. Say what I'd been up to as a way of proving to myself that each week hadn't been a total waste of time and do it in the style of an online punk fanzine, with links to music I was listening to, weird cartoons

I'd drawn, and any other odds and sods I wanted to include.

Another way of looking at it was that I was trying to structure my free-time like it was work so as to avoid having to confront that it wasn't, and I was also trying to start some conversations online – through the philosophy blog, through the Sabbatical 'zine – so I didn't have to live each week entirely in my own head and could let people know what I was doing to make sure I wasn't going crazy. If I were an *academic* sat reading all day about prisons, education theory, and the state, and coming up with my own theories about ideological manipulation and schools, whatever theories I ended up developing would seem like legitimate intellectual work. As a random, independent citizen just doing all that reading and writing alone in his home office, it was easy to feel like a lunatic conspiracist just shouting wildly into the wind.

I didn't need academia's permission to do my own philosophy work, but without its *legitimacy* it was easy to feel like, if not exactly a *fraud,* then like I was something fraud-adjacent, doing something mad and undeserved.

How was it fair that my wife had to go off to work each day to pay the bills while I was allowed to just sit on my ass, read books, and think deep thoughts? The work I was doing was good, and I was enjoying it, but I was also guilty about it, and missing the classroom every day.

*I have all I ever wanted*
*I am living out my dream*
*I getting what I hoped for*
*I am feeling so empty*

*So be careful what you wish for*
*And be careful what you dream*
*Because one day you might get it*
*And it might make you want to scream*

*I am doing all I yearned of*
*All my plans have come to be*
*I've achieved every aspiration*
*So why this uncertainty?*

*I wasn't careful what I wished for*
*I wasn't careful when I dreamed*
*Now I have just what I wanted*
*And yet it isn't what it seemed*

I hadn't even got through my first September by the time I knew for sure I didn't want this kind of freedom at all. That I wanted to be back teaching as soon as I possibly could. That I didn't want the pomposity and myopia of academic life now any more than I had when I had finished my PhD, but I did want to live a life immersed in, informed by, and *sharing* my love of philosophy with others. That I wanted students to teach again, and for them to teach me. That I wanted that beautiful dialogue that could only happen in collective learning environments; environments where the teacher was as open, curious, and vulnerable as their students.

I wanted the chance to finally be the teacher I hadn't allowed myself to be in my old job, insecure as I was about so many things in those early days of my career and getting lost in silly ideas of character that I could hide behind instead of simply giving voice to my concerns about, and opposition towards, regimes of school discipline and the entire project of coercive schooling. I didn't want to sit in an ivory tower and talk about teaching with people who had no idea what actually went on in a classroom, I wanted to be there on the ground actually *doing it* again.

Through working on a podcast about philosophy with other philosophy teachers around the country, I was given the opportunity to speak to some sixth form students about my work on anarchism at an independent school in Winchester and I jumped at the chance. The talk

I gave was fine, but the highlight was the extensive Q&A afterwards where the students grilled me about what I had said and put all my ideas through the ringer. I realised that for all my enjoyment of my research and writing in the preceding weeks, the few hours of preparation I had done for the talk had been where I'd really hit a flow-state of fulfilled productivity. I had always had my political objections to independent schools – all the obvious ones about inequality, unfairness, segregation, the damage they do to the surrounding pools of potential students in state schools and, of course, the historical damage their students seemed to have done to the country as they continue to bag all the top jobs in government and fail to understand the world outside of their private school bubbles and myopic ideas about social class – and yet… Hadn't I already been complicit in helping several students get into elite institutions like Oxford or Cambridge? Weren't they just as likely to produce the sort of person my prejudices told me populated private schools? Hadn't I been working at a fucking *grammar school* already for the last decade, with the only real difference between the two being the fees required by the independent sector? I had been more than willing to apply for jobs in higher education that were as equally unfair, unequal, and privately funded by fees as any independent school. If I was willing to accept a paycheque from a university which demanded its own extortionate tuition and perpetuated its own economic and educational inequalities, then why not a paycheque from a similar institution in secondary education too?

The answer had something to do with the idea that secondary education was compulsory whereas tertiary education wasn't, and that somehow the unfairness at this earlier stage seemed more impactful to me, and more wrong. But that unfairness was equally built into the grammar school system I had been working in previously. Although no fees were paid to attend it, it remained far more likely you would be able to pass the entrance exams and get in if your family had the money for tutors, books, computers, etc., and that when you were older you would do better in your exams if you didn't have to work a part-time job on top of your studies to contribute to the family finances. Privilege again. The grammar schools definitely poached all the top students in the area and pulled down the overall attainment of the local comprehensives, but I had squared all those objections away originally because of the fact that, sadly, it seemed like it would only be in the high-achieving and problematic grammar school environment that I would be able to teach something as niche and marginalised as philosophy. The same could be said of independent schools, where philosophy seemed to thrive not only as an A-level subject in its own right, but also as part of the International Baccalaureate programme which many of them were free to use as an alternative to the less expansive A-level approach. Part of being *independent*, for all its associations with money and privilege, also meant independence *from the state*. From many of the very same obligations imposed by Ofsted and the Department for Education that had been driving me out of the profession in the first place.

I realised that, despite working at a state school, albeit a state *grammar* school, for a decade, it had only been local *independent* schools – or less local ones like Winchester – that had ever invited me in to talk about interesting things like anarchism. That freedom from state control of education, even in a privileged setting, was precisely the sort of crack in the system in which alternative approaches could possibly thrive.

In my final days at my old job, I had been speaking to a head of Philosophy at another local independent school about his exciting new programme of Philosophy he was rolling out across the lower years in place of Religious Education. He had the freedom to do that in their context while I did not. When I looked into innovative schemes to bring philosophy to young people, like Northeastern University London's *School Certificate in Philosophy*, or the national Philosothon or Ethics Cup competitions, it was mainly independent schools who were doing them. As I found myself invited back to Winchester a few more times in October to teach some evening seminars online for

Black History Month on exciting topics like bell hooks on 'education as the practice of freedom' and Ruth Wilson-Gilmore on prison abolition, I noticed a job had come up at a local independent school for a maternity cover for their head of Theology and Philosophy. The ad made clear that this was a very philosophy-centred department and everything they said they did at the school ticked every box of my philosophical interests. The job started in January, giving me three whole months still to work on my research and writing if I got it, whilst also giving me an end-point to my self-imposed estrangement from the profession I was missing and a place to teach again.

If I didn't get the job, nothing was lost; I would be right back where I already was: stuck on my sabbatical. But if I got it – who knows? As a maternity cover it would only be temporary, but it would be a taste of teaching in a different school. A new start. A way of seeing if it was teaching I was really running from, or just my previous school.

I applied and got an interview for the following Friday. Again, the time I spent planning a lesson for the day on Aristotle's virtue ethics was a highlight of my week. Teaching the lesson itself when I got to the school was a joy. Being able to draw out the prior understanding the students had of Kant, Bentham, and Mill to put the Aristotle stuff we would be looking at into context and knowing that it was a lesson that, although planned, *couldn't* be planned as I would have to respond, in the moment, to whatever the students gave back to me, reminded me in an instant of that thrill you feel when you are working in the moment with your whole mind firing on all cylinders. I would ask them big philosophical questions, such as if doing the right thing was the same thing as being a good person, and, unable to know for sure how they might respond, had to be alert and ready to help midwife the conversation into something relevant from whatever thoughts they might give me. I had missed that buzz and energy, even if I hadn't missed having to wear a suit again and, yes, a tie.

I got the job.

Fuck.

After eleven years of endless self-contradiction as an anarchist rule-enforcer, atheist teacher of faith, and a punk rock rebel stuck conforming to endless professional norms even as I tried, in futility, to fight back, I was now going to have to add another inconsistency to my so-called values and work in an independent, selective, fee-paying school. That said, it was an independent, selective, fee-paying school where I had been asked by the Head during the interview about my anarchism and answered honestly and unapologetically.

'Are we going to be letting an anarchist into our midst if we give you this job?' he asked me.

'Yes, absolutely.' I replied, explaining my political beliefs while stopping short of showing him the anarchy A I have tattooed on my wrist.

I had been asked next if I was serious, as it says in my author bio for my book on anarchism, about 'subverting the system from within', and I confirmed that, indeed, I was. That my job was to make students ask questions and think critically and that, if I did it well, they would be asking questions about everything, including questions about the school and society at large. What was more subversive than being a Philosophy teacher? After all, hadn't Socrates been put to death for corrupting the youth of Athens doing exactly the same thing?

It was an interview where I talked openly and honestly about my disaffection at my previous school, criticised the latest trends in education policy, and even the very notion of professionalism, and I had still been offered the job. My assumptions and prejudices might be wrong about private education. Or, perhaps they are utterly correct, and this is the very privilege and inequality I don't think is fair: that only those who can afford to opt out of the stultifying state system get exposed to interesting teachers like *me*. But as I have said before, I got into teaching to share my love for philosophy with others, not to be a hero or a martyr for an education system – a *schooling* system – I don't actually believe in. In an imperfect world, as frustrating as it might be, this imperfect institution looks like a wonderful new environment in which to teach Philosophy, even if it might simultaneously symbolise everything that also needs tearing down.

On a political level it may have its problems, but what job doesn't when *jobs themselves* are the problem? On a personal level, it will be an interesting challenge to try and recreate myself and keep my newly rekindled passion for teaching alive in a new and novel environment after eleven long years in a place where I had grown stale. It will be nice to be able to teach new students as myself at last, and not as some self-defeating caricature of what I thought, long ago, a teacher had to be.

At least that's the plan.

I might simply end up hating it and go back to the drawing board. Back to the sabbatical. It's October now. I only just got the job last week. Tomorrow, I visit HR to fill in the final bits and pieces. Give them my ID documents and sign some forms. I still keep expecting the other shoe to drop. A social media check that discounts me for the role because I've sent too many tweets saying not only 'fuck the government' but 'fuck *this specific* government', or a DBS check that flags me up as being anti-police and therefore somehow, in the eyes of the police who do the judging, no longer fit to work with children?

Maybe I'll be prevented by PREVENT? Deemed too radical and extreme to be let inside a classroom because of my beliefs in the authentic democracy of anarchism? There's a lot that could go wrong before January, when I start. *If* I start. I won't quite believe it until it happens. But assuming it does happen, then, ironically, I guess now I have only until Christmas to try and get everything done. To try and enjoy the momentary freedom I have been given from teaching and check that I am making the right decision in going back. The research project on prisons and schools continues happily in the background, written now as a book for public consumption rather than a means to academic employment. I'd rather see it one day in the 'Smart Thinking' section at the front of a Waterstones than tucked away upstairs in their proper 'Philosophy' section, let alone sequestered within an unread academic journal. A book, perhaps, to change the world and not just change a line on my CV? But I have also become aware during my brief time away from work that I am very bad at simply relaxing and having fun. That with all these weeks stretched out before me in which to indulge and enjoy myself, I have been, instead, working perhaps harder than I ever used to work as a teacher? Next week will be October half-term, and I reach this mid-way point having not spent a single day of gifted unemployment doing nothing but reading a book, or watching movies, or playing video games. What is wrong with me? Why can't I switch off? Even this memoir, designed to take my mind away from all the heavy philosophical stuff I think about each day, saw me spending the free-time of my down-time primarily reliving my time at work, grieving for my long-dead parents, or raging against a broken world. Why did I choose to write this introspective memoir and not a light-hearted novel instead? Or just go for a lovely afternoon walk?

As a result of this realisation, I intend to do a bit more indulging in the things that make me happy over the next two months before the new job begins (if it begins) and not just immerse myself completely in prisons, punishment, and education all day long. There are other books on my shelves than weighty philosophical tomes, and I should treat a work of fiction or a book of poetry with as much priority as I do my non-fiction reading lists. I do hope to get my research project finished soon, but have made peace now with it perhaps not being completed before Christmas. My PhD took three years; why should this latest piece of longform philosophy be any different? I don't need to rush it to meet a deadline which exists only in my own mind.

However long it takes, is however long it takes. From what is written so far, I believe it will be very good indeed, but the most crucial research project of the last few months – the one I'm glad I have completed – has been the research I've unwittingly conducted on what I really want to do with my life. Because it turns out that I have put most of my energies into that and, as a result, I now know, against all the odds, that I think I really *do* want to be a teacher, even when I believed that I didn't.

Maybe the new job in January will be everything I have been looking for, and maybe it won't? Maybe I will be able to finally be the teacher I want to be there, or maybe I'll slip back all-too quickly into old and disappointing ways? Maybe I will find the cracks I seek in which to experiment with new and exciting anarchist pedagogies, atheist free-thinking, and punk rock unconventionality, or maybe the hope of independence beyond the state system will prove merely illusory and I'll have to seek other places back in the public sector where more fertile cracks might break through?

Maybe one day I'll leave teaching again for good?

All I know is that I won't know until I try, and that I have tried *not* being a teacher for a short while now and found it surprisingly wanting.

All I can do is take each day at a time. See how everything feels in a new and different environment. Another January 1st and another New Year's resolution to take another leap of faith, even though I'm an atheist.

I'll dip a toe in. See what comes from it. Teach a lesson or two. See if this thing goes anywhere interesting. After all, if it doesn't, I can always quit and do something else.

I guess I'll give it until Easter and see…

ACKNOWLEDGEMENTS

It is literally the second day of the Easter holidays 2023 as I write this and, yes, I am still working at that new school. Turns out I was right about the importance of different grass on the other side, even if it isn't entirely greener. The new job isn't perfect – what job is? But it's engaging me in all the right ways and I'm really enjoying being back in the classroom again. I've given it until Easter and now find myself hoping that the temporary maternity cover can somehow morph into something more permanent. As it stands, rather poetically given the start of this book, they can only promise me until Christmas right now, but I live in hope…

That's right – the start of this *book*. As you obviously know (because you're holding it in your hands), this fun little project I started last year as a bit of catharsis after the last decade of slog and grief *did* actually become the book I wanted it to be. Not only a book, but a *punk rock* book published by a *punk rock* publisher, so I should probably start the thanks here with David Gamage at Earth Island who confirmed my suspicions that this was something people other than myself might want to read and put his money where his mouth is. Which means I should probably thank Tim Cundle and Welly Artcore too, because they wrote some cool books with this publisher long before me and introduced me to Earth Island in the first place. I should probably thank the two of them too for letting me publish some of my wares in their 'zines, Mass Movement and Artcore, respectively, back in the day. Because of DIY 'zine-makers like them, Steve Scanner, Monk Dave, Pete Troll, and anyone else who ever allowed my teenage and young adult self to see his name in print by giving me a column in their 'zine (or website), I developed the sort of self-inflated ego which made me write a memoir about my life even though I am nobody you've ever heard of.

This book wouldn't have been possible without that punk-nurtured self-belief in the voice of the everyday. That, and Paul at Tippermuir

Books, who gave me my official start as a proper author of books when he published my philosophy book, *Authentic Democracy: An Ethical Justification of Anarchism,* in 2020. Thanks to him, too, for showing me I was a writer, not merely an academic.

That said, even with all my writerly tools, words will never be sufficient to describe all the ways in which this book, and my life, wouldn't be possible without the love and support of my wonderful wife. Every aspect of my anarchist, atheist, punk rock self has been embraced and made richer by her in ways too numerous to mention and impossible to convey in mere *language* over the many years of our relationship, and I could only write this book because she gave me the luxury of time to do it. I was only brave enough to quit a stable job when I had no other job lined up to go to (and no real clue of where I would end up) because, when I took my leap of faith, she was holding my hand the entire time. I hope she knows that whenever she feels she needs to tap-out on this ridiculous profession for a bit herself and write her own memoir, I will be there to return the favour.

The memoir itself could be seen as an extended thank you to my complicated and problematic parents, who, despite the flaws of their marriage, and their deficiencies to each other, never failed to encourage creativity and intellectual pursuit, and never once told me to grow up and stop dreaming. They're dead now, so maybe thanks are wasted on them, but their essential contribution must be acknowledged. As I read this back to myself, I couldn't help but think it read as a fucked up love letter to them both as much as it did a book about teaching, anarchism, atheism and punk. I still miss them every day. I guess Jello Biafra was right when he said there's no such thing as closure when it comes to grieving our loved ones.

The other survivor of our weird little family, my sister, continues to inspire me every day too. Writing this book was a form of therapy I wouldn't have been brave enough to engage in without her constant advocacy of good mental health and self-care. Chats with her and her partner, John over the years (and more recently attempting to interact with the fledgling verbal skills of their daughter, my niece, Willow, too) helped crystalise many of these events over time and always remind me that no job is worth losing your soul for (even for those of us who don't actually believe in souls). Their bravery and hustle in living the creative lives that they want and pursuing their dreams, even when obstacles are thrown in their path or people tell them it will be impossible, is truly something to shout about, and I'm grateful we get to be such a big part of their lives. That isn't always the case with siblings.

Beyond blood relatives there is also my extended mishpocha. My honorary godparents, Beth and Ed, who taught me that wonderful Yiddish word in the first place, were a huge part of my formative childhood vacations to the States (they were always the parents I wished I'd had when I didn't yet realise how lucky I was to have the ones I did), and they remain a significant part of my life now despite living thousands of miles away in Florida. And I wouldn't have ever picked up a bass guitar if it weren't for my best friend, Simon. Or studied Philosophy for that matter. More than friends, I think we were gateways to other worlds for each other when we were kids and his influence is all over this story despite him not even knowing I was writing it. Like Zelig, or my secret hero, Forrest Gump, he was there discovering anarchism, atheism, and punk rock right alongside me at every moment, raging against the same stupid school we both attended and is still a good person to rage alongside even now. If you want to read his take on our fucked up childhood, you should pick up his book, *The Killer You Know.* A surprising amount of it is basically true. Shout outs should also go to our fellow Academy Mortician, Tom. I reckon we must be due another reunion soon? I'll write half an EP if Simon wants to write the rest? Someone give Steve a call about the drums…

To all the students I have annoyed, confused, or otherwise been an asshole to over the years, I can only apologise. At the same time, everyone needs a teacher they hate and as I still remember all of mine, even after all these years, I guess I am honoured to be one of yours. It's part of our job to assume someone is saying nasty things about us when we're not around and you're entirely entitled to do so…just know that it was never my intention to be an asshole, or to annoy or confuse you. I am just a human being doing the best he can and all too often I have failed to be the teacher, or even the human being, I'd like to be. For those who I *did* manage to inspire, educate, or who otherwise enjoyed (or continue to enjoy) my lessons, however, thanks for getting it. You're the reason that even when I quit, I still couldn't quit. We also need to remember our good teachers too.

One such teacher, mentioned in the book, is my old A-level Philosophy teacher, Dermot. If Simon was responsible for the anarchist, atheist, punk rock bit, then I'd say Derm is largely responsible for the teacher bit. A constant source of wisdom and wit, I hope to continue haunting the best walks and coffee shops the National Trust have to offer with him for many more years to come. Our chats were invaluable in the forming of many of the thoughts in this book, and his own luck with emailing random publishers with manuscripts was what prompted me to first get in touch with Earth Island. I'd tell you to check out his book too, but he's far more private (sensible?) than I am and writes under a pseudonym.

I guess I should also mention the teaching colleagues who have helped keep me sane whilst working in an insane job. Both those explicit allies in the good fight of subverting from within, and those who just made working in schools more pleasant for them being there. I won't mention any names (because it is frowned on in teaching to be as public with your thoughts and feelings as I am unless you're trying to grease some career progression through Twitter) but hopefully you all know who you are. If I ever had a laugh in a staffroom with you, or a groan in a corridor, or planned something amazing for our students with you, then you're who I'm talking about. Especially the one (and only) colleague who came and asked me if I was alright during the COVID time when I very clearly wasn't. That act of kindness meant a lot.

Thanks go, too, to all the other anarchists and DIY-spirited radical thinkers and utopian daydreamers in schools, or anywhere else, trying to change the world as best they can from within the cracks of normal society and its harmful institutions. Another world is always possible so long as people like you and me continue to inspire and disrupt.

I also feel it's important to note that while the title of this book is *Anarchist Atheist Punk Rock Teacher*, dogma, ideologies, and the blind faith of team-sports are terrible things. While these are all titles I currently identify myself with and ideas I believe in, all thoughts are subject to change given the right compelling argument or new evidence against them. Hopefully you've seen throughout reading this book, or anything else I've written about anarchism, that even though I have the circled-A tattooed forever on my arm, I'm still open to the possibility that I am wrong. That maybe anarchy *wouldn't* work, that maybe there *is* a God, that maybe there's better music and communities out there than I've found through punk rock – certainly that there are better careers to have than teaching! Clinging on to beliefs and not being open to the possibility of being wrong is death. While, so far, I remain pretty sure that anarchism is the most legitimate form of political organisation we could have, the evidence for the divine is poor, punk rock saved my life, and that teaching is what I want to do to pay the bills, I do so only because of the current evidence and arguments I have at my disposal. We should always have the humility to be open to change if change feels necessary, even if what might need to change is our most deeply held beliefs. (That does, of course, necessarily include the idea that all beliefs might be subject to change: you have to also be open to the possibility that some ideas will end up being lifers or else you're not taking your own advice). I guess what I'm saying is that *my* anarchism, atheism and punk rock might not be the same as *your* anarchism, atheism, or punk rock, or that you might be an authoritarian theist who has never listened to punk rock in their lives, and that all of that is fine. We can still be friends and have a chat about life. We might even be able to change each other's minds about some things when we do. Never fear being challenged. Fear only the stagnancy of complacent thinking.

And finally, I would be remiss if I didn't thank you, too: the reader. The person who picked up this obscure book about a random person you've probably never heard of and decided to see what it was all about and have now read through right to the bitter end. Even the acknowledgements bit so many just skip over. You now know more about me than some of my friends do! Kudos to your curiosity and thank you for your time. I hope you enjoyed it as much as I enjoyed writing it and far more than I enjoyed living some of it. Now go out and make the world a better place.

DaN McKee, April 2023
www.everythingdanmckee.com

## About the author

DaN McKee is an anarchist, atheist, punk rock teacher of philosophy and religion who lives in the West Midlands with his wife, his cat, and way too many books. He is the author of *Authentic Democracy: An Ethical Justification of Anarchism* and has published academic philosophy papers on anarchism, education, punishment, and punk. Back in the day, when he wasn't writing angry political columns for UK 'zines Scanner, Fracture, and Mass Movement, he was bassist and singer/songwriter in UK punk bands Academy Morticians and Bullet of Diplomacy. These days he releases music under the name Strangely Shaped By Fathers and saves his angry political columns for his two websites: Philosophy Unleashed and EverythingDaNMcKee.

Ingram Content Group UK Ltd.
Milton Keynes UK
UKHW052139190623
423673UK00010B/63

9 781739 363833